SLOW BOAT THROUGH FRANCE

*Early twentieth-century steam power at work on the
Seine at Suresnes Lock, west of Paris*

SLOW BOAT
THROUGH
FRANCE

Hugh McKnight

DAVID & CHARLES
Newton Abbot   London

For my fellow travellers aboard *Avonbay*

BY THE SAME AUTHOR

Canal and River Craft in Pictures
Canal Enthusiasts' Handbook 1970–71 and No 2 (with David Edwards-May)
The Shell Book of Inland Waterways

page 2: Avonbay on the long climb to the summit level of the Canal de Bourgogne.

British Library Catalogue in Publication Data
McKnight, Hugh
    Slow Boat Through France
    1. France. Inland Waterways Description and travel
    I. Title
    914. 404838

    ISBN 0-7153-9407-X

Phototypeset by ABM Typographics Ltd., Hull
and printed in Hong Kong
by Wing King Tong Co Ltd
for David & Charles Publishers plc
Brunel House   Newton Abbot   Devon

Contents

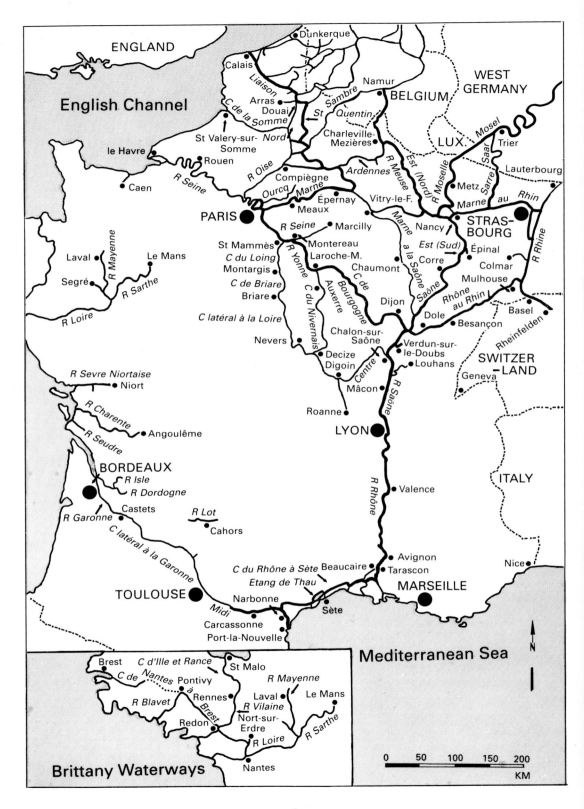

ENGLAND

English Channel

Dunkerque
Calais
Liaison
Arras
Douai
C de la Somme
St Valery-sur-Somme
le Havre
Rouen
R Oise
Caen
R Seine
Compiègne
Ourcq
Marne
Épernay
Meaux
PARIS
R Seine
Marcilly
St Mammès
Montereau
C du Loing
Laroche-M.
Montargis
C de Briare
Briare
C latéral à la Loire
Nevers
Laval
R Mayenne
Le Mans
Segré
R Sarthe
R Loire
R Sevre Niortaise
Niort
R Charente
Angoulême
R Seudre
BORDEAUX
R Isle
R Dordogne
Castets
R Garonne
C latéral à la Garonne
R Lot
Cahors
TOULOUSE
Narbonne
Midi
Carcassonne
Port-la-Nouvelle

Namur
BELGIUM
WEST GERMANY
Sambre
St Quentin
Charleville-Mézières
Nord
Ardennes
R Meuse
LUX.
Mosel
Trier
Lauterbourg
Metz
Sarre
Saar
Est (Nord)
R Moselle
Vitry-le-F.
Marne
au
Rhin
STRASBOURG
Nancy
Est (Sud)
Épinal
R Rhine
Chaumont
Marne à la Saône
Corre
Colmar
Auxerre
C du Nivernais
C de Bourgogne
Saône
Mulhouse
Dijon
Rhône au Rhin
Dole
Basel
Chalon-sur-Saône
Besançon
Rheinfelden
Decize
Verdun-sur-le-Doubs
Digoin
Centre
Louhans
SWITZER-LAND
Mâcon
R Saône
Geneva
Roanne
LYON
ITALY
R Rhône
Valence
Avignon
Nice
C du Rhône à Sète
Beaucaire
Tarascon
Etang de Thau
MARSEILLE
Sète

Mediterranean Sea

N

C d'Ille et Rance
Brest
C de Nantes
St Malo
Pontivy
R Mayenne
à Brest
Rennes
Laval
Le Mans
R Blavet
R Vilaine
Redon
Nort-sur-Erdre
R Loire
R Sarthe
Nantes

Brittany Waterways

0   50   100   150   200
KM

6

Preface

THIS is the story of a voyage nearly 4,000km long, from the Thames to the French interior. Travelling at a fairly gentle pace, we were on the move for 102 days, spread over a four-year period. Other inland waterways explorers sell up and devote their whole existence to such a venture but we had houses we did not want to leave and responsibilities that included earning a living or completing our education.

In sharing our experiences with fellow canal and river enthusiasts, one purpose is to demonstrate that ownership of a European floating holiday home is well within the capability of any moderately resourceful family. Admittedly, we were able to rely on inland boating expertise dating back almost four decades. Even this did not always protect us from a few alarming moments. But most of the time, our voyages were unworried and tranquil. Anyone tempted to follow our example and set off in search of rural France by water would discover some of the loveliest countryside in Europe, the best food in the world and a still vibrant network of inland navigations which are little touched by the sometimes destructive hand of tourism.

I must thank *Avonbay*'s co-owners, June and John Humphries, for the part they played in these adventures and also for reading the text and making a number of very useful suggestions; our various crews and the visitors we had on board at different times; the lock-keepers and professional boatmen for a genial acceptance of our invasion of their territory; my publishers; and my editor, Pam Griffiths, for allowing unusual freedom in the content and layout of this book; the editor of *Motor Boat & Yachting*, who originally commissioned several portions of the text; our friend and engineer Jim Macdonald, whose skill and enthusiasm kept us mobile with a minimum of worry; and finally, *Avonbay*. I never knew it was possible to become so fond of a boat. She is beautiful, comfortable, dependable and tough. What more could you ask of a little ship?

Opposite: *The inland waterways network of France totals 8,000km of rivers and canals*

Hugh McKnight
The Clock House
Shepperton-on-Thames
TW17 8RU   England

1
Introducing Avonbay

IT TOOK me thirty-eight years to cross the English Channel. The build-up was inevitable, if prolonged, and started one day in the summer of 1947 when my father returned from his office with an aluminium rowing dinghy roped to the roof-rack of the family's 1936 Ford 10. Now, four boats and many thousands of kilometres of inland cruising later, here I was, out of sight of land in mid-Channel, aboard twin-engined diesel yacht *Avonbay*. It was exciting and very slightly frightening.

Our first, originally nameless, vessel was berthed initially at Howlett's boatyard on the tidal Thames by Richmond Bridge. All four of us would make regular day-trips to gravelly beaches off Ham Common, downstream of Teddington lock. A move to the non-tidal preserve of the Thames Conservancy shortly followed acquisition of a bad-tempered Evinrude outboard motor. Regulations for the upper waterway demanded that all motorised craft must bear a name. Thus, the aluminium cockleshell became *Tiree Isle,* in consideration of our (slightly distant) Scottish origins.

Converted motor torpedo boats, and ex-landing craft – freely available in the immediate post-war years – shared the Thames with a wide variety of wooden cabin cruisers and small seagoing vessels. I would see these impressive craft daily from the public riverside park near our home in Strawberry Hill. Any notion of one day owning something of equal grandeur never crossed my mind. Horizons widened only very gradually. *Tiree Isle* was replaced in 1954 by a craftsman-built double sculling Thames camping dinghy, constructed of mahogany by Burgoine's of Kingston during the twenties. Based near our new house at Shepperton, this arrival with canvas tent supported on a series of iron hoops was capable of extended journeys. But for several years *Chérie* never strayed more than a day's return travel from home moorings, passing through Shepperton and Chertsey locks (2s (10p) motor launch ticket each), to find a wilderness picnic site in the gravel pits off Penton Hook weir stream.

A friend, several years older than me, had parents with a Bond Street fur business, a pre-war convertible Rolls Royce and a riverside house in Twickenham. Tied to a pontoon at the bottom of their lawn was *Yelka*, an elegant slipper stern launch. When, in 1957, David Mlinaric became a 7s6d (37½p) junior member of the Inland Waterways Association, I immediately copied his example, only vaguely aware that 4,800km of rivers and canals were waiting to be explored in England and Wales. IWA members were encouraged to blaze a trail through little-used waterways, so we penetrated the lower reaches of the River Wey Navigation in Surrey, explored on foot the weed-choked remains of the Basingstoke Canal and memorably failed to enter the Grand Union Canal at Brentford when *Yelka* ran hard aground on a falling tide off Isleworth.

1963 saw the purchase – for £150 – of a romantic but elderly 6m gaff-rigged cabin sloop which came complete with a useless air-cooled engine. Renamed *Dorymouse*, she looked a brave sight under full sail. More often, her mast and spars lay on deck and suitably repowered she penetrated much of the British inland network from Essex to Yorkshire and Leicestershire to the Westcountry.

Active involvement with the Inland Waterways Association brought new friends: among them John Liley on the staff of *Motor Boat & Yachting*. When he was offered the use of a motor cruiser in central France for a fortnight in the autumn of 1968, I enthusiastically accepted a berth. Peter Zivy, a French Anglophile who spoke better English than most natives, owned the only fleet of hire boats then available on French waterways and was seeking publicity for his venture. Our jaunt comprised a circuit of the Nivernais, Yonne, Seine, Loing, Briare and Loire canals. Here, we discovered a world akin to British canals back in the thirties: we met several hundred 350-tonne capacity *péniches* and a handful of ancient wooden barges, bank-hauled or drawn by animals. Suddenly, I had found a practical outlet for the previously useless French learned at school.

The next spring, Michael Streat and John Humphries, both friends acquired through the English canal world, established Blue Line

Cruisers (France) Ltd by opening a hire base at the junction of the Canal du Midi and the Canal latéral à la Garonne in Toulouse. Thirty of us crewed the first seven boats from Bordeaux docks. The party included two viscounts and their ladies, Gerald Norman, Légion d'Honneur, former Paris correspondent of *The Times* and Dr Charles Collins, owner of a Dunkirk Little Ship. Each evening, we would gather in a canalside café to admire ourselves on television as the saga of '*L'Invasion Anglaise*' unfolded. The rest is history: after three changes of ownership, Blue Line is the largest hire cruiser fleet in the world and the waterways of France have experienced an undreamed of prosperity directly resulting from that £50,000 investment at Toulouse in 1969.

Almost every year afterwards, while keeping our own canal boats in England (I was soon to buy an 1895 motorised ice-breaker called *Parry II*) I would join June and John Humphries and their four small girls for a summer holiday boating in France. As chairman of Blue Line, John took no fees from the company, accepting the use of a cruiser in lieu. The firm expanded in the wake of our exploratory cruises as we sought new bases. When we discovered the idyllic Alsatian forests of the Canal de la Marne au Rhin near Strasbourg, we were doubtful if pleasure craft could ever operate without severely disrupting the constant flow of commercial barges passing through radar-controlled locks. Nevertheless, a Blue Line yard was established at Hesse, and there are now more than a dozen, spread through eleven regions. Slowly, the French have copied this British example and as freight traffic has declined, large numbers of pleasure cruisers are welcomed as the economic saviours of a beautiful and historic network.

Until the mid-seventies my navigational skills and expertise had been tested by nothing more taxing than the estuary of the Medway or the lakeland expanses of the Shannon and the Caledonian Canal. At this point Grant came into our lives. As Sir Robert Grant Ferris MP, Deputy Speaker of the House of Commons and ardent explorer of European waterways, he was known to me only as one of several distinguished vice-presidents of the Inland Waterways Association. That was to change when he invited June, John and me as guests aboard his magnificent 18m motor yacht *Melita*. Some years afterwards, shortly before becoming Prime Minister, Margaret Thatcher was to enjoy a cruising holiday on the same vessel. John saw service on naval convoys to Russia at the end of World War II, so declined to join the ship in Majorca, preferring to board at Arles in the more predictable waters of the Rhône. A paid crew of two was already installed when I flew out from London with Grant for the voyage to the French coast. It was decidedly rough and despite *Melita*'s stabilisers we were all quite ill except for Douglas, the deckhand. The weather forced us to seek shelter in Barcelona before running down the Costa Brava and into the mouth of the Rhône at Port St Louis.

We stayed until a little south of Paris and learned much about the ways of large seagoing motor crusiers. Although already planned, our departure at St Dizier was not inappropriate for the previous evening a serious fire had erupted in the engine room. June reached for the nearest extinguisher, only to be chided by our host: 'Don't use that big one. It always makes a mess!'

Boating with Grant came with its full share of excitements. Several years later, *Melita* was replaced by the no less beautiful but smaller *Melitina*, a sophisticated Nelson 42 with a top speed of around 18 knots. By now enobled, Lord Harvington was determined to cross Europe from the Rhine to the Black Sea by the inland route; as completion of the Rhein-Main-Donau Canal was still more than a decade in the future, his plan was to take *Melitina* by motorway from Nuremburg to the Danube. We joined him for a three-week segment between the Rhine Gorge and his craning operation. My most vivid recollection of that journey was of narrowly avoiding a bow-on collision with a fast-moving 2,000-tonne barge in the lock cut at Schweinfurt.

Meanwhile, summer cruises had continued each year on the waterways of France. In 1983 we began on the Saône at St Jean-de-Losne, headed northwards up the Canal de l'Est and continued down the willow-fringed Meuse to Verdun. Here, there were large numbers of immaculate steel-hulled motor yachts from Holland and Germany. Our plastic Bermuda cruiser was possibly one of the originals from the 1969 inaugural progress. It had seen better days. In spite of our experience (even expertise) we felt rather inferior. Both *Parry II* and the Humphries' canal tug *Clevanda* had by now been sold, for our interests were increasingly directed towards Europe. Six weeks after our return to England, we became joint owners of *Avonbay*.

Avonbay was discovered neglected and unwanted in a gravel pit off the Thames at Penton Hook, the same gravel pit I had visited as a twelve year old during summer Sunday picnics in *Chérie*. It was here that I had first hoisted the tan sails of *Dorymouse* and hoped that no one was watching to witness my tentative boat handling attempts. During the intervening years, the largest inland marina in Britain had been established in the workings. Although we knew with accuracy the sort of boat we were seeking, the search was fully expected to take six months. In spite of obvious advantages in being able to visit remote waterways, a trailed cruiser would be too small for the five or six people who would normally comprise the crew. I love converted ex-freight barges, especially snub-nosed Dutchmen. But these are rarely to be found much shorter than 20m overall.

We drew up a list of requirements. Everything pointed in the direction of a cruiser not unlike *Melitina*. Seagoing so that she could reach mainland Europe under her own power; preferably with a steel hull to withstand inevitable contact with river bottoms; comfortably within the 3m air draught and 1.8m water draught dictated by the confines of the smaller French canals; equipped with twin diesel engines for greater peace of mind and manoeuvrability; and priced below £20,000 after improvement and modification. Buying new seemed a non-starter, for Dutch-built production craft of 12m in length only answered our specification at upwards of £50,000.

It is still difficult to believe our fortune in that our ideal was sitting alongside the brokerage pontoons at Penton Hook Marina. *Avonbay* was the first and only vessel we considered. Only five years old, she immediately impressed with her distinctive lines, recalling an overgrown police launch or a pilot vessel. Much later, in the South of France, an admirer asked if she was indeed *un bateau pilote*. Rather than explain otherwise, we assured our quayside friend that she was and he was delighted to be proved correct. In fact, *Avonbay* is a slightly lengthened version of the Western 35, designed purely for pleasure cruising or (with an open stern cockpit) for sea fishing. Almost 12m overall, the hull and totally enclosed superstructure were of Corton steel. A haze of green moss covered her magnificent teak decks and rust streaked the dark-blue hull and white cabin sides. No one had loved her for rather a long time.

Designed by naval architect Robert Tucker, she featured a pronounced curve across her long foredeck and from beam to beam on the cabin roofs. Sliding doors each side provided access to a spacious wheelhouse/saloon where we were later to entertain up to twelve to dinner. By night this area was transformed by several deft movements as a huge folding bed was unfurled. Lifting hatches in the floor revealed a pair of 1.5 litre Leyland diesels installed in their own engine room; here you would need to be a dwarf to describe the area as spacious, but at least there was ample room for stowage of spare gear. Gradually, we were to find corners for a barbecue and charcoal sack; quantities of paint, oil and grease; a folding shopping trolley; spare fenders; a large tool chest and all the other necessities vital for carefree cruising. The helmsman's place was on the port (left) side behind an impressive display of instruments, duplicated for each engine. Illuminated compass and depth-sounder completed the navigational equipment.

Several steep steps led down to the forward cabin: I clambered in and a collection of small spiders made for the furthest recesses. At the entrance was a compact loo with wash basin, facing a large hanging locker. Twin V-berths both had their own ample stowage and shelves, with a chain locker for the anchor cable in the extreme bows.

Moving to the stern, a second large loo was discovered to starboard, complete with wash basin and shower tray; opposite, another hanging locker provided plenty of space for clothes. A passageway opened up into the third cabin, fitted out as galley: gas water heater; full-sized domestic cooker with oven; sink and refrigerator were all installed. To port, what at first seemed to be a single berth could instantly be pulled out to create a generous double bed. Across the back of the boat a locker opened to reveal a steel box for bottled gas, some slightly intimidating hydraulic controls to the twin rudders and a heap of concrete ballast bricks.

Throughout the interior, little expense had been spared in lining surfaces with richly varnished mahogany. This decor became positively lavish in the saloon, where the curved ceiling was covered with attractively grained veneer. The basic finish was to a very high standard. There were several features which were rather tasteless: fitted cushions throughout were covered with serviceable dark-brown waterproof fabric; the floors had been treated to an alarming tile design in bright orange linoleum and the many small curtains featured a similar (but ill-matched) pattern. By the time we had completed our fitting out, these few defects were rectified in our effort to create a fair imitation of the carriages of the Orient Express. Finally, the name *Avonbay* exactly reflected our intention to indulge in widespread river cruising but with the possibility of putting to sea when desired.

Refitting completed, Avonbay *now boasts an outside steering station and inflatable dinghy slung in davits*

It took ten minutes to convince me that *Avonbay* was exactly what we wanted. But what would potential joint owners June and John make of her? Excitedly, I reported the find to June (John prefers to spend weekday afternoons as senior partner at his City law practice), drove 15km to Wimbledon to collect her and youngest daughter Diana for an immediate inspection and we arrived back at Penton Hook within a couple of hours. June positively likes boats; she is also a highly competent interior decorator; given the right equipment she can create gourmet feasts afloat in a pint-sized kitchen. Matters such as engines, gas and water supplies and navigation aids are of very little consequence. It would be up to me as the most technically responsible member of the triumvirate to ensure that these boring aspects of cruising life functioned to perfection. Would she approve of *Avonbay*?

Seen from above, Avonbay *has unexpectedly slim lines. Unlike many similar craft of her type, the bow cabin is located entirely below deck level, providing generous sitting space outside*

Earlier, I had selected two neighbouring craft with similar specifications and prices. Both looked sleeker and quite characterless. I would also show these to the inspection party, thereby cunningly enhancing the boat I had already chosen. This ploy was an utter waste of time. Thirteen-year-old Diana, who had practically been born on a narrow boat at the 1970 IWA National Rally in Guildford, pushed past us in her excitement, found the bow cabin within seconds and said, 'That's mine!' June's enthusiasm was of the contemplative sort, for she was already deciding on furnishing materials and where to hang pictures.

It remained to win John over. First impressions would be important, for the deal we struck was that he would finance the purchase, I would spend much of the coming winter in carrying out modifications and we would share expenses of new equipment and running costs. June and I had at least persuaded him to take a look the following Saturday. I talked hard about *Avonbay*'s obvious qualities of seaworthiness, how fine she would look in her newly applied naval colour scheme and how suitable a vessel she was for a member of the Board of the Thames Water Authority.

Jim Willis, the broker, started the engines. This was the first time we had seen them running and I was secretly horrified at the roar which filled the wheelhouse. Fortunately, John seemed not to mind. I made a note to cover the floor with a generous layer of underlay prior to arrival of the fitted carpets. She handled beautifully as we glided away from the mooring and I remembered with gratitude those exciting voyages aboard *Melita* and *Melitina* which had made us familiar with the control of such a boat. We decided to buy, subject to survey.

A long-standing canal friend, Jim Macdonald would have been the obvious choice of marine surveyor. John's legal foresight counselled against employing him on the basis that we would not want to involve him in any form of dispute should any faults materialise in *Avonbay* at a later date. An unknown and independent surveyor was therefore selected. On the appointed day, the expert arrived, poked around within, tore some floor covering in an abortive attempt to inspect the inside of the hull, glanced alarmingly briefly in the direction of the engines with the comment that they were not really his responsibility and signalled to the waiting crane driver to haul her ashore. Underwater, the hull was found superficially rusty, but (after a few blows with a hammer) perfectly sound. Most of the resulting written report featured defects like corroded interior light switches. *Avonbay* was deemed to be 'in very good condition commensurate with age'.

Buying a boat does not involve quite the same complications as house purchase, however, there were documents to sign as well as transfer of the registration papers. As both vendor and buyer were solicitors, there was every chance of a suitably legal transaction. One final meeting was arranged between broker, previous owner and the purchasers. We learned a little of *Avonbay*'s past, although many tantalising gaps remained to be filled during the next two years. She had cruised from the Severn Estuary to France (a not insignificant voyage), enjoyed a brief career as a hire cruiser in Burgundy, been brought back to Brighton Marina, failed to find a buyer, and then moved to the Upper Thames where she had remained on the market for more than six months. The asking price had already fallen from £16,000 to £14,000. On our production of a £2,000 estimate for cleaning off and painting the hull, we clinched the deal at £12,000. We wanted her, the vendors obviously didn't and were relieved to have made a sale. Both parties were very happy. If they had not produced a photograph showing themselves on board in France, we would have believed their ownership and use of the boat with some difficulty. I already appeared to know more about the equipment installed than they did. The seller's wife made two contributions to discussions. (a) 'The brass steps by each doorway to the wheelhouse look lovely when polished.' (She was absolutely right.) (b) 'There is something a bit wrong with the fridge.' (Again, she was quite correct. Some weeks later we discovered most of the relevant machinery to be missing. This was no problem, however, as June had by then been promised a much improved new model, complete with freezer compartment, as a Christmas present.)

Mid-October was a good time to acquire a boat, for it provided six winter months to make everything perfect for our inaugural cruise the following Easter. Some weeks were to pass before the marina was able to haul *Avonbay* into its cavernous hanger for professional refurbishment of the hull. Meanwhile, as much detachable gear as possible was taken home for attention. Next priority was to remove all traces of rust from cabin tops and sides, a dusty task with power

In good weather, living accommodation is virtually doubled by ample space on a variety of levels. The small stern deck provides convenient stowage for a pair of bicycles

sander that had to be carried out without spoiling the slowly emerging glossy dark-blue paint of the hull. The building was cold and dark so heat and light were imported by positioning photofloods on deck.

Just before Christmas, I was informed that *Avonbay* would shortly be returned to the water and another boat take her place indoors. My labours ended with a final fling of six consecutive days. Brass name plates, each a metre long, were screwed into position. Inspired by those on continental barges, that on the stern proclaimed our port of registration to be Littlehampton.

We visited the International Boat Show in Earl's Court with greater than usual interest. A shopping list included VHF radio telephone, brass hatches for bow deck and stern cabin, dinghy davits, pair of folding bicycles and decorative brass interior lights with matching miniature switches. An afternoon's excursion to Southampton resulted in the purchase of a secondhand manual anchor winch, luxuriously padded helmsman's chair (lately removed from a cross-Channel car ferry) and a stainless steel and teak swimming ladder.

Fitting out continued at weekly intervals, greatly assisted by Jim Macdonald: both engines were stripped down and provided with new heavy-duty 12V batteries; lifebuoys replaced; and new tensioned safety wires threaded through the stanchions. In common with the inhabitants of gipsy caravans and canal narrow boats, further brass decoration appeared: a horn and Francis searchlight from *Parry II* and a mushroom ventilator over the galley. Jim arrived with his mobile welding set and fabricated steel grab rails. These also provided a secure stowage for our selection of boat hooks and a vitally useful boarding plank made by bolting a length of timber to an aluminium ladder.

Strangely, we lacked internal doors between cabins and to all the storage cupboards. This was rectified by a friendly joiner working with a quantity of brass locks, knobs and cabin hooks. Now it was time to introduce a carefully contrived colour scheme for the interior. The bill for recovering all upholstery in dark-blue velvet Dralon was £900. Working single-handed one Saturday, I cut and laid matching deep pile carpet throughout, learning late in the eight-hour operation that success is best achieved by use of a very sharp knife. June's sewing machine worked overtime making two dozen curtains in a pastel blue print. The same material was chosen for cushion covers, duvets, fitted sheets and pillow cases. Table china and even cutlery handles were selected in a similar colour. Pride of place in the saloon was given to an early twentieth-century framed watercolour by H.C. Fox RBA, showing a horse-drawn barge ascending the River Arun and so reflecting our inland waterway interests as well as the nearby Littlehampton port of registry.

During our *Melitina* cruise across Sweden in the spring of 1984 we had admired the shiny golden balls atop many public flagpoles. What could be better as a decoration for our own ensign staff at the stern? A selection in different sizes was located in a Motala hardware shop. Fashioned of thick, coloured glass like Christmas tree baubles, ours provided a finishing touch of real class. Initially, we flew the red duster to which all British yachts are entitled, until John realised that his membership of the Royal Naval Volunteer Reserve entitled him to apply to the Secretary of State for Defence for a warrant to use an undefaced blue ensign. As there are fewer than twenty British yacht clubs so honoured, this move considerably enhanced our prestige in home waters or when meeting compatriots abroad. More often it resulted in total confusion as to our country of origin.

Avonbay's circumference was already ringed with heavy-duty black D-shaped fendering. As further protection for her topsides, we hung four air-filled white fenders to port and a similar number to starboard, instituting a rule that these would be lifted on deck at all times except when coming alongside or working through flights of closely spaced locks.

A rarely exercised bonus for members of the Thames Water Authority Board was provision of a free mooring. John applied for his and we were directed to a floating pontoon alongside Molesey Lock at

Left: Jim Macdonald at work on the new outside steering station. Right: Eric Diggins, certified compass adjustor, uses his pelorus (a rotatable compass dial fitted with sighting mechanism) to check inaccuracies on our own equipment, shortly before we set sail for France

Hampton Court. Being regarded by the river staff as something akin to an official inspection craft, we made frequent journeys along the Thames that summer, celebrating birthdays on board, entertaining several Members of Parliament and taking the Thames Chairman for his first excursion afloat. Arriving at TWA headquarters in Reading, John sprang ashore and with the tone of authority befitting a Board member, announced to the nearest employee 'We're taking on water.' Our surprise was considerable when several men shortly came rushing from the building carrying a portable pump, thinking that we were about to sink on their frontage! I explained that we merely wished to top up the drinking water tanks.

Equipped with steering in the enclosed wheelhouse, *Avonbay* emerged as less than perfect in fair weather. The crew would be lying on deck sunbathing while the hapless helmsman (usually me) sweltered within. Once again, Jim came to our aid by adding a second, outside, steering station aft of the saloon. Wheel, hydraulic pump, throttle controls and basic instruments all had to be duplicated. No fewer than ten additional pipes and cables were added, not counting electrical connections. Now the captain commanded a much enhanced all-round view from his folding seat on the stern deck. With practice and judicious use of engines in forward and reverse gear at the same time, it was possible to manoeuvre with impressive accuracy. All our improvements demanded a revaluation for insurance purposes; the resulting figure was more than twice the original purchase price.

Anxious to test our abilities in more demanding waters, we mounted an expedition into the Thames tideway during Diana's October half-term holiday. Although lifelong residents of Greater London, we were fairly unfamiliar with the fast-flowing reaches through the City. For several days 'home' was a berth in St Katherine's Dock, one of few satisfactory pleasure craft marinas in the capital. Behaving like tourists, we fed the ravens at the Tower, gazed out towards the distant sea from the high-level footway on Tower Bridge and entertained a succession of visitors on board.

As a second winter approached, I enrolled for two local authority night-school classes. The course in marine diesel engine maintenance never started for lack of support, while I withdrew from navigation tuition after the fifth session, unable to guarantee weekly attendance over a six-month period. We would have to reach the Continent on a combination of commonsense and the basics gleaned from articles in the technical press.

2

Hampton Court to Calais

A SATURDAY morning in late May. We woke at 3.50am and were through Teddington lock by 4.15am, just as dawn was breaking. Excitement was intense. Our impressively early start was dictated by the state of the tide which we intended to have in our favour for the entire run to the Medway Estuary. Food supplies had been loaded at Molesey the previous day and we had cruised past the twisted Tudor chimneys of Hampton Court Palace, tinged red in the sunset.

It was almost high water at Strawberry Hill, the broad reaches of the Thames lapping at the lawns of Radnor Gardens, my childhood playground. Familiar buildings passed by: my first school at Pope's Villa; Twickenham Embankment with chlorine-tainted memories of the public swimming baths; Jacobean Ham House, glimpsed through the trees; Marble Hill House and then the heights of Richmond Hill. Round a slight bend, Richmond's grey stone bridge came into sight. With me on board were June, John, Diana and her schoolfriend Auriole. A pause while the gates of Richmond Half Tide Weir were raised and then on to Isleworth, Syon Park and Kew Gardens, a remarkably rural reach for somewhere so close to London. The river stretched out ahead like a placid lake; for a time *Avonbay* was the only

A nineteenth-century lifeboat goes to the aid of a vessel in difficulties on the Goodwin Sands

19

moving object in this tranquil picture.

Firmly believing that marine engines benefit from gentle treatment, we had by now instituted a golden rule never to exceed 2,000rpm (slightly more than half power), except for emergency bursts. The two Leylands purred away almost silent from the decktop steering station, giving us 8 or 9 knots by the time we found the tide ebbing off Hammersmith at 7am. To port was the Georgian terraced house of dear old A.P. Herbert, who loved this tideway so much. I once helped him hand-feed the terrapins in a small pool at the end of his riverside garden after he had presided over the AGM of the Inland Waterways Association. London sleeps late on Saturday mornings: we noticed few people and little road traffic until the Lower Pool was reached at 8am. Commercial river freight is now negligible and in 1985 the redevelopment of Docklands – Europe's biggest urban building site – had hardly started. The Thames seemed strangly unused and neglected.

We surged onwards, noting Wren's grey spire of St Anne's, Limehouse close to the entrance of the Regent's Canal, gateway to the secretive waterways north of London. Navigation was deceptively easy as we ticked off the buoys, one by one, on the chart. Blackwell Point was a highlight, for here we used the VHF radio telephone for the very first time and obtained an instant response: 'Avonbay calling Barrier Control. Do you read me?' 'Barrier Control to Avonbay. Please pass through the green channel.' Ahead, nine silver-topped piers of the massive flood barrier spanned Woolwich Reach from shore to shore. We followed instructions and headed for a 60m gap identified by illuminated green arrows.

Onwards from Tilbury where the waterway widened, coastal shipping increased in frequency, although we were more affected by the wash of fast-moving pleasure craft. With the tide starting to turn, we passed the Nore Sand buoy at 2.25pm and set a course across the Sheerness Middle Sand and the mouth of the Medway. Feeling ridiculously brave and confident in such an expanse of water, we were somewhat chastened when a windsurfer nipped under our bows! Confirming that we had calculated our tides with satisfying accuracy, a strong flow now carried us past the marshy shores of the Lower Medway.

For many years, we had known and greatly liked General Sir Hugh Stockwell. After the political fiasco of Suez, where he had commanded the intended invasion force, he retired to a cottage on the nearly moribund Kennet & Avon Canal in Wiltshire. He was to devote the last twenty-five years of his life to fighting for that beautiful waterway's restoration, declaring: 'I had to lose one canal in 1956 and don't intend to lose another!' Another of Hughie's dictums was: 'Time spent in reconnaissance is never wasted.' June and I had acted on this excellent advice shortly beforehand and made a car tour of the tidal Medway to locate a suitable mooring for *Avonbay* before embarking on the slightly worrying Channel crossing proper. Some establishments claimed to be full to capacity or so lacked interest in our enquiries that we saw no reason to give them our custom. Gillingham Marina boasted an impressive security system and attractive clubhouse, membership of which was included in the £85 mooring fee for four weeks.

In a single day, we had travelled 117km from Teddington; France was appreciably closer. Up to now, we had never been more than 2km offshore. The next stage would be rather different, as we took a broad sweep round the Kent coast before heading for mainland Europe. Many engine difficulties result from dirt in the fuel. Heavy weather can shake up all kinds of rubbish that lurks in the bottom of diesel tanks, so Jim and I paid a visit to Gillingham to carefully clean fuel filters and give the machinery a final check. As they had come to know *Avonbay* well by now, we were delighted when Jim and his wife Mig accepted our invitation to join us for the sea passage to France. I had complete faith in his ability to cope with any engine failure we might suffer. Distress flares were added to the safety equipment.

Settled weather was slow to arrive, but towards the end of June conditions seemed reasonable. On Friday 21, I drove with June to the Medway, met up with Mig and Jim, transferred my car to a safe park in Dover and waited for John to come in by train from the City. At high water, *Avonbay* was switched from the mudberth, fuelled up and moved to a floating buoy well out in the river. Passing ships and a strong wind gave us a rather uncomfortable night afloat.

Next day, the forecast was dubious, so rather than suffer another twenty-four hours bouncing on the buoy we spent the Saturday cruising up the Medway through Allington lock and on to East Farleigh, upstream of Maidstone. Arrangements had been made for the Allington lock-keeper to lower us back to the tideway at 5am, Sunday. Bright and calm conditions convinced us we could try to run for Ramsgate or even further. A forecast obtained over VHF radio was encouraging and we were off Garrison Point by 8.30am. Rather than risk the muddy waters of the Swale inshore of the Isle of Sheppey, we headed for the shipping lanes of the Thames Estuary and continued due east down the well-buoyed Princes Channel as Whitstable, Herne Bay and the Isle of Thanet slipped past, well to the south. Several magnificent sailing barges provided interest and we had no difficulty in locating the East Margate buoy before turning down the coast to the North Foreland lighthouse. Now running into a choppy sea, *Avonbay* was pitching considerably. The antique ship's bell in her wheelhouse tolled endlessly: no one could be bothered to wrap a cloth round the clapper. Spare cushions were hastily pushed into the crockery cupboard and bottles stowed with care. Everyone, I noticed, had gone a little quiet. Lack of experience and little knowledge about how much punishment our boat could take suggested an early halt in the safety of Ramsgate's outer harbour. True, we had noted several tiny open fishing dinghies tossing at anchor well out to sea, but it wasn't worth taking any unnecessary risks.

On checking prospects with British Telecom's Marineline forecast, any immediate notion of going to France had receded. John, Mig and Jim departed for their respective Monday morning work activities. This left June and me to pack the boat up, recover the car from Dover and so would begin the weary weather-watching process all over again. It was rather depressing. Many are the tales of cruising holidays dominated by long periods bottled up in port.

Next morning, to my surprise, investigations over the harbour wall revealed a near glassy calm. It was not at all in keeping with the latest telephone forecast (Force 3-4, gusting Force 5). June came to look. I consulted the crew of a Fisheries Protection launch, indicated *Avonbay* and asked them for any opinion. 'Go now,' they suggested. 'It won't get any better!' Hardly waiting to consider this advice (which subsequently proved to be perfectly accurate) we cast off. Coastguard and Customs had already been notified of our planned movements. That was the last contact *Avonbay* had with English soil.

My chart of the Dover Strait provides a vivid record of that Monday's voyage. Coffee-stained and bearing pathetic little pencilled rings as we recorded each buoy, it shows our course out of Ramsgate, into the Gull Stream and down the coast at a safe distance to Deal. To port were the notorious ship-wrecking Goodwin Sands, parts of which briefly dry at low water. My family tree, researched with some accuracy, clearly traces my descent from Godwin, Earl of the West Saxons, in the eleventh century. While saddened at not being linked with a more likeable personality, I was fascinated to learn of a legend claiming that this treacherous area once formed an island in the Earl's estate. We decided that now was not an appropriate moment to explore.

Midday saw us off the South Goodwin lightship. Dover's cliffs faded astern in a haze as we set course for Cap Blanc Nez, hopefully making due allowance for tidal streams. By now the sea was producing a long, lolloping swell: we rode this comfortably, rarely taking any spray on deck. There was no hint of the French coast, some 24km (15 sea miles) south-east.

After dozens of car-ferry crossings on the Dover–Calais run, I was firmly convinced that all the while one or more passenger craft would be visible. Never mind any navigational inaccuracy: we would merely follow the ships! After a while, we realised with growing surprise that not another vessel was in view anywhere. June scanned endlessly with the binoculars. No land; no other traffic. Was it possible to get things wildly wrong and finish up in the North Sea or the Atlantic? There was plenty of time to consider all the possibilities.

Just about the time when France and England were equidistant and there was consequently no difficulty in deciding whether we should continue or turn back, the waves started to grow much larger. Soon, there were white horses and deep troughs. Steering now demanded total concentration, taking each wave bow-on, while attempting to stay on the correct course. I throttled back to around 5 knots, but this only slightly reduced the endless pounding as we crashed into one wave after another. Water poured over the foredeck, sluicing past the wheelhouse doors. I was heartily glad that *Avonbay* was totally enclosed: there is no doubt that an open boat would have been overwhelmed. The pronounced curve of the decks threw the sea off quickly, but it was worrying not knowing how much of this treatment we could stand. A hovercraft appeared at high speed, seeming to be making straight for us. We altered course for several minutes to avoid a collision. Then nothing more in sight for a whole hour.

The decision to leave Ramsgate had been mine. We hadn't even telephoned John to say what we were up to. Just once, instead of rising over an oncoming wave, *Avonbay* buried her nose in it. Looking through the toughened glass of the windscreen, there was nothing ahead but water for a full five seconds. That was the worst moment. Fortunately June never fussed or questioned my ability to cope. Later, we agreed that we had both been secretly rather worried! By now, the unfixed steering seat which had threatened to fling itself across the wheelhouse had been dismantled and stowed. For the remaining hours of the passage, I stood at the wheel, bracing myself with one hand on the instrument panel bulkhead. Moving about the boat was only possible by crawling on the floor. To have ventured outside would have been suicidal, resulting in being washed overboard within seconds. Had we needed to abandon ship, the dinghy could never have been launched amid this turmoil. The stern loo now began to fill by siphoning sea in from outside. As the safety cock is situated deep inside the engine room, June quietly pumped the bowl clear every ten minutes. All the time, I fervently hoped that the engines would keep running: to go below and try to clean filters or bleed the fuel lines in these conditions was too dreadful to contemplate. Wonderfully, the machinery thudded away without missing a beat. By any standards, the sea was rough and having no sight of land or shipping emphasised our isolation.

Suddenly, we noticed the orange hull of a Townsend Thoresen ferry, fast approaching from astern. It was the ill-fated *Herald of Free Enterprise,* which was to sink off Zeebrugge with such tragic loss of life just twenty months later. Assuming she, too, was bound for Calais, we were greatly encouraged and after she had overhauled us we followed in her wake until she disappeared from view. But there was still no hint of the French coast. June was glued to the binoculars and eventually announced with due elation that she thought she could see a buoy. She was right! According to the chart, it should have been the RCW marker, with Cap Blanc Nez beyond to the south-west. Half an hour later, we were close enough to read its lettering. *Avonbay* was dead on course!

Until this journey and close study of the chart, I had never before realised during all those car-ferry crossings that Calais Harbour can only be approached by running for several km close to the coast to avoid shallow water. We rounded another buoy and entered the narrow channel leading north-east past sand-dunes to our destination. Now there were numerous passenger vessels passing in each direction. *Avonbay* felt like the filling in a sandwich as these monsters raced by on each side. By this time the sea was reasonably quiet, so it was possible to leave the wheel for a moment, clamber on deck and hoist a French courtesy flag. I also ran up a yellow Q flag, requesting Customs clearance as soon as we were in port. This was totally ignored by the authorities: a disappointing reaction for us beginners, for we were trying hard to behave in a manner appropriate to our blue ensign. We could see the sharply pitched red-tiled roofs of waterfront buildings and the Gothic bell tower of Calais' *Hôtel de Ville.* Real French children waved from the pierhead at the harbour entrance. A complicated array of light signals controlled shipping movements; unable to interpret them, we rounded the stone groyne and slipped into the quiet water beyond, hoping that a ferry was not about to emerge.

The view ahead was thankfully familiar. Car-ferry terminal to port and the locked entrance to the Bassin de Ouest to starboard. It was just on 6pm, eight long hours since leaving Ramsgate. Written application to the harbourmaster had already reserved a berth for *Avonbay*, so we secured to the bottom of a weed-festooned ladder. June was first ashore, followed a second later by me. We had arrived in France!

Steady rain was falling; it was cold and windy. Enquiries soon indicated that we had missed being able to enter the *bassin* at the top of the tide. We made for a telephone kiosk to ring home with our news. A few seconds later, June had John on the line: 'Darling, you were quite right about the weather. We have taken your advice to pack the boat up and will come home tomorrow.' The tease fell flat as John answered: 'I suppose you're in Calais.' He was as pleased as us and throughout that day had been visualising our slow progress across the Channel. We were really thrilled to have made it and our long summer cruise to Burgundy was suddenly a reality. It had been the most exciting day of my life. What better now than a celebration dinner ashore? Le Channel restaurant beckoned from the nearby Boulevard de la Résistance. But after such conspicious success so far, it seemed unwise to leave faithful *Avonbay* tied to a quay on a fast-falling tide. We decided to eat our first meal of the day on board.

In the Outer Harbour, several buoys were laid where boats could await opening of the *bassin*'s tidal gates. All except one were already occupied by fishing vessels. I started the engines, June positioned herself by the pulpit with a boathook and we made for the vacant buoy as a cruiser appeared with identical intentions. Just like two cars racing for the same parking meter, the other boat arrived first, failed to grab the ring and backed off for a second try. Now it was our turn to demonstrate some boatmanship. June deftly threaded our bow warp through the buoy and made fast. The opposition breasted up on an unoccupied fishing boat. Game, set and match to *Avonbay!*

A ghastly night followed. For reasons best known to the harbour authorities, a dredger started operations nearby in the early hours. Added to this was the wash from car ferries manoeuvring a short distance away, so we rolled diabolically. About 1am, I scrambled out of bed to stuff cushions back in the crockery cupboard. It seemed extremely unfair to be thrown around in harbour almost as badly as at sea! Our suffering came to an end at 5.20am with high water and the opening of the Bassin de Ouest gates. Contact was duly made with Capitaine Henri and a 1,400 francs payment made for a month's mooring to a pontoon. This could have been avoided by using the unsupervised public quay opposite, but we decided to buy peace of mind. An early lunch ashore, then it was time to board a taxi for the short trip to the ferry terminal to return to England. We had been in France for less than twenty hours. Although due to return in under five weeks, we hated abandoning *Avonbay*, a plucky little ship whose performance had been faultless.

Calais Hôtel de Ville, seen from the canal that leads into the French interior

3

The Liaison

Vegetable punts in the Clairmarais network of waterways at St Omer, early twentieth century. The scene had changed little ninety years on

FREQUENT brief journeys through Calais had suggested it was ugly and over-filled with British day-trippers. My dislike of the town increased when I consumed my worst French restaurant meal at the greatest ever cost. These opinions changed on making our thankful landfall in June. Then, when five of us arrived by car in late July to start a 1,065km voyage to Burgundy and found *Avonbay* in fine shape, we had to agree that it was perhaps not such a bad place after all. No contact had been made earlier with French Customs, so John and I drove to their office near the lighthouse. Unless they have goods to declare, arriving foreign pleasure craft are excused Customs inspection; but we were anxious to obtain written evidence of entry to France. Thus, we could avoid payment of French Value Added Tax amounting to 18.6 per cent of the boat's estimated value, provided she was to be used for less than six months in every twelve during the next three years. After that, brief export to another country would begin another tax-free cycle. A bored Customs officer listened to our request for an official stamp on a document we had prepared. 'Not necessary,' he repeated several times. We tried a new approach: 'Perhaps you could kindly stamp the paper as a souvenir?' The officer beamed, complied with our request and we thereby saved several thousand pounds.

June's shopping habits long ago earned her the name of 'Mrs Squirrel'. Never sure when we would find the next food store, she begins each cruise by loading several trollies at a supermarket, meaning that subsequent purchases are restricted to fresh food supplies. We returned to the Bassin de Ouest with sufficient food and drink to last for several weeks. Sadly, a costly but unexchangeable British gas cylinder was discarded in favour of two French ones, so taking care of fuel for cooking and the fridge. I drove across town to a recommended garage where the car was to be parked under cover until collected by friends and taken to Burgundy, ready for our return to England. Advance payment of 533 francs was requested, a substantial amount for four weeks storage. When next seen, the previously spotless paintwork was splattered with mud, suggesting it had enjoyed some illicit adventures in the Calais hinterland during our absence.

At 10.45am the next day, the single set of tidal gates at the mouth of our *bassin* opened, followed by a rush of fishing boats and cruisers. All except *Avonbay* headed out to sea. We turned right, ran up the harbour and straight through the now level chamber of the Écluse Carnot into another large *bassin* beyond. This in turn leads to the Canal de Calais. We moored for a final visit to the shops. Calais is the country's leading passenger and vehicle port and the seventh biggest freight harbour. Our small motor yacht seemed very vulnerable as huge container ships jostled at the quays. By the time we were ready to leave, our *péniche*-sized Écluse de la Batellerie had closed for lunch. Charles de Freycinet, Minister of Public Works, 1877–9, devised a programme for the enlargement of several thousand km of French waterways, making them suitable for Flemish barges, loading 300 tonnes. The resulting Freycinet Act has given its name to a standard lock size, admitting barges 38.5 x 5m. This was the first of many hundreds we were to negotiate.

There is nothing very remarkable about the 29.5km of Canal de Calais, opened in 1681 under Louis XIV. But for British visitors it provides an undemanding introduction without the difficulties of other Channel connections at Dunkerque, Gravelines or the Somme and Seine estuaries. Few *péniches* were encountered that afternoon as Calais fell away behind. We were in a typical flat Flanders landscape. All this had been English for 210 years; Henry VIII's Field of the Cloth of Gold, scene of his meeting with François I in 1520, lay to the south between Guines and Ardres. However, our concentration was fixed on matters practical rather than historical, for long stretches of the waterway were thick with wrinkled carpets of rotting duckweed. Soon, both water intakes were blocked and the engines began to overheat. Much of that afternoon, I crouched in the engine room, cleaning one filter after the other as we alternated between the two motors. Not a very auspicious beginning. We hoped that conditions would soon improve. Small groups of red-brick cottages with tiled roofs appeared on the banks, under a leaden sky.

Regular canal travel in France during sixteen years should have prepared us for indifferent weather, especially here in the north. But somehow I always envisaged this first voyage in *Avonbay* would begin with a hot sun beating down on deck, necessitating frequent halts to plunge into the pellucid water. Day after day, a Gallic heatwave would follow the wisps of early morning mist. By 9am it would be too hot to wear more than the skimpiest of bathing costumes (and there are waterways in the south where we were to discover boaters who dispensed with even them!) The Canal de Calais obviously did not understand our requirements; indeed the weather was not to greatly improve until we arrived in Paris. It would be false to claim that this did not matter; that we equally appreciated the softened colours of the French countryside with buildings enshrouded in a fine drizzle. We minded quite a bit and were to put in some ambitiously long daily runs in the hope that the sun would appear once we were a little further south.

Le Pont d'Ardres is a curious X-shaped bridge spanning a four-way water crossroads at the head of the Ardres branch. Now rebuilt in concrete, it was originally a most elegant stone complex known as the Pont Sans Pareil. As a seventeen year old, I vividly recall staggering over it under the weight of a Union Jack decorated rucksac, during the early stages of a hitch-hiking expedition to Spain.

Several times we noted various red-brick buildings of some antiquity. Pierced at intervals by tiny open windows, we first assumed them to be fortifications. Eating ashore that evening we were informed that they were designed as forcing houses for raising chicory, an explanation sufficiently unlikely that it could have been correct. Dinner, taken in a waterside restaurant after the canal's sole lock at Henuin, was a bizarre affair. We were the only customers in a large dining-room, claimed by Madame to normally be packed with holiday-makers who came for the fishing. All started well enough, until the service became progressively slower. Our hostess was seen to have a rather unhealthy relationship with a bottle. Dessert was produced with some difficulty: by then she could barely stand unaided. Another prolonged delay and coffee was literally thrown onto the table. Her addition of the bill owed little to the normal laws of arithmetic – Madame made several wild stabs towards an acceptable total and was genuinely thankful when John relieved her of the task. In this lonely spot, she was no longer equal to running the business single-handed. We wondered what tragedy had placed her in this situation. Next morning, she had regained her composure and was energetically

Opposite: *Waterways from London to Paris. Route shown in bold is the course taken by* Avonbay

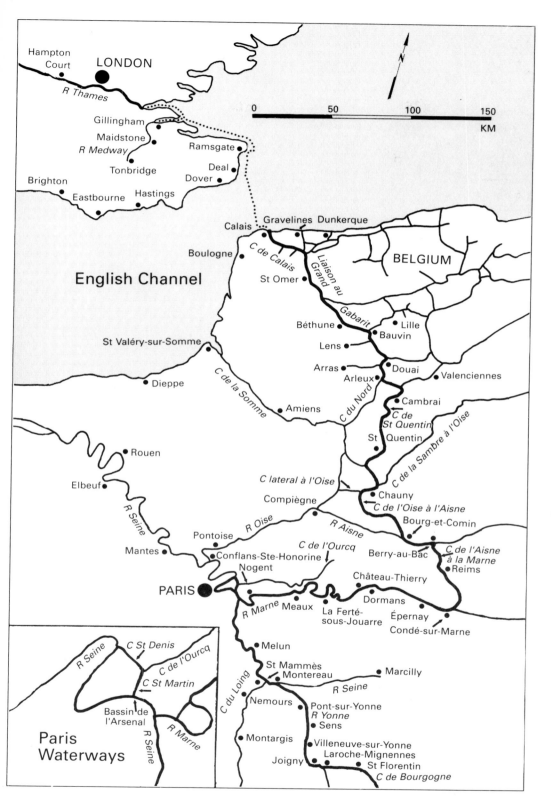

LONDON

Hampton
Court

R Thames

Gillingham

Maidstone

R Medway

Ramsgate

Tonbridge

Deal

Dover

Brighton

Eastbourne

Hastings

English Channel

Calais

Gravelines Dunkerque

Boulogne

C de Calais

BELGIUM

St Omer

Liaison au Grand Gabarit

Béthune

Lille

Bauvin

Lens

St Valéry-sur-Somme

Arras

Douai

Arleux

Valenciennes

C du Nord

Dieppe

Cambrai

Amiens

C de St Quentin

St Quentin

C de la Sambre à l'Oise

Rouen

C lateral à l'Oise

Elbeuf

Chauny

Compiègne

C de l'Oise à l'Aisne

R Oise

R Aisne

Bourg-et-Comin

R Seine

Pontoise

C de l'Ourcq

Berry-au-Bac

C de l'Aisne à la Marne

Mantes

Conflans-Ste-Honorine

Nogent

Reims

PARIS

Château-Thierry

R Marne

Meaux

Dormans

La Ferté-sous-Jouarre

Épernay

Condé-sur-Marne

Melun

C St Denis

R Seine

C de l'Ourcq

C St Martin

St Mammès

Marcilly

Montereau

C du Loing

R Seine

Bassin de l'Arsenal

Nemours

Pont-sur-Yonne

R Yonne

R Marne

R Seine

Sens

Montargis

Villeneuve-sur-Yonne

Paris
Waterways

Laroche-Mignennes

Joigny

St Florentin

C de Bourgogne

29

laying tables for an influx of clients that we suspected would not materialise. Her parting gesture was to pick a large bunch of sweet peas from the garden. These she brought to the quayside as a present for the British sailors on *Avonbay*.

Turning right at a T-junction, we entered the canalised River Aa. This soon merged with the Liaison au Grand Gabarit (Large Gauge Link Waterway), comprising a succession of old enlarged navigations extending 180km from Dunkerque to the Belgian frontier beyond Valenciennes. Sizeable direction boards lined the bank, emphasising that we had left a country lane for a motorway. Huge tonnages of goods, including coal from the main colliery area of France, are carried by close-coupled barges propelled by powerful pusher units, small coasters and the ubiquitous 350-tonne capacity *péniches*. Unwelcoming sloping sides of concrete are attacked by almost constant wash, making difficulties for pleasure craft intent on mooring. Advance planning was now necessary to locate suitable overnight halts, ideally in the smaller side canals remaining from sixties modernisation. Such possibilities are clearly marked on the highly detailed *Carte Guide* published with commentaries in French and English. The series covers most routes nationwide; although expensive, no explorer should venture afloat without them.

St Omer is one of several historic towns now bypassed. Rather than double back through a lock giving access to this agreeable place, we remained on the through route, catching glimpses of a network of tiny

Le Pont d'Ardres, a highly unusual waterway junction on the Canal de Calais. This exquisite engraving is taken from A Treatise on Inland Navigation or the Art of making Rivers navigable, of making Canals in all Sorts of Soils and of Constructing Locks and Sluices, *by Charles Vallancey (Dublin, 1763). The complex bridge has since been reconstructed in concrete* (Courtesy, David Horsfall)

waterways threading through the Audomarais, a swampy expanse mainly devoted to cultivation of vegetables. Here, small punts complete with boatman can be hired for a root-level tour of onion fields and cabbages.

Infrequent locks provide chambers 144m long with an average rise and fall of about 4m. Selecting the appropriate VHF channel from the *Guide*, we called up keepers by radio telephone, more often than not arriving to find gates open ready to receive us. Small pleasure craft were specially catered for by at least one pair of floating bollards set in the chamber walls: once our lines were attached, they rose with the water.

British canal engineering techniques are rarely encountered on the Continent, for most of our navigations remained firmly fixed in the eighteenth century while those abroad were being enlarged and modernised. A notable exception is the impressive Fontinettes vertical lift at Arques. Twin *péniche*-sized caissons are suspended in a lacework of cast iron, replacing a flight of five rather shorter eighteenth-century locks. Edwin Clark won the design competition with his proposals for a device to overcome the 13.13m ascent. His very similar Anderton lift, connecting the Trent & Mersey Canal with the Weaver near Northwich, had successfully begun operations in 1875. Les Fontinettes was inaugurated some thirteen years later and remained in service until it was ousted by a 3,000 tonne capacity lock in 1967. The lift survives as a tourist attraction, complete with barge aloft in one of the raised tanks. Tours are available at certain times.

The new waterway provided a graphic impression of the direction now being taken by French inland water transport. Readings off the echo-sounder showed a consistent depth of more than 5m in the centre, enabling giant barge units to roar past at high speed. Smaller 350-tonne *péniches* were experiencing hard times here as elsewhere. Dozens lay idle, two or three abreast at Béthune.

A small Freycinet chamber lay disused alongside the big Cuinchy lock. Its keeper was installed in a modern concrete eyrie; we much preferred the old control cabin, a delightful (if derelict) structure of cast iron and glass which would not have looked out of place as a Victorian garden conservatory.

From the *Guide*, we identified an overnight escape from the *mêlée* of the canal by entering an old portion of navigation leading to the centre of La Bassée. Sure enough, there were newly installed pontoons almost directly outside a supermarket and within 200m of a cheap and agreeable restaurant. We tied up, soon to be joined by a large group of teenagers, armed with drinks and a music cassette player. Sensing that amiable banter would degenerate into rowdy vandalism with the onset of darkness and the effects of alcohol, it seemed we might be in for a

PAS-DE-CALAIS   CANAL D'AIRE

ÉCLUSES DE CUINCHY

LILLE	BRUAY	101	BÉTHUNE	012
DOM	ÉCLUSE	1359	AIRE	319
LILLE	TEMPS DE GARE	5045	SAINT-OMER	4953
DOUAI		3651	DUNKERQUE	9247
PARIS	LA VILLETTE	5821	CALAIS	9359

disturbed night. Several years before, while car-camping near the Marne, I had been the target of a nocturnal group of wild motor cyclists. Such an experience was not to be repeated. On moving on again, we fortunately discovered a convenient gravel wharf at the Bauvin entrance to the Canal de la Deule.

Next day, steady rain did little to enhance the colliery area leading to Douai, a city where tourist souvenirs include brass miners' lamps and little sacks of chocolate wrapped in black cellophane like lumps of coal. More barge docks, crumbling warehouses in *art deco* concrete and occasional hints that the authorities were introducing rudimentary pleasure-boat facilities gave us no reason to linger.

Arleux marks an exceptionally wide junction at the start of the Canal du Nord. We could see several dozen barges moored up the line before the first lock. While this would have offered the quickest route to Paris via the Oise, we were becoming weary with modern concrete channels, for the Nord was completed only in 1965. Work was well advanced by the outbreak of World War I but severe shelling caused widespread destruction. By 1960, chronic congestion on the parallel Canal de St Quentin brought the project alive again. We chose the smaller, older and more intimate St Quentin route. From the water, Arleux appears to consist of little more than a barge chandlers, run by the Arnoult family. This kind of establishment was once common on French canals. Few now remain, so we agreed it was our duty to inspect their stock. Fuel and water (not always easy to find) were laid on at the jetty. Ashore, a well-filled provisioning shop topped up our fresh food supplies. Among the tinned peas and crates of beer were massive brass-bound barge steering wheels, heaps of chunky anchor chain, buckets, steel cables, rubber gloves with which to handle them, waterproof suits, boots and a wide selection of huge brass horns of the type that can alert lock keepers 3km off. It was disappointing that *Avonbay* was fully equipped.

On a shelf between tins of grease and a pile of bargeman's caps stood a large glass case containing an exquisite horse-drawn model *péniche*. Complete in every detail down to the rows of tiny copper fastenings in the wooden planking, I wanted it more than anything I had seen since discovery of *Avonbay* some eighteen months before. Fortunately, the proprietor firmly said it was not for sale: had it been, I might easily have come away 5,000 francs poorer!

At last the weather brightened as we continued down the Liaison past a succession of lakeside villages frequented by anglers. Faced with a choice of routes at K3, we chose a longer course via Le Bassin Rond. The canal widened into a broad pool at Étrun, with sailing dinghies, motor boats and the first hire craft we had seen since Calais, forty-eight hours earlier.

Opposite, above: *Charming though derelict, this nineteenth-century keeper's cabin stands alongside the Écluses de Cuinchy, Canal d'Aire, now absorbed into the Liaison au Grand Gabarit.* Below: *Les Fontinettes vertical boat lift, dating from 1888. Note péniche in the raised caisson, left. The structure has been replaced by a modern deep lock*

4

Napoléon's Canal

NORTHERN France has some charming countryside and the Canal de
St Quentin is an unusually pleasant waterway. Its other great
attraction is a passage through the Grand Souterrain or Bony Tunnel.
At 5,670m, it is the longest canal tunnel now open in Europe (or as far
as I know in the world).

Before reaching the St Quentin proper, beyond Cambrai, five
duplicated locks had to be negotiated on the Upper Escaut. In 1964,
shortly before much traffic was siphoned off by the Canal du Nord,
this line was handling 8 million tonnes of goods annually. Traffic has
since reduced greatly, but it remains an efficient route where lock
delays are rare. While timber platforms forming guides at each end of
the locks were dangerously decayed and the banks frequently in need
of repair, we generally recorded 2m of water under the boat. Keepers
were both efficient and friendly, the one at Thun-l'Évêque selling us
cabbage and beans from his garden.

On the outskirts of Cambrai, we passed a pair of rusting cast-iron
gates set between crumbling stone pillars. Beyond the undergrowth on
the other side could be seen a beautiful white *château* set in its own
park. We thought no more of this at the time until eighteen months

Helping a donkey
ashore from his
stable aboard a
berrichon *barge,*
1897

34

later when we were returning from a cruise to Alsace and leaving nothing to chance, it had been decided to book one night in an hotel. Anywhere within a 50km radius of Cambrai would have suited. We consulted a guide book with care and chose Le Château de la Motte Fénélon – after all, Monsieur Michelin did award the restaurant four crossed knives and forks! Driving through the municipal housing estate which occupied part of the *château* grounds, provided some disappointment. The Easter cruise had been beset with problems; now it was snowing. We were seeking a little luxury.

Then, ahead in the dying light we saw our hotel: a superb eighteenth-century mansion, grand without being huge. 'Time for a swim before dinner,' I told the girls, recalling mention of an indoor heated pool. A very young man languidly came to the reception desk, visibly annoyed that we had interrupted his television programme. He confirmed our bookings and casually mentioned that the restaurant was closed. This we refused to accept and the subsequent meal – although of a high standard – was rather a strained affair. Expecting to be conducted up a grand staircase to our rooms, we were instead given instructions to reach a series of prefabricated huts in the snow-covered grounds. En route, we passed the swimming pool, a small tank of brown water on which the previous autumn's leaves floated. The accommodation was ice cold. 'No, it is not possible for you to sleep in the *château*,' we were told. And 'No, there are no other guests tonight.' After a long drive, we couldn't face searching for an alternative establishment, so decided to make the best of a very bad situation. When settling our considerable bill next day, I asked why there was no mooring stage on the canal by the watergate; no welcoming sign to attract passing pleasure boaters to what was, after all, an exceedingly good restaurant. 'Good gracious,' came the reply. 'We wouldn't want that sort of person coming here!'

Alongside the second of the two Cambrai locks, we tied up in a basin for the night. The city has long ago recovered from savage bombardment in World War I and exploration detained us well into the following morning. My favourite feature was a *boulangerie*, with ornate *art nouveau* façade, lovingly decorated in cream.

Climbing swiftly towards the summit, the waterway penetrates hilly terrain. Between *écluses* 12 and 13, a one-way system round the island at Pont des Grenouillères, will long be remembered as where we glimpsed an otter, gleaming in the water ahead. Few barges hindered our progress so that as the day wore on we realised there was every chance of catching the 7.30pm tunnel tow at Vendhuile. There was then no *Carte Guide* covering the St Quentin and navigational details were scarce. Latest information suggested that commercial and pleasure traffic would link to form a *rame* and be drawn by electric chain tug through the Grand Souterrain, along the cutting which follows and into the 1,098m Lesdins Tunnel at the far end. To be thus under tow for over 20km might take eight hours, so we anticipated an exciting night.

At the Écluse Bosquet, last lock before the summit, the keeper asked us to make all reasonable speed, for the tunnel tow had already departed, half an hour ahead of schedule. We caught up with the *rame* a little before 7pm, finding that tug, three *péniches* and a small French sailing cruiser were about to disappear underground. A line was flung to the sloop at the rear and made fast to the bollard on *Avonbay*'s foredeck. We silenced the engines and found ourselves gliding effortlessly towards the portal. Too many fatal cases of asphyxiation have taken place in canal tunnels lacking ventilation systems to allow motors to be used. Sodium lights at 50m intervals provided illumination, while timber fenders prevented damage should we steer too close to the towpath. It was all rather different from the rabbit hole of our own Harecastle Tunnel in the Potteries, where a sagging roof

The view from our deck as Avonbay *joins the tail of the obligatory tow through 5,670m Bony Tunnel, Canal de St Quentin*

used to brush the cabin top of a narrow boat, until greater headroom was provided by removing the towpath. Of roughly similar age, the Grand Souterrain offered ample clearance between our superstructure and the line of power cables suspended above. We were surprised at how quiet it was; the *péniche* crews had retired below for their evening meals. The only sound was a distant clanking as the electric tug dragged itself forward, hauling up a submerged chain and spewing it out astern. Some form of tug propulsion was introduced here in 1867; although presumably of a later vintage, the design of our apparatus was obviously ancient, being a double-ended barge with numerous small square windows running the length of the gunwales.

It is claimed that on one record-breaking occasion no fewer than seventy-four barges formed a convoy, representing a freight total of perhaps 22,000 tonnes. Any speed comparison with towpath snails would have resulted in a fair contest! Well inside, we noted the legend 'John Liley, 1982' painted in large and neat Gill Sans on the wall. Was the former editor of *Motor Boat & Yachting* an advocate of canal graffiti, or had this been executed by another hand?

Bony Tunnel had long prevented completion of this vital route between the Seine basin and the Escaut. Building schemes were started and abandoned throughout the eighteenth century, one plan being for a single bricked bore 14km long. Eventually, Napoléon decreed that work should recommence. A stone plaque at the southern end records 1802 as the starting date. It was finished eight years later and the whole line inaugurated by the emperor himself. There is a story relating how passage of the tunnel was so awe-inspiring a prospect that no one was prepared to volunteer to take the first boat through. The authorities offered a reward comprising a toll-free pass in perpetuity and the bargees were practically fighting each other on the towpath for the honour. A wooden vessel was duly selected and remained in active use nearly a century later, doubtless rebuilt so many times that little of the original craft remained.

The German army drained each of the two tunnels during World War I, creating underground stables, hospitals and a command centre, all connected by shafts to other fortifications in the Hindenburg Line. Apart from occasional concrete block houses, there is little now to be seen of the destruction achieved around Cambrai during the final months of 1917. A corridor between the St Quentin and (uncompleted) Nord canals was the setting for the world's first full-scale tank battle.

We emerged into a gloomy steep-sided cutting, clothed with mature trees, at 8.45pm. It was almost dark although, after nearly two hours underground, we had no difficulty in passing the northbound tow and selecting a mooring. Our tug captain came down the towpath with the news that all boats would continue under their own power and pass directly through Lesdins Tunnel. 'Could you please be under way at 6.00am?' Slightly disappointed not to be hauled off into the tunnel it was nevertheless good to be able to get on with a late dinner.

Heavy rain fell in the night. By morning, rivulets of water were trickling through the ferns to form a morass on the towpath. We trundled off into a grey dawn. Riqueval Bridge, first crossing of the summit cutting, is a soaring stone arch, looking much as it did in one of the World War I's most dramatic photographs – Brigadier-General J.V. Campbell VC is seen addressing troops of the 137th Brigade of the 46th Division. Helmeted men are shown in their hundreds, massed on the skyline and clinging precariously to the treeless muddy slopes of the canalside. A few are clearly wearing life jackets, even though the canal bed is drained. We couldn't help wondering how many of these British Tommies were to reach home. How would they have reacted had they been able to look sixty-eight years into the future and witness *Avonbay*'s blue ensign sliding past?

Using both engines, we cruised slowly through the second tunnel, our speed dictated by the preceding barges from yesterday evening's convoy. Now we were dropping through a succession of locks towards the valley of the Oise. Payment for the tow probably included a contribution for that latter part of the summit crossed unaided. As any form of charge for pleasure-craft use of French waterways was extremely rare, this bureaucracy merely amused us (see note on planned cruising licences, page 199). An impressive receipt, issued at Écluse 22, recorded '*passage spécial de Riqueval*' of '*un yacht, voyage de Calais à St Jean-de-Losne*' for a total of 66 francs. Beyond, at St Quentin, we moored in the *port de plaisance* and walked 600m to a pleasant square dominated by the town's gothic *hôtel de ville*.

Ten more duplicated locks took us through farming villages, past a junction with the Canal de la Somme at St Simon and down to the railway sidings and industry of Tergnier. Here, we could have turned left for the River Sambre and the Belgian frontier near Maubeuge. Well ahead of schedule and our intended arrival date in Paris, we consulted the *Guides*, discarded plans to reach the Seine by way of Compiègne and the Oise and settled on a much longer route through the cathedral city of Reims. This comprised a series of moderately scenic canals, eventually leading to the River Marne. That evening, lock closure prevented progress beyond a scruffy town called Chauny, so we tied up near a side lock used by barges to reach factories on a short isolated reach of the upper Oise.

Deep gloom descended in more senses than one. Our internal lights lacked their normal brilliance; the pump supplying water to the sinks sounded unusually tired. There must be an electrical fault. Knowing far less about marine mechanics than is desirable, I try to keep *Avonbay* in commission by carrying out a rigorous daily maintenance programme. Up to this point, the boat had been wonderfully trouble free. Recalling hours of hand-cranking an evil-minded petrol engine on *Dorymouse* or failing ever to fully comprehend the antediluvian blowlamp-fired Seffle semi-diesel unit aboard *Parry II* (one of its endearing tricks was to fire backwards, a trait only normally discovered when engaging forward gear and obtaining rapid movement astern!) it was sheer delight to be able to press the starter buttons and enjoy day after day of carefree boating. But the complications of a twin-engined diesel yacht are similar to the combined complexities of a house and a car. There is rather a lot to go wrong.

Lying on my back with my head in a locker behind the inside steering wheel, I identified a tangle of melted wires under the port engine instrument panel. Given this situation with a car, I would immediately summon the nearest garage. But our wiring is unique to *Avonbay;* there was no boatyard anywhere in the vicinity; and it was Sunday morning. John firmly belongs to that school of thought which believes in everyone being master of his own trade and employing experts to sort out what you do not understand. I wanted to attempt repairs myself rather than struggle with acquiring outside help and all the attendant linguistic difficulties. By lunchtime, the burned wires had been replaced. Only time would show if the flat battery was receiving its charge.

Another junction at Abbécourt and another change of direction. Now we were heading south-east along the Canal de l'Oise à l'Aisne, a 48km linkline completed as recently as 1890. Until that day, 4 August 1985, John had regarded *Avonbay* with a degree of benign amusement. He was genuinely happy that she provided June, me and the rest of the family an amount of pleasure that was fast becoming obsessive; he didn't, however, totally share our enthusiasm. The Abbécourt lock-keeper changed all that. 'Do you have many pleasure craft through here?' John asked him as the lower gates closed. 'Yes, a reasonable number,' he replied, pressing a button to raise the upper paddles. 'But few *bateaux importants* like yours!' From that moment, John has been master of the smartest little ship on European waterways.

Our electrical malfunction remained. A decree was passed forbidding all but essential use of the taps. Candles were produced; early bed seemed likely. Realisation was slowly dawning that one battery of the pair (used for engine-starting, windscreen wipers and navigation lights) was unaffected. I discarded a scheme to link the two, in case this made us totally immobile. A solution was urgently required.

The canal climbed through woodland and meadows via a series of interlinked radar-controlled locks. To British eyes, these space-age developments really are remarkable: 300m before a chamber, sensors lurking in the reeds detect a passing boat and prepare the lock accordingly. Traffic signals variously command 'stop', 'go' and 'Monsieur Radar knows you are there, is doing his best but is not quite ready.' The act of leaving one lock flashes a message to the next so that it can be filled or emptied as required. In case of accident, a red-painted rod brings the entire operation to a halt. This bears the words '*Alarme. Tirez!*' In one instance a rude child had added the scrawled legend '*Vos culottes, Madame.*'

As the system was designed for 38m barges, small motor cruisers do not always arouse Monsieur Radar from his slumbers, and more subtle techniques must be employed. Variants include switch bars near the gates which must be pushed for a full ten seconds. If all normal measures fail, central control can be summoned by canal telephone. Within minutes, a generally helpful employee will arrive aboard a blue corrugated van to perform magic acts on an illuminated panel. You wave goodbye, only to find with embarrassment that the same man must be summoned half an hour later. Most remarkable is the apparent total lack of vandalism. Much of the delicate cabling and switchgear would be wrecked within hours in similar unsupervised situations on English canals. One regret must be the gradual disappearance of the traditional lock-keeper, someone to accost with a few halting (and doubtless reasonably inane) words of French. On these 'improved' routes we miss the varied selection of livestock and a chance to buy garden fruit and vegetables. But Monsieur Radar does provide an ingenious solution to one-time overmanning.

We enjoy eating ashore. Locks close at 7.30pm in summer, so visits to a restaurant are an enjoyable way of passing the evening and making contact with local people. Quite small villages support restaurants with at least the same frequency as public houses are found in England. Research begins with the *Carte Guide*, perhaps followed by investigation on the ship's bicycles. Invariably, the greatest value is obtained by selecting a cheap establishment and ordering the best meal they can provide. Attempts to economise at a grander place almost always result in poor quality. So it was that we stopped beyond the bridge of Anizy-le-Château. The rest of the crew installed themselves in a small family-run hotel, while I telephoned Jim in England for advice on the electrical troubles. His diagnosis pointed to the importance of securing professional help without delay. On returning to the party, I took my place at the table only to be informed by a

Opposite: There was still dew on our teak deck as we set out early one morning to cross the vast expanse of the Étang de Thau on the French Mediterranean coast near Sète. John, left, Diana steering and Charles, right, all contrive to look unconcerned as the author perches precariously on the pulpit to take this fish-eye lens view

Overleaf: Blue velvet, varnished mahogany and polished brass in Avonbay's saloon/ wheelhouse. The trapdoor in the carpet provides engine-room access

young and quite attractive waitress (wearing unmatching earrings): 'Monsieur, you may not sit there. This table is reserved for the English family. If you wish, you may eat with me in the kitchen!' Startled by this proposition, I perhaps demonstrated insufficient gratitude for the implied favours on offer. Subsequently, I was treated with haughty indifference for the rest of the evening. In due course, a single man entered from the street and after a brief word sat at a table in the back with 'my' waitress, whose name, we learned, was Sabine. Glimpses through a half-open door showed that his meal consisted of entertainment considerably over and above the food and wine consumed.

Meanwhile, John had been selected for special attention and received larger portions than any of us, served with knowing winks. Sabine was enjoying herself. Always prepared to be adventurous when eating out, I ordered *profiteroles des escargots*, having previously only encountered such choux pastry accompanied by chocolate and cream. 'Did you enjoy them?' asked Sabine, as she cleared the plates. 'Certainly,' I answered. 'It's the first time I have eaten snails served this way.' 'Good,' came the reply. 'It's the first time we have cooked them this way!'

Sections of narrow-gauge railway lines set in the towpath were a reminder that at one time many hundreds of kilometres of French canal had been equipped with small towing 'mules'. These were made available to the owners of lumbering unpowered barges that were tug-hauled on river navigations. Most widely found in the north and eastwards to Alsace, they first appeared as steamers in the 1870s; later electric and diesel units chugged backwards and forwards along the single tracks. Where engines met head on, tow ropes were exchanged. Early problems arose from the paths being shared with horses and a reluctance of engine drivers to work the traditionally long hours demanded by the boat people. Although efficient, such methods of traction reduced all traffic to the speed of the slowest bank-hauled barges. Eventually, by the mid-forties, two companies held a monopoly: Traction de l'Est in Alsace and CGTVN (Compagnie Générale de Traction sur les Voies Navigables) on other routes. Sometimes, rail-less tractors were developed with pneumatic tyres. The end came suddenly, as recently as 1973, when subsidies were withdrawn. The few remaining horse-drawn barges had by then been retired and a handful of unpowered *bâtards* were seriously delaying self-propelled *péniches*. I recall seeing just one tractor in action in the autumn of 1968; its prosaic duty was to pull horse-boats across the Guétin aqueduct on the Canal latéral à la Loire, the animals being led round by road bridge, an equally hazardous operation in view of the heavy lorry traffic. Rusting engine sheds, sets of points and weed-

Opposite, above: *Michael Streat at the helm, as we begin the long descent to the Saône down the Canal de Bourgogne. The hilltop settlement is the twelfth-century fortified village of Châtauneuf-en-Auxois (see page 73)* Below: *Sunbathing – Paris style – on the Quai des Tuileries. With good reason, the French describe such costumes as 'le Minimum'!*

grown rails can still be found, together with several preserved locomotives in places such as Toul and Strasbourg.

We reached the summit of the Canal de l'Oise à l'Aisne at the ninth lock in the village of Pargny-Filain, a windy spot with dinghy sailing on a reservoir and a swimming beach. Beyond lay the Tête Oise or Oise end of the 2,365m Braye-en-Laonnois tunnel. This is a modernised bore, boasting ventilation fans, traffic lights linked to close-circuit television and illumination. We passed through astern of a Dutch cruiser, dropped down a further four locks and joined the Canal latéral à l'Aisne at Bourg-et-Comin. 19km of level water would now take us by evening to Berry-au-Bac, where a hire cruiser company offered the best hope of effecting repairs to *Avonbay*. Surroundings were heavily wooded and festooned with wild clematis as the chalk-laden River

One of the last French examples of towpath traction was seen at Le Guétin, Canal latéral à la Loire, in 1968. The boat, normally hauled by a pair of animals, was a narrow beam berrichon, *loaded with 100 tonnes of cement. Progress was painfully slow.*

Aisne twisted through loops on our port side.

Champagne-Navigation's offices were in the town, some distance from the moorings. I arrived in teeming rain by bicycle as the proprietor was coaxing life into a patio barbeque. Desperately dredging my memory for words of technical French, I explained our predicament. The nearest electrical engineer, I learned, would be found in Reims, a short day's travel down the Canal de l'Aisne à la Marne.

Next morning, Electricité de France had provided Berry-au-Bac with a power cut, rendering the Aisne–Marne Canal's first lock inoperative. While waiting for something to happen, we sauntered round the little waterway junction town, gazing up at the black hulls of empty *péniches*. Opposite our mooring was one of those sell-you-everything bargeman's shops, bearing the name of Monsieur Brasseur. In *Cruising French Waterways*, I had published a photograph of the establishment showing chalked inscriptions advertising the day's bargains from rabbits to cherries. My glowing report read: 'As the years pass, these fascinating shops sadly decrease in number, so all readers are urged to help in the survival of this example by taking on galley stores.' 'Come on,' I said to the crew. 'This is one place we don't want to miss!' Needing little more than a couple of loaves, June, John and the girls followed me inside. '*Deux baguettes, s'il vous plaît, Madame.*' 'They are all sold,' she announced in an unexpectedly surly tone. As more than three-dozen sticks of bread stood arranged in wicker baskets, this information was difficult to credit. We asked for something else, but the staff were too preoccupied even to listen. Had Grand-père Brasseur been tortured in the last war? Did these shopkeepers take us to be German? Perhaps they illogically disliked all pleasure-boaters. Maybe my written testimonial had produced such a startling upturn in profits that they could now afford to ignore most customers. Never before had French tradespeople treated us so rudely. We left enraged and mystified, thinking evil thoughts.

Still in this mood, we directed our energy at the lock-keeper who was taking advantage of the power cut to hoe his cabbages. Surely, we suggested, the lock could be worked manually. Three *péniches* and several cruisers waited at each end of the chamber. He was heavily outnumbered. Reluctantly, items of gear were gathered from a store and bolted into position on the gates. Years of button-pushing had sapped his energy, but we insisted he must continue. Eventually, the gates were cranked open by hand; an upper paddle wound up and *Avonbay* rose to the top level. Altogether, we had waited more than four hours. We left quickly, just in case the power should suddenly be restored and the keeper's labours shown to have been pointless.

5

Champagne

THERE was a certain feeling of having done it all before – recently. The Canal de l'Aisne à la Marne features an ascent to its summit level, a 2.3km tunnel and a fall through further locks to the southern end. So does the Canal de l'Oise à l'Aisne which we had just passed through. Sometimes it was necessary to pause while we recollected where we were. All efforts were concentrated on reaching Reims, where Monsieur Lecomte runs a barge shop on the northern outskirts by the commercial Port Colbert. First, we topped up with diesel fuel, thus hoping to acquire his interest and co-operation. Unhesitatingly, he appreciated *Avonbay*'s electrical situation, called up his colleagues, Electronic Service 51, by radio telephone and agreed to our remaining on his moorings while repairs were carried out. Notwithstanding it being late afternoon, Michel Gavatz and his assistant were on board within half an hour.

A horsedrawn barge approaches Chalifert Tunnel on a canalised section of the Marne navigation near Meaux. Note the scrap of sail hoisted on the mast (which must shortly be lowered for the subterranean voyage ahead). Circa 1914

We were immediately impressed by the way in which they removed their shoes before setting foot on our saloon carpet. These were men well used to working on immaculate *péniches*. Methodically they tested circuits, exuded confidence and departed for the night taking with them one alternator and a heavy-duty battery for further consideration in their La Neuvillette workshop. Accustomed to the capacious engine rooms of freight barges, they were like a pair of giants in a doll's house, crouching in the bowels of *Avonbay*. Two further visits later, their task was completed the following day, having – amazingly – replaced the British-made alternator from stock and fitted a new battery. We were charged a very fair 2,879 francs; nevertheless, it had been an expensive short-circuit.

Able to relax for the first time in several days, we raided a canalside supermarket and moved the boat to a noisy mooring surrounded by fast roads close to the city centre of Reims. It is generally supposed that Reims takes its name from Remus, whose brother Romulus founded Rome. Certainly, the capital of Champagne has flourished for more than two thousand years. Once we had escaped from the ceaseless whine of the canalside Paris–Metz *autoroute* and walked several hundred metres, we found ourselves standing in awe before the magnificent thirteenth-century cathedral of Notre Dame. This is one of the finest Gothic churches in existence, vast but somehow friendly. Badly damaged throughout World War I, much of the medieval glass survives; where windows had to be replaced, they were designed by Chagall in a rare demonstration of how modern art can sometimes blend successfully with the old. We bought and lit candles, by way of contributing in a tiny degree to the maintenance of this wonderful structure, perhaps also as an acknowledgement that our fine boat had safely carried us from England to the heart of the Champagne country.

Hereabouts are the northernmost of the French vineyards, covering about 27,000 hectares of undulating chalky soil. When travelling through France I am always astonished that a market can be found for so much wine. Although our support for the industry is enthusiastic, how such huge quantities of fermented grape juice can be consumed is beyond comprehension. Production of champagne alone now exceeds 180 million bottles each year.

Seven supposedly automatic locks conducted us away from the city. Often their switchgear failed to work as designed and willing staff would arrive to release us. Eventually, we reached our next great tunnel, Billy-le-Grand, named after an unimportant hamlet in the fields overhead. The keeper, installed in a concrete box above the southern portal, had an enviably pleasant job, watching television screens transmitting pictures of boats approaching each end of the bore. Being young and athletic, he was both able to attend to lights controlling the one-way traffic and to scamper up and down a long flight of steps to tend several fishing rods on the canal bank. As we passed, he returned our wave by lifting a keepnet containing enough fish to supply a busy restaurant.

Condé-sur Marne brought us to a T-junction with the Canal latéral à la Marne. We turned right and headed westwards, direction Paris. It had been a warm afternoon, so once moored to an unloading gantry in the village of Mareuil-sur-Ay, June, Diana and Auriole joined me in the milky waters of the canal for a refreshing swim. John had disappeared with his wallet and returned looking pleased with himself. Without revealing what he had been up to, he requested that the shopping trolley be produced from the bilges and I set off with him to a small building surrounded by vineyards. This was the sales office of Marc Hébrart, producer of fine champagnes. We came away with three cases, including a *rosé brut*, at a discount price of 47 francs per bottle. All were duly stowed with the ballast to be consumed on special occasions when we had company on board or to mark a noteworthy bit of navigation. The penultimate bottle was shared with German and Swiss friends eighteen months later, in celebration of our conquering the Rhine Gorge.

Next day began disgracefully early, for I woke to our first misty sunrise since leaving Calais. June was aroused to record it (with great success) on her ciné camera, while I took a series of stills. How very different from the gloomy April downpours chosen by Georges Simenon when he used this immediate area as the setting for his murder story *Le Charretier de la 'Providence'* (1931), translated as *Maigret Meets a Milord*. Everything is there in closely observed detail: Lock 14 at Ay; the small town of Dizy, further down the canal; Épernay, along the D201 on the far side of the River Marne. Not much has changed geographically, more than half a century later. It is an atmosphere-charged novel of streaming rain, down-trodden horse boatmen and a clear indication that French canals were an even more insular world than they are today.

Every true waterways explorer is attracted by the concept of cruising to the absolute limits of navigation. So, on leaving the canal, we turned back on our tracks to follow the uppermost 5km of the River Marne to a *port de plaisance* in Épernay. Several British and German cruisers made us welcome, while the proprietor did his best to book us on a tour of the Moët et Chandon champagne house, featuring rides by electric train through extensive underground chambers. The weather had finally improved: we preferred to enjoy the unusual sensation of soaking up some sunshine. Almost 180km of peaceful River Marne lay ahead, through eighteen locks and a pair of short tunnels, with the magnet of Paris at the far end. It was a lazy five-day voyage through woods and meadows, unremarkable but always likeable.

Long ago, some unthinking waterways engineer installed locks on the Marne with chambers composed of sloping sides. The first three at Cumières, Daméry and Vandières are of this pattern. Although sturdy *péniches* can happily rub their way to the lower level, we were fearful for our somewhat exposed twin propellors. Approaching the first, we

Boundary stone in a vineyard on the banks of the Marne

held back to allow the barge *Polissonne* to enter ahead. M. and Mme Guy Tinnes of St Mammès happily agreed to our suggestion of lying outside them, so we had ample opportunity for sharing experiences as we travelled in company for the remainder of the day. The Tinnes expressed great interest in our Mareuil champagne purchase. We offered them a bottle, receiving in return a box of fifty small cigars purchased in Belgium. Then their photograph album was produced so we could admire pictures of their parents' boats and of *Polissonne* breaking ice on Dutch canals. A young couple with two small sons, they loved their wandering existence, obviously worked hard and appeared to make a good living.

Vineyards clothed the right bank down to Dormans, where we selected a deep quayside mooring outside the municipal swimming pool. A long search eventually produced a well-above-average restaurant – the Hostellerie Demoncy. Not only did we want to eat ashore, but a mains power point was urgently required for June's 16mm ciné camera batteries. These were left on charge overnight and happiness was consequently restored to our film-maker. Much later, an ingenious transformer was fitted, enabling *Avonbay* to carry out this vital function. Experts tell us that in spite of excellent results, the arrangement contradicts established 12V practice. Dormans provided a serviceable galvanised ship's bucket and gave us a disturbed night as unusually noisy trains thundered past on the opposite bank.

At first, the Marne was a wild and deserted river, with little commercial traffic and fewer pleasure craft. Everywhere, however, small fishing punts were noted tethered to the bank, often with a protective roof of corrugated iron sheeting. We passed little villages with complicated stone churches, received an inspection from a red squirrel when moored to a tree for lunch and generally enjoyed the remote peace of it all. Château-Thierry, birthplace of La Fontaine, offered a good mooring by the bridge beneath the imperious stare of a slightly fierce nude effigy of La Marne personified. One hundred and eighty-five steps (we counted them) led to the ruins of a castle built for Thierry IV, last but one of the Merovingian kings of the Franks in the eighth century. On Côte 204, overlooking the town, is the massive World War I memorial, commemorating the first American offensive in the middle of 1917.

One night was spent anchored off a rocky bank in La Ferté-sous-Jouarre. By now, locks were electric and progress was rather faster. Hardly visible, the little Canal de l'Ourcq approached from time to time on a higher level to the right. This curious navigation was opened in the 1820s, to convey raw water from the River Ourcq to Paris. With locks only 3.2m wide but 58.8m long, freight craft had the same slender proportions as English narrow boats. Once, there had been an inclined plane connection with the Marne at Trilport. Following development of the Paris canals for pleasure cruising in the early eighties, consideration was given to the creation of a new lock, relinking the waterways. Such a move would be of little interest to *Avonbay*, whose draught, beam and height above water all exceed the permitted limits. Hire cruisers and passenger vessels now ply the Ourcq along its 108km length from central Paris to a terminus at Port-aux-Perches: a journey that I was able to make in a borrowed boat several years later.

Recent history was made on the Marne at Poincy, when, in the fifties, Peter Zivy created France's first-ever hire-cruiser fleet, Sainte Line. He subsequently moved operations to the Canal du Nivernais at Baye and, like many pioneers, is largely forgotten by newcomers to the inland waterways leisure industry. Now long absent from the boating scene, Peter's contribution was unique and at the very least should have secured him membership of the Légion d'Honneur. But a prophet is without honour . . . we had fond memories of his London taxi and the red-painted replica of a British telephone kiosk on the Poincy quayside.

Family life aboard a Canal de l'Ourcq flûte, *early twentieth century. Today, the waterway is one of the narrowest – and least travelled – in France. Its upper reaches in the Marne valley are intensely rural*

10 VARINFROY (Oise)
Le Pont, vue d'aval

Edit. Loiseleux

Meaux, cathedral city and capital of Brie, spreads around a loop of the river and is effectively bypassed by the first of several canal cuts. We cruised several hundred metres up the natural course to make fast to a newly erected floating pontoon right in the heart of town. Retracing our route, it was then necessary to lock into the 12km Canal de Meaux à Chalifert, before stopping for the night in Esbly. Here, shopping was convenient; we brought out the trolley to exchange a gas cylinder (widely available in hardware shops and garages) and discovered that some banks can behave in an unexpectedly provincial manner, unwilling to contemplate any form of international dealing, whether by Eurocheque or VISA credit card. The river was rejoined after passage of a 290m tunnel at Chalifert.

Now the closeness of Paris was increasingly evident. Gone were the deserted reaches: we started to enjoy being something of a spectacle. Knots of onlookers gazed from bridge parapets and locksides; opulent *fin de siècle* mansions, not infrequently constructed in Franco-American 'creepy' Gothic, graced the banks, amid fine trees and lawns. Another canal between Vaires-sur-Marne and Noisy-le-Grand provided a brief encounter with our friends the Cowley family aboard their smartly converted 1932 Sheffield keel barge *Danum*. They were travelling upstream, so our conversation was limited to twenty seconds at an ever-increasing volume. It was to be two years before we met them again in Nancy and could enjoy a more civilised talk.

A four-year bridge-building scheme was noisily in progress by the Île aux Loups in Nogent-sur-Marne. *Avonbay* slipped through the narrow channel, turned back upriver at the far end and secured for the night in a *port de plaisance*. Dinner was provided at a charming little restaurant whose patio tables overhung the river and were frequented by some of the best-fed ducks in the whole of France. The waitresses worked under the duress of carrying food from the main building on the far side of a moderately busy road. A significant mortality rate seemed probable; on our night, the staff escaped uninjured.

For the first time since leaving Calais, sixteen days earlier, the next day began really hot and sunny. Hardly a ripple disturbed the river's glassy surface. What superb conditions for our arrival in Paris! Surroundings progressively became more urban. While we could easily have selected a secure mooring out here and commuted to the capital by public transport, we had taken the precaution of reserving a berth for several days alongside the Place de la Bastille. We pressed on with growing anticipation: the 600m St Maur tunnel cut through the neck of a huge river loop; down 4m in a massive lock and soon after we had joined a convoy of barges through the Écluse St Maurice at Charenton. Beyond a final three bridges lay the Seine and one of the most exciting cities in Europe.

6

Paris

STRÖME EUROPA'S.

LIEBIG COMPANY'S FLEISCH-EXTRACT & PEPTON.

Seine.

PARIS.

The Seine in Paris. One of a series of beautifully printed cards issued with Liebig Meat Extract, illustrating European rivers, 1898. The company produced about 2,000 similar sets of Trade Cards between 1872 and 1974

AS A REGULAR visitor to the French capital since the age of fourteen, I had acquired a fair working knowledge of its museums, churches, secondhand bookshops, rubber-wheeled Métro system, frantic Boulevard Périphérique motorway and riverside quays. Notre Dame, the Eiffel Tower, the Louvre and the pavement cafés of Montmartre were all reasonably familiar. But having fourteen-year-olds Diana and Auriole with us, the entire range of sights awaited rediscovery.

The moment we joined the Seine, commercial traffic was brisk: 350-tonne *péniches* chugging past, much larger push-tow barge units and – worst wash-makers of all – the ultra-modern steel and glass passenger vessels whose hectic activity produces conditions similar to boating in a giant food mixer. I have seen ocean-going sailors succumb to serious seasickness within ten minutes of mooring up in a small boat at the old Touring Club de France jetties by the Pont Alexandre III.

Our first priority was to refuel. Not having studied the *Carte Guide* with the required close attention, we were sternly reprimanded by the crew of a police boat for attempting to run downstream of the Île de la Cité at a time when passage was reserved for upstream craft. Trying not to appear too crestfallen at this rebuke, we asked their advice on where to buy diesel and were directed to a floating establishment immediately below the double-decked Pont de Bercy. This information being confirmed by the *Carte Guide*, we tied alongside and waited.

There is a widespread opinion that Parisians can be brusque to the point of rudeness; that people from anywhere else in France could almost belong to a different race. The proprietor of the fuelling station had ignored us for a quarter of an hour and was so uncooperative when I winkled him out of his office that, had there been an obvious alternative, we would have taken our custom elsewhere. When he did speak, it was at such a speed as would have perplexed a native. I could hardly have received a worse reaction had I been a beggar asking for a crust of bread. Eventually, I understood that we must wait for the arrival of a mobile tanker barge, currently supplying a *péniche* upriver.

Just above the Île St Louis, a lock lurks on the north bank, providing access to a canal network, owned and maintained by the city authorities. This is the way into the Canal St Martin, joined in turn by the Canal St Denis. Once known collectively as the Canal de la Seine à la Seine, they provide a heavily locked but shorter alternative to the 30km of river between this point and St Denis. Thus, a watery circuit of the city is possible, very much as London can be ringed by boat, using the Thames, Grand Union, Paddington Arm and Regent's Canal back to the Thames at Limehouse. Until 1982, this Parisian route, although commercially exploited, was so beset with permission difficulties that few pleasure boats ever made the effort to penetrate its secrets. All that is now changed and summer passenger craft cruises from the Seine to the Bassin de la Villette and beyond to the Canal de l'Ourcq are a rightly popular tourist attraction. Private boats are welcomed too. The Port de Paris Arsenal, a broad pool, has been skilfully equipped as possibly the most agreeable city centre marina in Europe. There are flower gardens, a children's play area, café, harbourmaster's office and even a DIY launderette for boat-owners. Mooring rates seem expensive until you consider shore-based accommodation prices in Paris. It is even possible to purchase a thirty-year lease for a residential mooring at a cost rarely approached in value by the smallest *pied à terre*.

We nosed into the entrance, blew our horn and the lock gates beneath a railway bridge began to open. Our every move was being noted on closed circuit television. A mooring was indicated and we took our place among a selection of French, British, American, Dutch and German craft. Having had cars broken into twice in the city, I was particularly interested in security arrangements. Throughout the day, a sad-faced *gendarme*, the very image of Peter Sellers' Inspector Clouseau in uniform, paced the gravel walks, intent on blowing his whistle should any member of the public dare to set foot on the unusually well-manicured lawns. He was kept busy. Sometimes, he would pause outside *Avonbay*, gazing longingly for five minutes or more. We offered him a drink, which, after much thought, was rejected with a gloomy '*Pas en service!*'

One warm night, I was awoken at 2am by sounds on deck. Without even waiting to put on a pair of shorts, I rushed outside to discover a thief in the act of making off with our dinghy. I screamed at the youth, who amazingly turned out to be English, made a grab for him and he fell clumsily half in the water, half on the catwalk to which we were tied. Within seconds, my shouts brought a patrol van with guard dog alongside. Lights appeared in the windows of neighbouring boats. At this point I thought it advisable to retreat within, satisfied that the criminal had been apprehended. There seemed no point in encouraging the headline: 'British yachtsman arrested for indecent exposure'!

Perhaps I need not have worried. Recent years have seen a remarkable relaxing of moral standards and Paris has never exactly been noted for prudery. Earlier that very day, we had seen sunbathers of both sexes along the riverside Quai des Tuileries, apparently wearing nothing at all. Closer inspection revealed them to be dressed in what the French so graphically refer to as *le minimum*. The thinking seems to be that what can pass in St Tropez is OK for Paris too. Curiously, if there was any offensive element, it was to be found in the throngs of voyeurs ogling from the street parapet above. Several years earlier, while driving down a main road in the Forêt de St Germain near the Seine–Oise confluence, my eye was drawn to a number of parked cars in a lay-by. Some men were gathered round a group of theatrically dressed girls. Supposing a film was in production, I pulled up to watch. The ladies, I now saw, were wearing little more than scanty underclothes and in one case just an unbuttoned clear plastic raincoat. Bargains were struck and a couple would make off into the woods. A year later, I happened to pass down the same broad highway (it is, after all the most direct road between Paris and the National Waterways Museum at Conflans-Ste-Honorine). The grassy verges were quite deserted. Rather than fail in an attempt to prohibit the 'trade', the authorities had imposed a total ban on parking! All very French.

One highlight of our stay was a dinner cruise on the Seine by *bateau mouche*. This would serve to assist our own navigation when it was *Avonbay*'s turn to explore the urban reaches. For a charge of 450 francs each, we hoped it would be good, but the service, delicious food, musical entertainment and views of the city as dusk fell could only be described as magical. With a single evening to fill, there could be no better choice than to spend it afloat. Our space-age vessel was equipped with rows of powerful floodlights, casting a brilliant glow on each bank. Young couples under the bridges who might once have been content merely to hold hands appeared quite unconcerned as we passed.

Another night, we had booked seats for the dinner/show at what used to be called the Lido in the Champs Élysée. By no stretch of the imagination could this be described as conforming to any Anglo-Saxon notion of family entertainment. Yet the dancing girls performed with glorious good taste in so much as that was possible adorned with a few ostrich feathers and a scattering of sequins. The staging and special effects were remarkable. I still want to know how a fully grown tiger was made to vanish before our eyes while caged on the end of a rope high above the stage.

During our stay, we walked until exhausted, returning gratefully to the calm of the Bassin de l'Arsenal. Here, there were exciting little tasks to perform such as changing engine oil, painting our new bucket and generally keeping up with domestic chores. We had worked hard at seeing Paris and still there are places I want to visit: the vast Père Lachaise cemetery where Piaf, Oscar Wilde, Chopin, Proust and Molière are among the tens of thousands buried amid architectural grandeur. Twenty years after my first abortive attempt, I have never to this day managed to join a conducted tour by boat of the sewers. We were sixteen months too early for the wonderful Musée d'Orsay, a railway station transformed into a temple of nineteenth-century art. Fortunately, a meeting with my French publishers shortly after the inauguration, made a visit possible.

Moorings in central Paris at the Arsenal Bassin, Canal St Martin

Seen from afar, Paris appears as a sea of modern high-rise towers, serving only to emphasise the beauty of the old, original buildings at its heart. The Paris of *Le Ballon Rouge*, with tall, grey houses under a cluster of slate and zinc rooftops, still survives reasonably intact. But why do we have to endure such insensitive expressions of late twentieth-century design as the transparent pyramid planted in the Louvre courtyard? We made a visit to the Pompidou Centre, believing reports that here would be seen a flowering of all the best in youth culture. The most that can be said of this British-designed structure (which looks as if the builders departed long before completion) is that a memorable view is obtained from the rooftop restaurant: a view that thankfully lacks the Pompidou Centre itself.

Down on the banks of the Seine, all can be forgiven, for there are few capitals which make such an enjoyable use of their waterfront. The amalgam of houseboats, barges, classical bridges, stately buildings and plane trees all reflected in the brown water is the very essence of Paris.

Three days was long enough to see plenty before there was any chance of becoming disenchanted with city life. John and Auriole sadly departed for England on Saturday 17 August. Michael Streat, *ancien fondateur* of Blue Line Cruisers (France), flew out from London for the latest in a long succession of waterway journeys. Thirty-five years earlier, he had been among the organisers of the legendary first National Rally of Boats in Market Harborough. Then, with his wife Pat, he ran a pair of hotel narrow boats in the English Midlands. Development of his pioneering Blue Line Company at Braunston near Rugby made him managing director of the largest canal marina in the country, with a fleet of hire cruisers and three pairs of the last regular freight narrow boats in service. Then came his successful creation of the French hire fleet. Once that was sold, he became involved with a leading American operator of French hotel barges. Michael probably knows more about the business of inland waterways than anyone else. He is also a talented writer and an amusing companion.

Before heading southwards for Burgundy, I persuaded the crew that a fascinating day could be passed exploring the northern fringes of the city by water. So we paid our mooring dues and left the Bassin de l'Arsenal at 9.45 am, immediately plunging into a tunnel that conducts the Canal St Martin under the Place de la Bastille. About half of this 4.5km waterway is hidden underground, the result of covering the Voûte Richard Lenoir (1884–92) and the Voûte du Temple (1906–7) in order to create boulevards above. A ghostly light percolates from shallow ventilation shafts overhead, providing brief glimpses of trees seen through a lattice of iron grilles. Emerging into daylight, we faced up to the two-rise Écluses 7 and 8 du Temple. It was a tight squeeze to pack in *Avonbay*, a pontoon-shaped Belgian cruiser named *Eglantine* and the tripping vessel *Patache Eautobus* (an amusing Gallic play upon words which appealed to us). Keepers working the mechanised gate and paddle gear were frankly unwelcoming, perhaps recalling recent times when their lives were untroubled by private pleasure boats. Paperwork was issued, to be inspected at each lock. The passenger craft skipper became agitated at the prospect of falling behind on his tight schedule and prevailed on the keepers to let him work ahead on his own. As once-only visitors we could hardly complain at such favouritism even though we had arrived first. Much time was lost as a result, endlessly working the engines forward and astern, waiting in centre channel while traffic descended.

Our journey took us through an unchanged old-fashioned Paris, close to the Place de la République and the Gare de l'Est. People watched through railings as we passed; a tramp blearily looked up from his mattress in a bridgehole. Two elderly swing bridges opened up ahead and appealing iron footbridges – *passerelles* – with shallow treads arched above. Sunday morning sunlight filtered through the branches of ancient horse chestnut trees. Slow progress through eight lock chambers dictated that we stopped for lunch in the wide Bassin de la Villette, start of the Canal de l'Ourcq. Michael recalled seeing a horse-boat work through here in 1954, an image which might partly have fired his enthusiasm for French canals. The far end was barred by a monumental iron lift bridge, the Pont de Crimée, dating from 1885. Chunky winding wheels supported cables at each corner, while the deck rose in a horizontal plane when activated by a boat pausing in front of a sensing device. We carefully read a sheet of French

River life on the Seine, early twentieth century. Artist unknown

instructions dispensed at the previous lock, noting that to pass through on red and green lights would make the mechanism very angry and 'thus provoke interruption of the navigation'.

Turning sharply to the left, we entered the Canal St Denis, whose seven duplicated locks would lower us 24m to the Seine, over a distance of 6.6km. The first chamber, Pont de Flandre, of exceptional depth, appeared to have no exit: merely a solid bar of stonework. Only .when the water level had fallen considerably was a single gate visible, pulled sideways by a hydraulic ram. Work was well advanced on converting a new but never used abbatoir into La Villette Cite des Sciences et de l'Industrie, a showplace for twentieth-century machines, computors, robots and all manner of cleverness. Most dominant feature is La Géode, a massive silver ball, containing a semi-spherical cinema screen. Between five and six million visitors were expected to flock annually to this remarkable exhibition: in concept, it all appeared rather similar to the Pompidou Centre.

While the St Martin exuded nineteenth-century charm, we found little to admire on the St Denis. Bisecting a region of drab slums inhabited by sad figures from the former French colonies, the banks were littered with wrecked cars, scrap heaps and untidy builders' yards. Paperwork was inspected and stamped at each lock before finally being surrendered together with a 30.80 franc payment, covering navigation on both waterways. With some relief, we rejoined the Seine in the late afternoon and headed back into Paris.

This is not a river for the faint-hearted. Barges and *bateaux mouches* weaved in all directions. *Avonbay* assumed her normal sedate speed, held station on the starboard side and made a regal progress upstream. Once we were through the Écluse de Suresnes, suburbs became more tightly packed. There was intense interest everywhere we looked: scores of highly individual houseboats, converted from *péniches*; a coloured saxophonist playing his sad lament on the Pont Mirabeau; the small scale Eiffel Statue of Liberty on the tip of the Allées des Cygnes island. By now, buildings were tinged with the gold of an August sunset. The Eiffel Tower was bathed in floodlight. Pont Alexandre III, most flamboyant of all the city's bridges, encrusted with classical bronzes and elaborate lanterns, alone made this journey worthwhile. We hugged the tail of a passenger launch in the narrows past Notre Dame, assuming that they were abiding by any one-way timed traffic system. Unnecessary delay in the gathering dusk might leave us searching for a safe mooring in pitch darkness. Already, it was too late in the evening to lock back into the Bassin de l'Arsenal. Eventually, a pair of steel piles was located in tranquil waters a little way into the River Marne. Only with the coming of morning was it apparent that we had spent the night by a sewage outfall.

7
Seine and Yonne

ONCE clear of Paris, the upper Seine is not unlike the Thames, but with a tiny number of pleasure craft and nearly constant commercial traffic. Sand and gravel are leading cargoes, dredged both from the river and from a series of extensive pits alongside. An intriguing aspect of this trade is that quantities of the material are conveyed in both directions, suggesting that healthy competition exists among ballast companies. Disregarding all ideas of self-preservation, hired rowing boats from several towns drift about with a total lack of interest in the most elementary rules of navigation.

Five huge electric locks were each shared with several thousand tonnes of shipping: there was always ample space for us at the back. By evening, the best deep-water mooring to be found in Melun was under a road bridge, opposite the island-based city prison. Faces appeared at barred windows and waved with surprising cheerfulness as we tied up. To attempt to dine out on a Monday evening in France can be a mistake – certainly it was here. The only nearby restaurant open for business appeared to specialise in African cuisine. Ordering was conducted with difficulty, as the staff spoke extremely poor French. My main course choice, named *poulet columbo*, seemed to have been prepared by launching a portion of chicken into boiling water and serving it on a bed of damp rice. We would have done so much better to have stayed on board.

Canal boat cabin, 1895. From L'Illustration magazine

All this was forgotten in the warm sunshine of the following morning. Some distance after Écluse La Cave, June began to create a buffet lunch. The ship's bar had been opened. Tranquil scenery appeared as the Seine skirted the eastern fringe of the Forêt de Fontainbleau where Louis XV had employed a fleet of Venetian gondolas to transport his deer hounds across the river. Shortly after the Pont de Valvins, we noticed an enchanting little restaurant on the port side. Decorated in black and red with a thatched roof, the building bore the sign 'Restaurant Plaisance-sur-Seine', and stood in wooded grounds at the very edge of the water. Notwithstanding our half-prepared meal in the galley, we unanimously agreed that investigation was called for. While not quite yet the regulation noontime hour for eating, several clients were already installed at tables by the river. Gently, *Avonbay* came alongside; ashore, a waiter reached for our lines with one hand while offering a menu with the other. Several customers came to admire the boat, so we decided to stay, at this stage having no notion of the most unusual nature of the establishment.

A series of small streams and pools intersected the garden, generously stocked with fat trout and salmon-trout. Fishing rods were supplied to the customers who proceeded to catch their meals in a hopelessly unequal contest. June and Diana were horrified: while they enjoy eating such fish, they prefer not to associate the cooked item with a glassy-eyed creature swimming along. Several words were therefore exchanged with the chef. He immediately understood the problem and produced four fine specimens of salmon-trout already gutted. While we tackled a delicious selection of *crudités*, these were cooked over a charcoal grill. To complete the meal, there were freshly picked little strawberries – 'a late variety' – served with slightly sour clotted cream. Most surprisingly, the feast was accompanied by our favourite Rhine hock, an almost unheard of aberration in a country firmly convinced that foreign wines are best avoided.

St Mammès marked a junction with the canalised River Loing, one of a chain of waterways leading south to meet the Saône at Chalon. This Bourbonnais route is generally considered the easiest and quickest way to reach the Mediterranean from the Seine. We were instead bound for the Canal de Bourgogne, more heavily locked but scenically magnificent.

Over a hundred *péniches* lay on moorings, sometimes reaching ten abreast into the stream. They were not the first idle barges we had encountered on this journey: the prospect of securing profitable cargoes grows bleaker each year. Sometimes the frustration arising from patently unfair railway subsidies results in smouldering resentment exploding into bitter 'strikes', when the boat families block navigations from bank to bank at key points throughout the network. Pleasure cruisers have been seriously affected by such actions and only the previous year a German girl had been accidentally shot at and wounded while her motor yacht was attempting to break through a *péniche* blockade. Now, there was talk in the waterfront cafés of organising another *chômage*. Less than three weeks after we passed through, all Seine traffic was brought to a standstill. In counter-protest, the manager of a passenger boat company handcuffed himself to the rails of a barge.

Now we had joined part of the circuit explored in my first ever French cruise in the autumn of 1968. Apart from the advent of hire cruisers, little had changed during the seventeen intervening years. The once awe inspiring, even frightening, huge lock of Varennes no longer appeared threatening. Further unemployed barges lined the river nearly continuously to Montereau, where it was time to turn south into the Seine's larger tributary, the Yonne. Given several additional days, we would have stayed on the Seine for a further 68km, reaching the head of navigation at Marcilly, discovering villages visited by the artist/writer Robert Gibbings during a famous rowing boat journey (*Coming Down the Seine*, 1953).

The Yonne is a wide, normally well-behaved river, equipped with voluptuous weirs and unusually big locks which are, for the most part, unmechanised. Providing links with the Bourgogne and Nivernais canals, where cargo boats are virtually extinct, there seems little prospect of further hand-worked locks being converted to power operation. Keepers actually mount bicycles to travel between top and bottom gates. As considerable physical exertion is needed to pass a single boat through, there is an understandable tendency towards economy of effort. Thus, you may be kept waiting up to an hour for the arrival of another craft with which to share the chamber. Two notable features are long iron levers mounted on the gates, thrown sideways through 180° to activate paddles; and sloping sides, a troublesome characteristic shared with the upper Marne. In spite of notices requesting all boats to moor up (*amarrage obligatoire*), where possible we held station in the middle of the chambers, running slowly ahead on both engines when the water entered. However, avoiding contact with the locksides made it difficult to put anyone ashore to help the keeper with his work. Several times, we were ordered to make fast on the pretext of showing papers: much tiresome fending off with boathooks then followed. Taken as a race, the Yonne keepers are not a particularly jolly bunch. Some strove to enhance their official status by wearing caps bearing an anchor and the initials P and C, denoting their importance as employees of the Département des Ponts et Chaussées, the government body charged with waterway control and upkeep.

A mere two locks had painfully been negotiated when the 7.30pm closing time approached. So, we selected a woodland mooring remote from any hint of civilisation, carried our folding Japanese barbeque from its hiding place in the engine room and enjoyed a splendid lazy meal on the towpath as the last rays of the sun twinkled in *Avonbay*'s brasswork.

Another hot day followed. In the long artificial cut at Courlon, we had risen to the upper level of Écluse 13, when the keeper disappeared into his house without a word. Normally, boat crews only operate equipment under the supervision of staff. In this instance, I really thought I was being helpful in winding the top gates open. As we prepared to leave, the keeper reappeared, fuming. 'You speak French?' he barked. 'Don't you know there's half an hour lunch break?' I replied that it might have been polite had he reminded us. We glared at each other. He then retreated, so we motored out into the pound beyond. Robert Aickman, founder of the Inland Waterways Association, used to tell the story of a canoe arriving at a very decrepit lock on the then derelict Southern Stratford Canal. Quite literally, this was the first craft to request passage in more than a decade. A keeper was, however, still employed, doubtless an oversight by the management. Together with the canoeist, he struggled to prise the rotting gates apart, finally remarking: 'If any more boats come through here, I'll pack the job in!'

Although the grain harvest was in full swing in vast undulating fields all around us, little of the crop seemed yet to have found its way onto barges. This was traditionally the start of a busy time for Yonne commercial traffic, but many lay empty on the quays at Sens, their crews making the most of the hot afternoon by refurbishing immaculate paintwork or splashing in the river itself. To port, the asymmetric cathedral of St Étienne dominated the city; begun in the mid-twelfth century, it is the earliest of France's great Gothic churches and inspired reconstruction of the choir at Canterbury.

Two empty gravel barges, *Diese* pushing *Noë*, caught up with us at the next lock, St Bond. It appeared they would continue through several more locks, so we gratefully made fast to one and thus avoided contact with the sloping chamber sides. These *péniches* represented the lower end of the *batellerie* hierarchy. Engaged on a boring and repetitive short-haul contract, they were poorly maintained and crewed by an uncommunicative, downtrodden couple. Several naked children would appear at the wheelhouse doorway, never daring to move further into the potentially dangerous world outside. We recalled similar families clinging to an age-old way of life on working narrow boats in England: battering along in ruinous craft, displaying little of the pride associated with the gleaming homes of Number One owner/operators. A combined length of 76m ending with the towering bows of *Noë* would have given the helmsman a very restricted view of oncoming traffic, had he not rigged up an ingenious system of pole-mounted mirrors, throwing an image onto a glass mounted above the wheel.

In spite of appearances to the contrary, the push-tow hammered upriver unexpectedly fast; we clung to his wake, working through Écluse Rosoy and just failing to reach Écluse Étigny before closing time. That evening, as the trees turned to black silhouettes against the fading light, calculations with the *Carte Guides* showed that we still had to travel 275km through no fewer than 197 locks if we were to reach journey's end at St Jean-de-Losne on schedule, eight days hence. Too many factors, among them car delivery, ferry tickets and the start of the school term precluded any adjustment. One of the eight days would effectively be lost entertaining my prospective German publishers; there was also some doubt as to whether the Canal de

The Yonne's sloping-sided lock chambers are potentially hazardous to paintwork and the propellors of twin-screw craft. This is St Aubin

Bourgogne locks would be available on the Wednesday. Earlier lethargy now disappeared with our waking in darkness at 5.50am, ready for the 6.30am lock opening. Halts were only permitted during the keepers' lunch breaks. Otherwise, we forced on for thirteen hours a day. Shopping was achieved by bicycle, the shopper catching up with *Avonbay* down the towpath. We really were to pay for all those idle moments earlier in the cruise. And to ensure that this rigorous programme was maintained, Diana hung up a check-list in the saloon, identifying every lock and our required arrival time there.

Very early morning on the river can be enchanting. We had left Étigny with navigation lights burning, while wisps of mist curled off the water. Later, an orange sun played hide and seek among the poplar trees and cast a pink glow on the ancient brick fortification tower in Villeneuve. Our barges roared off into the distance, like cardboard cut-outs against the sunrise, before abruptly turning into a gravel pit to load their next cargo. From then on, the beautiful Yonne was ours alone to enjoy.

Two shotgun explosions startled us at Villevallier lock, followed by the whine of a circular saw. Noticing an assortment of domestic fowl, Michael wickedly suggested that the keeper had felled a poacher and was quickly preparing a coffin. The keeper appeared from behind a chestnut tree, both barrels smoking. We asked what he had fired at, only to receive the enigmatic reply: '*C'est à faire peur!*' Who, or what, was the intended target of this fear, we never discovered.

Joigny rises sharply from its waterfront, with the church of St Jean standing high above a jumble of fifteenth and sixteenth-century timber framed houses. Many have been expertly restored in recent years, removing stucco cladding to reveal ancient wooden beams. Among the most elaborate, the House of the Tree of Jesse was being refurbished when we moored briefly for lunch. Michael bravely set off in search of a new pair of trousers, quite happy to grapple with the complexities of continental measurements. I made a rapid expedition to the far side of the waterway to record on ciné and stills *Avonbay* moored at the town quay. An aged fisherman (he looked at least ninety) was in the process of hurling himself and a bicycle laden with rods and keepnet down the precipitous bank to a little wooden rowing boat. As the operation seemed fraught with danger, I helped him aboard, ignoring the mumbled protests. He was a cantankerous old boy, who resented my assistance with fierce independence. Without any word of thanks, he paddled off into midstream, there to enjoy an afternoon of his own company. Quite clearly, it could only be a matter of time before he plunged into the Yonne, heavy bicycle, fishing tackle and all. The episode worried me considerably.

8
Burgundy

GIVEN the very limited time left to us, the idea of passing through 189 locks on the Canal de Bourgogne was a daunting prospect. Step by step, we were to climb up 114 chambers before reaching a summit level at Pouilly-en-Auxois; there, on the watershed between the North Sea and the Mediterranean, we would begin the descent towards the River Saône. Those initial 114 rising locks would be the most difficult, for *Avonbay* would be facing a fierce cascade of water each time the upper paddles were opened. Early on, we dispensed with twin ropes ashore, substituting a labour-saving single fixed line between our centre cleat and a bankside bollard. Just one crew member looked after the boat, running slowly ahead on both engines and steering slightly towards the near wall. The remaining three of us were released to help keepers open the gates or cycle ahead in an effort to prepare the next lock before the boat came gliding round a corner to start the process all over again. Fortunately, this waterway is equipped nearly from end to end with a well-surfaced towpath. After several energetic days, June was heard exclaiming with considerable feeling: 'I thought this was intended to be a boating trip, not a cycling holiday!'

Building of the Canal de Bourgogne commenced in 1775, but it was not until the early days of 1833 that the first barge was to reach the Saône direct from Paris. Locks were laboriously lengthened to conform to the 38m Freycinet standard between 1878 and 1882. Up to

On-board stabling of a Canal de Berry barge, 1897.

67

1968, tractors still hauled unpowered wooden barges along the southernmost section, from Dijon to St Jean-de-Losne; about the same time, the through route was nearly severed when a motorway scheme was proposed, using part of the canal bed. Pleasure cruising was then negligible, while commercial traffic was in a sharp decline. Closure was narrowly averted and although the A38 Dijon spur is sometimes uncomfortably close, the canal fortunately survives intact. During a first voyage in 1974, we met numerous commercial barges, trading across the summit and drawn through Pouilly tunnel by electric tug. Now, the *péniches* are almost extinct except at the extreme ends of the waterway. There are, however, large numbers of hire cruisers and hotel barges; as it was peak season, we feared we would experience a slow passage.

Rather than view the next few days as a nearly impossible task, we began to regard it as a challenge. After all, had I not once tackled the Grand Union Canal's flight of twenty-one Hatton locks single-handed between midnight and 4am? When cruising the Canal de Briare as guests aboard a large motor yacht, our host had raced off down the towpath by motor bike to alert the next keeper. We relaxed, throttled back and took several minutes longer than expected to travel the pound. Irate, the captain returned with a squeal of brakes shouting: 'What do you think I'm doing this for? Fun?' We certainly were here for fun, even if it was sometimes necessary to remind ourselves of the fact.

Our direction changed to south-east as we left the Yonne at Laroche Mignennes and entered the first lock of the Canal de Bourgogne. Copious paperwork issued here included details of the arrangements for Wednesday travel, shorter Sunday lock hours, a questionnaire requesting comments on the standards of service offered by canal staff and a traffic census card to be stamped at specified locks. Processing of the resulting information would keep several civil servants employed for months.

That night, *Avonbay* halted in the village of Brienon, precisely on schedule. Dinner was delayed as a pair of extremely keen French waterways enthusiasts came on board. Although reluctant to wake early next day, we were on the move at 6.30am and had already worked four locks by the time we were sweeping over the Armançon aqueduct and into the St Florentin basin shortly after 9am. Here was a most animated scene: an unladen *péniche* was reversing in order to turn at a winding hole. Several hire cruisers were being prepared for the next customers and breakfast was in progress on the hotel barge *Argonaut*. We moored alongside to fill our water tanks and began to chat to some of the American holiday-makers taking a stroll on the imitation grass deck.

Returning from a cycle expedition with Diana to the *boulangerie* in

Percey, I arrived back at the canal just too late to prevent another oncoming hotel barge filling a lock which by all reasonable standards of behaviour should have been ours. We glared at the English crew in their spotless white shorts and uttered a few choice remarks about wasting water. Michael, recently a passenger on such a vessel, recalled the words of a stewardess, conducting a party round Reims cathedral. Pausing before a magnificent example of medieval stained glass, she turned to her charges with the comment: 'Right. There's your Crucifixion. OK?'

Passing through Tonnerre, the keeper confirmed that we must call at the Ponts et Chaussées office to organise special arrangements for travelling the following Wednesday. A young lady asked that we telephone with our position on the Tuesday. We could either take our chances by joining a (free) convoy which might include a number of boats and consequently be slow; alternatively, the nearby hire cruiser company would sell us a 400 franc pass, entitling us to our own personal mobile lock-keeper. As this suggestion seemed more reliable, I parted with the cash and received tickets in quadruplicate: one to be surrendered immediately, another to be taken back to the office and the remaining two to be retained until later.

Rarely more than 2km apart, locks kept us busy until early evening, when we reached Tanlay, again precisely on schedule. Given other circumstances we would have visited the sixteenth-century *château*, reputedly one of the finest in Burgundy. But after a cooling swim, there was work to be done: Heidi and Wolfgang would be driving from near Frankfurt to meet us for a cruise next day. This would be a first meeting with my prospective German publishers, a small but reputable firm specialising in maritime books. *Avonbay* would have to look her very best if the required translation contract was to materialise!

Everyone was awake early: there was a four-course lunch to buy and prepare; the brasswork to polish; carpets to sweep; bottles of Mareuil champagne to put on ice; silver goblets to clean and a determined effort made to transform the boat from a holiday home into a floating hospitality centre. It was unfortunate that I was still dressed in a swimming costume, scrubbing oil stains off the hull, when a German car pulled up on the quay. To our delight, Freddy Soler, a mutual Swiss friend with an inland waterways travel agency, had come too.

Our guests seemed to enjoy their outing, taking turns to steer. It soon became clear that it was not a matter of 'if' the book should appear but 'when'. Throughout, I was anxious to appear relaxed and unhurried; we lingered over lunch for two hours and when the visitors departed in mid-afternoon, we had progressed a mere 11km through five locks. Eighteen months later, Heidi and Wolfgang were to be our navigators when *Avonbay* made a very exciting descent of the Rhine Gorge, while a year after that, Freddy was unexpectedly back on board in Alsace. *Cruising French Waterways* duly appeared as *Frankreichs Flüsse und Kanäle*. The home team of June, Diana and Michael had all worked splendidly.

Now there were just five days left to cover 165km with 154 locks. Allowing ten minutes for each lock and keeping within the 6kph permitted cruising speed, we might just achieve this target. Sleepily, we presented ourselves at the first lock of the day, exactly at 6.30am. Hardly remembering this was a Sunday, and in any case not having found time to study printed information dispensed back at Laroche, we were surprised to find no keeper. Not quite for the first time on French waterways and slightly fearful of the consequences, we worked ourselves through, feeling thoroughly naughty. Arriving at the next lock, we were offered the information that keepers would not arrive for duty until 9am with a two-hour break for Sunday lunch. We moored and regretted all that lost sleep; when eventually allowed through, nothing was said about our earlier misdemeanour.

Bourgogne locks feature their own distinctive gear, painted in this area in an appropriate shade of Burgundy. In addition to fierce windlass-operated gate paddles, sturdy cast-iron ground paddles, bearing a dial with 'O' (*ouvert*) and 'F' (*fermé*), speed the process. These are generally worked by the keepers alone. A elegant scissor-like iron lever activates the gates, rather in the manner of a cranked balance beam.

By evening, *Avonbay* lay beyond Montbard, south of lock 56, Venarey. In six hours, we had dealt with twenty-two locks and were alarmingly behind schedule. All the while, the rolling countryside was steadily becoming more beautiful. Keepers' cottages, built in stone from a design of 1794, now sported a charming ornamental oval dormer window in the roof, each seeming like a classical pavilion, misplaced from the park of a great *château*. A herd of creamy Charollais cattle made their way down the towpath to a group of farm buildings.

With a degree of luck and some exceptionally hard work, we might just reach the Pouilly summit level in a single day: fifty-five locks spread through 38km. June spent much of the time cycling ahead, preparing one lock after another and filming the boat. Her edited result gives little hint of how we struggled. It all comes over as an idyllic progress through summery France. Even when not under pressure, this is an impressive series of locks: fifteen in a closely stacked series at Pouillenay; the six of Chassey; twelve at Marigny. After that, gaps are a little wider, but there was rarely time for refreshment, beyond snatching a cold drink.

Diana and I decided to cycle for fresh bread at Pont Royal. I harboured the ulterior motive of making a flying visit to the newly established little canal museum at the port. 'Don't wait for us,' I told June and Michael. 'We'll catch you up at the next lock.' Eleven years had passed since my last journey through the canal; perhaps we were punch-drunk with locking. Whatever the reason, I totally forgot that we were now on the Bourgogne's only long pound: 10.5km through the St Thibault cutting. Bread and museum mission accomplished, we struggled down the overgrown towpath. Have you ever tried cycling through long grass? Sometimes, there was a distant view of *Avonbay* rounding a bend. We took to a village road, getting slightly lost. 'Why hadn't they stopped for a few minutes?' we wondered with growing anger. 'It's obvious that we shall take ages to catch up!' It came on to rain. Really heavy stuff. Soon we were drenched. Eventually, the runaways slowed enough for us to overhaul them. I passed the rest of the afternoon in an alcoholic daze, partly to warm up, mainly to drown my frustration. The 7.30pm closure saw us five locks short of the summit at the end of thirteen hours of remarkable progress.

Dawn brought thick fog, reducing visibility to less than 50m. As a lemon-yellow sun broke through the mist at 8am, we cleared Écluse 1, obtained permission to navigate the one-way 3,347m tunnel and swept into the broad summit level basin of Pouilly-en-Auxois. At a height of 378m above sea level, we were at the parting of the waters between the Atlantic and the Mediterranean. There was no time to re-explore the town where much had changed on the canal since our first visit in 1974. Hire cruisers, private craft and hotel boats lay at moorings by the landscaped quay. When we bought *Avonbay*, I carefully measured her air draught, making it fractionally over 2.74m. The tunnel features overhead electric wires, the power supply for an ancient chain tug, now lying virtually disused outside. While headroom is officially 3m, the tumblehome is acute. *Avonbay* rapidly loses air draught either side of her centre, but there was always a lingering doubt that she would pass through. At best, I reckoned we should have to dismantle all deck gear, including searchlight and outside steering wheel. One possibility was to pay a reputed 300 francs to be floated on board a curious vessel fitted with sluices like lock paddles; use of this *bac* would effectively place us 0.6m lower. But it was designed for unladen flat-bottomed *péniches*, rather than V-shaped hulls like ours. There was uncertainty about it still being available; even if it was, twenty-four hours advance notice would surely be demanded. Equally, we could turn round, working through all those locks again . . .

The wires spanning the stone-lined approach channel progressively sagged. Theatrical flashes of sunlight pierced the fog. As we entered, it

was obvious there was ample space – perhaps a full 0.6m clear. The official measurements had erred on the side of pessimism. I steered on top, however, in the knowledge that if we were to foul any obstruction, my head would be the first object to make contact (with the electric wires). The tale is told of British prisoners during the Napoléonic Wars being used on labour gangs to cut their way through Pouilly hill. Confined inside the workings, they were promised their freedom when the job was completed. Few are said to have escaped and many corpses are claimed to be buried behind the stonework. Our headlamp lit up the interior with great clarity. Every 10m, plaques recorded the distance travelled. We were through in twenty-five minutes and out into an invisible basin at La Lochère, where the first of the descending locks was totally concealed in white mist.

Notwithstanding a widespread belief on French waterways that mere boat skippers cannot be trusted to operate locks unsupervised (as happens on most British canals), a remarkable experiment had begun two years earlier to modify a series of locks south of the tunnel to DIY operation. In this way, savings in the annual maintenance costs exceeding 20,000 francs per kilometre would be achieved, without, we were assured by the management, any keepers being dismissed. They gave us a booklet – in English – featuring cartoon-style drawings showing how it was all to be done. Quite what was the reasoning behind depicting us pleasure boaters as one-legged pirates escapes me! Actually, all is delightfully foolproof. Gate sluices are dispensed with, the iron-encased ground paddles being used instead. One, painted red, fills the chamber; another, blue, empties it. A locking device on a chain secures one gate to its twin and minute electrical contacts sneakily sound alarm buzzers if you fail to follow the correct sequence. We were treated to a lesson by Madame at the first of the ten locks and although all were empty against us, we shot through in record time to be rewarded at Vandenesse with a superb view of the twelfth-century fortified hilltop stronghold of Châteauneuf-en-Auxois.

Châteauneuf is one of the most romantic little towns to be found near a French canal. Perched on a crest above the cornfields, travellers by boat or dashing past on the A6 *autoroute* see little more than the sheer castle walls and a row of turrets capped in rusty red tiles. Down the centuries, a succession of families have been in possession from Jean I of Châteauneuf, who took up residence in 1175, to Georges de Vogüe who gave the site to the nation in 1936. Inside the fortifications and protected by the great castle itself, a maze of little streets, market place and houses dating from the fourteenth century will be found in varying states of dereliction. Some once proud residences have degenerated into barns for cattle, while in recent years others have been restored as weekend and holiday homes. A small hotel/restaurant

A chain tug emerges from the northern end of the tunnel at Pouilly-en-Auxois, circa 1912. Note the overhead electric wires. This same vessel remained in regular service until the 1970s

73

(providing excellent food), several craft shops, a grocer's and an antique shop are indications that Châteauneuf is recovering from many years of slow decline. The population fell from 377 in 1859 to 63 in 1975. Even now, it is an isolated place, reaching into the clouds: several centuries ago, before the advent of cars, electricity or barges on the canal, it must have seemed to exist on the very edge of the world. Never before, have I discovered a place with such an intense sense of history; yet it remains a living town, little affected by the few tourists who make their way up a 2km hilly approach from the waterway below.

Many legends survive from the last 800 years. One of the saddest concerns the strikingly beautiful Catherine, last of the original Châteauneuf line, who was condemned to be burned alive in 1456. Unhappily married to Jacques d'Aussonville, she took as her lover Giraud de Parmentier, steward to her husband. The two decided that Jacques would be better out of the way, so Giraud made the journey to Épinal to procure poison with which to lace a cake. Catherine herself baked the lethal concoction on 24th November 1455. The husband took a large bite and conveniently fell dead on the castle flagstones. All would probably have passed without suspicion had a greedy servant not helped himself to a slice, with equally fatal results. At her trial, Catherine was sentenced to build a chapel in expiation before being roasted at the stake. The *château*, confiscated by Philippe le Bon, Duke of Burgundy, was made over to Philippe Pot the following year. It was he who carried out an extensive building programme, creating the structure which survives to this day.

On 3 December 1870, a fierce engagement took place outside the walls between the French army and 7,000 Prussians; 400 of the invaders were killed or wounded. Little subsequently seems to have disturbed the peace of Châteauneuf. Wild flowers fill crevices in the narrow alleys and the houses slowly crumble. Nothing would have pleased us more than to tie up, order a taxi and take lunch at the Hostellerie du Château. But this time, we could only admire from afar. Some weeks later, returning to Burgundy to close *Avonbay* up for the winter, we drove over the hills in our elderly green Bentley, arriving at the town as the last rays of an October sun were casting long shadows in the Rue de la Porte du Bas. The air was thick with wood smoke from a dozen log fires. We spent a comfortable night, untroubled by the ghosts that must surely linger here. Catherine de Châteauneuf is at peace.

Winding along the valley of the River Ouche, the canal typifies everything that is best in inland waterways. Small, stone-built villages, charming lock cottages, lumpy grazing populated by contented cows . . . the next twenty-eight locks to Pont-de-Pany could have kept us amused for a week. We passed them all in a long afternoon.

Next day was the dreaded Wednesday closure. A really kind keeper's wife and her two young children had propelled us into the evening by cycling ahead for half a dozen locks and staying more than an hour after they should have gone off duty. Such unheard of disregard for regulation time-keeping was rewarded by an intentionally generous 150 franc *pourboire*. We were, however, now nine locks ahead of where I had arranged to meet our personal 400 franc lock-keeper. One of the canal staff implied that we had been idiots to pay any money when a regular (free) convoy would take us down to Dijon. It was all highly confusing. In the event, we were the only boat in the 'convoy', an efficient operation starting at 9am in the company of two young men equipped with a towpath van. Our no-nonsense locking was matched by their quickness, meaning that the scheduled lunch point was reached an hour early at 11am. To suddenly switch from frantic activity to two hours of relaxation came as a rude shock. Alongside the canal, the narrow-gauge track of a little

The day that we worked through fifty locks in the seemingly endless climb towards the Pouilly-en-Auxois summit level. Here, Avonbay rises in one of the Pouillenay chambers. We all agreed that the Bourgogne is a ravishingly attractive assault course

rebuilt mineral railway is gradually being extended out from Dijon. I discovered Michael deep in conversation with the enthusiastic founder of this tourist enterprise; doubtless he had failed to even notice the comical comparison between his tiny diesel locomotives and the massive streamlined TGV trains that periodically emerged from a tunnel where the Paris–Lyon line clung to a hillside several fields away.

After lunch, we were placed in the charge of a young overweight keeper, who conducted us through nine locks amid a cloud of motor-cycle dust.

Banks of modernistic flats appeared on the skyline. Ahead, the spire of Plombières-les-Dijon church sparkled in a mosaic of multi-coloured Burgundian tiles. We arrived at the city's canal basin, lately transformed into a fine *port de plaisance* complete with black swans, and moored (free) to a pontoon for the night, taking care to ignore a troublesome boat-owner who appeared to consider that *Avonbay* should tie up elsewhere. Across the water an obelisk marked arrival of the first barge, 152 years earlier. On this visit we saw nothing of the fine Palace of the Dukes of Burgundy, the famous mustard shop or any of the other attractions of the city. It was sufficient to have arrived, safe in the knowledge that our last remaining day's boating would see us at the planned destination, on time. This was a cause for celebration, so we took a taxi for an evening of unashamed luxury at one of Dijon's best restaurants – Le Chapeau Rouge.

Our final day to the Saône was notable for delays caused by heavy freight traffic. No one approves of working *péniches* more than I do; with a payload up to 350 tonnes, not only must they make economic sense but they bring life and purpose to a canal for twelve months of the year. Much of the Bourgogne is a delightful plaything for pleasure craft during the summer season only. But how we cursed the hold-ups at each of twenty-three locks, never quite long enough to make mooring worthwhile. So we manoeuvred backwards and forwards for a quarter of an hour at every one. Barges painfully struggled ahead; others pressed hard on our tail. Fortunately, it was a blissfully sunny day, some consolation on a tediously straight length of waterway, cut like the path of an arrow for 29km across the Plaine de Brazey. We were thrilled to reach the *gare d'eau* in St Jean-de-Losne just 180 minutes before lock closing time; after thirty days of boating from Hampton Court, 1,400km travelling through 343 locks.

In later years, *Avonbay* would visit more exotic countries, perhaps recording greater annual distances. Plans are now being formulated for a voyage right across Europe to the Black Sea, via the inland Danube route, once the Rhein-Main-Donau Canal link is finished in 1994. Nothing else, however, can match our sense of achievement in reaching St Jean-de-Losne on 29 August 1985.

Opposite: *June steers through the early morning mists of an August day. On the River Yonne at Villeneuve.*
Overleaf: Avonbay *was one of seven pleasure cruisers packed, sardine fashion, into the tank of the Arzvillers inclined plane boat lift, Canal de la Marne au Rhin. Difference in levels, top to bottom, is 44.5m*

9
Floods

HOW it rained! France was wetter than could be thought possible, as I spent a diabolical thirteen hours driving alone from London to St Jean-de-Losne. Most of the journey down the *autoroutes* the car was bombarded by muddy lorry spray. It was 20 March and I had gone out a week ahead of the rest of the crew to prepare the boat for an Easter trip to Alsace. Arriving after dark, I directly made for the welcoming Auberge de la Marine to enjoy a well-earned dinner.

More than ten years earlier, we had 'discovered' St Jean and its huge *gare d'eau*, a great basin off the Saône where freight barges once gathered. Then, apart from a group of pleasure cruisers and a graveyard for ancient wooden *péniches*, the place had been deserted. Following our suggestion, Blue Line later opened a hire-boat base. Now, in the highly efficient hands of German-born manager Charles Gérard, the operation was flourishing with up to fifty British-built cruisers moored around an ingeniously converted Rhône barge, whose stern had been adapted into a drydock.

During the five months since we had last seen *Avonbay*, a new diesel-burning Webasto central heating system had been installed. Pipework conducted draughts of hot air to vents in each cabin, making her suitable for use in almost any weather. Although trapped in thick ice for much of January, she had survived the Burgundian winter

Opposite, above: *With searchlight gleaming through early morning fog as a warning to any approaching boats, we climb away from the German frontier towards the summit of the Canal du Rhône au Rhin* Below: *Lutzelbourg: a characteristic Alsatian town on the Canal de la Marne au Rhin*

81

splendidly, apart from a series of bursts in the copper water supply pipes, where it had proved difficult to completely drain them.

Requiring the car at the end of our journey, I drove to Hesse on the Canal de la Marne au Rhin near Sarrebourg, returning to the boat using a combination of trains and two rather expensive taxis. This tedious exercise lasted twelve hours. All chores completed, I looked forward to the arrival of June, John, Diana and Auriole. Their journey from London was achieved by flying to Paris, catching the TGV express to Dijon and taking a taxi for the final leg. All was now ready for our start on Good Friday morning.

Plans for the summer were to explore southern Germany on the rivers Neckar and Main. 'Why not take in Switzerland as well?' someone had suggested. The notion of travelling to the Rhine's upstream limit of navigation immediately appealed, so the year's itinerary expanded into a three-country tour. The only extra equipment required would be a Swiss courtesy flag. I had expected such a request to bring Captain Watts' Albemarle Street chandlery to a speechless standstill. However, with mortifying indifference, the sales assistant assured me that one would be in the post within a week. And so it was, just as if British motor yachts set sail for cuckoo-clock country every day.

Our idea was to follow the already familiar highest reaches of the River Saône, take the Canal de l'Est (Branche Sud) through the Vosges forests and run down the Nancy–Strasbourg canal. Here, at Hesse, *Avonbay* would be poised just two days from the Rhine, for the start of our summer adventure. This first leg comprised 365km with 148 locks.

It was still raining. The much-swollen Saône had undergone a sombre transformation from the sluggish summer mood that we knew so well. The coloured tiles of St Jean-de-Losne's church roof disappeared astern. All was unusually deserted: none of the normal old men seated in fishing punts, no children swimming from little sandy beaches nor blue-and-white hire cruisers. Just a bleak and leafless landscape under a grey sky. In total contrast, we relaxed in our centrally heated saloon, pleased at the ease with which the boat surged into a strong current. Evening brought us to Apremont lock, at the beginning of one of a series of artificial cuts, characteristic of this winding river. We moored to a sloping grass bank; on setting sail at dawn, it was encouraging to detect a positive fall in water levels. But it was still raining. Under these conditions, canals are infinitely more reliable than rivers. The lockkeeper appeared less than pleased to be woken at 7am by a mere pleasure cruiser. He worked us through in complete silence. We were determined to be off the Saône as quickly as possible.

That day is best remembered for cold rain, wind and a deserted radar-controlled lock of Scey, paralysed by a power cut. Tunnels were encountered at Savoyeux and St Albin, while the magnificent medieval *château* of Ray-sur-Saône reminded us of happy earlier voyages, exploring shady backwaters, swimming, and lazing in butterfly-filled meadows. This time, we saw a bright-eyed otter and perhaps twenty kingfishers. By 6.45pm, the little town of Port-sur-Saône had been reached, just fifteen minutes before the lock would have closed for the night, leaving us out on the dangerously swollen river. We moored on a canal by the town bridge together with three laden barges and a hire cruiser.

St Albin Tunnel on the upper Saône. From Philip Hamerton's The Saône *(1887)*

The following morning was Easter Sunday, clocks had unexpectedly moved forward an hour and all locks were closed. It was not until later that we realised that this enforced delay would threaten to ruin our holiday, as we could easily have reached Corre and the safety of the Canal de l'Est by evening. Lunch was taken at the Restaurant de la Marine, dinner across the river in La Pomme d'Or. On board, we admired our German-style Easter tree, decorated with painted wooden rabbits, chicks and eggs — souvenirs from a boating trip into Bavaria. More heavy rain fell in the night. To our surprise, the *péniches* were still lying beyond our bows when we woke next day. Ahead, closed stop gates, keeping flood water out of the canal, now barred upriver progress. The towpath ditch had grown into a sizeable stream, and all around, fields were inundated.

Trees stood midway across a river several hundred metres in width. It would have been possible to canoe for long distances over normally dry meadows. Somewhere, in the recesses of my mind, the situation was strangely familiar: then I remembered the Great Flood in *Winnie-the-Pooh*, when Piglet was marooned in his tree-house and Pooh floated to the rescue on an empty honey jar. Christopher Robin daily took his umbrella and put a stick at the edge of the water; in the morning he couldn't see his stick any more, so he put in another. We similarly marked the level and found it was rising hourly. A football field was now a lake; soon the river itself would be breaking into our canal. I consulted the local navigation office: not surprisingly, they offered little prospect of our being able to continue until well into the week. That afternoon, I cycled 8km to the next barrage to verify conditions upstream. The needles of Conflandey weir had been totally drawn, leaving an ugly 10-knot maelstrom alongside the lock chamber. It rained heavily as I rode 'home' through streaming woods, arriving drenched, cold and dispirited.

Port-sur-Saône is a pleasant little town, much like hundreds of other little French towns. A good spot for an overnight halt, but badly lacking in resources to keep us amused for what was to be eight days!

John, tired of waiting, abandoned ship on the Wednesday, adamant that time would more profitably be spent in his London office. Not that the rest of us had scope for an unlimited stay in France.

By this stage, we were well known to all the shopkeepers as 'the English refugees caught by the floods'. Credit cards at the ready, we devised new plans for filling in time. International money transactions appeared to be beyond the experience of Port-sur-Saône's banks, so we taxied into Vesoul. Even here, it was necessary to instruct the staff on

Burgundy and the North East. Avonbay's French travels shown in bold

how to provide French cash on a VISA card! One day was spent taking lunch at the wildly expensive Château de Vauchoux. This gastronomic treat began with *paté de foie gras*, served (curiously, we thought) with a very sweet Sauternes, *écrevisses* (freshwater crayfish) in a cognac and cream sauce, *noisettes d'agneau, Charollais* steaks, two further wines (the red Bordeaux being served in half-bottle sized balloon glasses) and an excellent range of desserts. For the four of us, the bill amounted to 1,660 francs, hardly surprising when a single bottle of Alsatian wine cost 200 francs (we subsequently found an identical supermarket example at just 20 francs). Stylish eating is an important ingredient of the French way of life, so we tried to justify the experience in the interests of research.

One morning, there was a slight reduction in water levels. The Ponts et Chaussées office suggested a move might be possible by the weekend. Then came more rain. Our second Sunday in Port-sur-Saône arrived. Three courses of action were possible. Either we left *Avonbay* here; or returned to the greater security of St Jean-de-Losne as soon as conditions allowed (so achieving nothing at very considerable expense and severely curtailing our summer cruising programme); or we might just continue to Hesse, putting in a succession of thirteen hours a day. This last possibility met with universal approval even though it involved complicated telephone calls to change hotel bookings and car ferry tickets for the homeward run. Nearing the end of another lunch in La Pomme d'Or, the girls – who had returned early to the boat – came running back to breathlessly announce: 'The *péniches* have gone!' Paying for a French meal is generally a prolonged affair. This time, we were out of the building within sixty seconds, racing over the long and windswept river bridge back to *Avonbay*. We launched into the still fierce current, badly slamming the wall of Conflandey lock whose lower entrance was behaving like a millrace. It was a relief to be on the move again and 32km later our friends on the *péniche Darligan* suggested we moored to them for the night at the mouth of Ormoy lock. Before daybreak, we had negotiated the illuminated chamber just like the professionals. With remarkable kindness, *Darligan*'s skipper signalled us to overtake him shortly before the final river lock. He obviously realised that we would soon be well out of his way. With a long series of canal locks ahead, several days were to pass before a similar overtaking opportunity would materialise. The previous night's present of a bottle of whisky had more than paid off. At 7.45am, Corre came into sight; the flooded River Saône was behind us.

10
Vosges and Alsace

AFTER a cold and cheerless winter, the southern Canal de l'Est displayed few hints of springtime. Drifts of snowdrops decorated the lock cottage gardens; occasionally, we noticed a hardy daffodil in flower. All was very different compared with the hot days recalled from our last journey down this woodland waterway.

For much of the passage on *Avonbay*, mobile keepers accompanied us up the valley of the Coney and through the stone-lined narrows at Fontenoy-le-Château. Here, an obligatory halt was made to visit the *boulangerie* of Monsieur Pérochon, where wood-fired ovens still produce village bread supplies. Hour by hour we improved on the planned schedule, so that by early evening nearly thirty locks had been negotiated.

Ready to move well before daybreak, it was exciting to see the powerful searchlight of a descending barge gleaming through the pine trees ahead. Thirty minutes passed before it was our turn to climb to the 10.9km summit level. Needing fresh food supplies, we paused briefly at Chaumoussey, where a high embankment is pierced at intervals by damp tunnels, providing a link between parts of the village. Hurriedly, shopping was nearly finished when a northbound *péniche* surged by. Determinedly, we caught him up, never expecting an invitation to overtake, as a descending series of locks would shortly

Storks nest on a Strasbourg chimney stack

86

be reached at Golbey. To our amazement, the skipper waved us past, one hand extended to take the bottle of red wine which he quite rightly expected in return.

Running through a bridge hole, an alarming grating sound was heard from the port engine propeller shaft. Subsequently, we discovered a length of barbed wire caught beneath the boat. Not daring to lose our place in the convoy, we continued on one engine alone. No amount of prodding with a boathook would release the obstruction, and for the rest of that journey we were restricted to the use of the starboard motor. With water temperatures close to freezing, I was not volunteering to dive in! A frogman removed the wire some weeks later at Hesse.

One night at Charmes was followed by a long plod down the uppermost reaches of the unnavigable Moselle, running in spate by the side of the canal. Two further lock flights on the dejected Nancy Branch eventually brought us to industrialised moorings on the Canal de la Marne au Rhin at Laneuveville-devant-Nancy. Constant freight traffic was feeding a Solvay chemical works in Dombasle-sur-Meurthe, providing a vivid impression of flourishing water transport as it must have been forty years earlier. More than thirty *péniches* painted in their company livery were lined up at the quays. We sped through a series of automatic, duplicated locks, dropping in one chamber while a barge rose alongside. The oily towpath, smoking chimneys and blackened trees might have belonged to the heyday of the Birmingham Canal Navigations.

American Henry C. Rowland passed this way some years before World War I (*Across Europe in a Motor Boat*, 1908). He was making a pioneering voyage from London to the Danube delta, where Limehouse-built *Beaver* was totally wrecked on a Turkish beach. The power unit was a brute of a twin-cylinder paraffin engine, designed for use in Danish fishing boats and nicknamed 'Dan'. Starting procedure involved aiming a pair of blowlamps at the cylinder heads for ten minutes. Seventy years later, I was struggling with a similar lump of Scandinavian machinery installed in my converted canal ice-breaker. West Germany now begins at the waterway's far end, beyond Strasbourg but in Rowland's day, Lorraine formed part of the Prussian Empire: it was even against the law to teach French in local schools. Canal boaters crossed the border at the village of Xures, where *Beaver* was presented with a great wooden plank, bearing the word *Vorfahrtsrecht*. This granted them precedence over all other traffic; merely cruising for pleasure, Rowland not infrequently waived the privilege, for 'it sometimes hurt our consciences to take the right of way over some poor devil of a canal boat captain who had been waiting patiently for hours.' Today, the situation is quite properly reversed.

Reminders of one-time German rule can be found everywhere. A village named Lagarde is followed by Gondrexange, and later by Xouaxange, Schneckenbusch and Brouderdorff. Inhabitants widely tend to disclaim affiliation to either France or Germany, firmly stating themselves to be Alsatian.

Rapid progress brought *Avonbay* to the hamlet of Port Ste Marie, a well-chosen stopping place with convenient restaurant. In the morning, lines were frozen solid, requiring blows with a sledge hammer before we could untie. Strange weather for mid-April, we thought, shivering; within hours, we were steering through a blizzard.

Sixties improvements to the waterway were designed to alleviate barge saturation. Five standard locks were replaced by a concrete tower at Réchicourt-le-Château, rising menacingly on the far side of a lake into which the canal was diverted. After an interminable wait, a green light beckoned. We entered, attached two ropes to a single floating bollard and held on tight during a massive 16.4m ascent to the upper level. Plenty of deeper locks occur on the great rivers; never before had we been through one like this, with a width suited to *péniches*. We might have been boating in a lift shaft!

Arriving in Hesse, Blue Line's manager, Philippe David and his English-speaking secretary made us extremely welcome. Engineer Alain Blanck could hardly take his eyes off our polished brasswork; we subsequently learned he was a vintage car enthusiast. The boat would be in capable hands during the next six weeks. Despite our long hold-up in Port-sur Saône, the journey from there had taken only four and half days. Driving off through the snow, we had to admit we were quite pleased to be homeward bound.

Towards the end of May, summer had at last come to eastern France. Accompanied by my mother – who had not been near Germany since Hitler was in power – we planned a gently unambitious trip, making a return journey down the nearby Canal des Houillières de la Sarre. Rather in the way that the name Leeds & Liverpool Canal conveys no idea that England's last surviving trans-Pennine waterway is among its most attractive, the Sarre Coalfields Canal doesn't sound very inspiring – 72km with thirty locks – it passes through remote countryside before crossing the German frontier where the first spoil tips are located. Until 1992, there would be no through route via the River Saar to the Mosel near Trier, although a series of big locks were already under construction. For the present, traffic was light, travelling lock-keepers unusually friendly and I was pleased to realise that *Avonbay* was not difficult to work virtually single-handed. The best scenery is found between the Marne–Rhin junction and

Mittersheim, past a succession of lakes and dense woodland. We quickly reached the border in Sarreguemines, but decided against exploring the short available reach of German Saar, for which I had not arranged an extension of insurance cover. One night, we had dinner ashore with two couples from North America. Devoted Francophiles, they were enjoying their latest annual canal cruise. We got on surprisingly well, considering that Abbe introduced herself as a doctor of psychology and a leading member of MENSA (the club for those of above average intelligence)! On returning to Hesse, I commissioned Alain to crane the boat out for a thorough shotblasting and paint job on the hull. We would want to look our best when navigating the Rhine to Switzerland.

Late July. June, John, daughters Evelyn and Diana and I returned to be greeted with good news and bad news. First, *Avonbay*'s dark-blue hull looked immaculate; moreover, the bill was very reasonable. Second, the Arzvillers inclined plane boat lift, first change of level in our chosen direction, was *en panne* for the next four days. With no alternative route to the Rhine, we would have to be patient. One day was pleasantly passed driving through coniferous forests to the superb Alsatian town of Colmar. Originally, the plan had been to make a detour there by water. Back at base, a constant stream of cruisers and *péniches* passed, so we fuelled, watered, provisioned and set sail to take up our place in the queue.

The authorities had halted all traffic in the Altmuhle basin, 8km short of the incline. A red traffic light glowed beyond a workboat, purposefully moored bank-to-bank. Half a dozen *péniches* lurked at the head of the blockage, with fifteen or sixteen Dutch and German cruisers. A careful note was made of boats already there, while new arrivals were recorded during the next two days. It was blisteringly hot, so the assembled company spent much of the daylight hours plunging into the canal. Our nearest neighbours were a Dutch family aboard the ex-Customs' launch *Brandaris*. The heavily bearded owner had been born on a barge and resolutely refused to accept the lesser status of pleasure boatman. More than once in the days that followed, he would insist on right of passage over other craft: we clung to him like a leech and benefitted considerably. He was something in the Rotterdam entertainment industry and filled the countryside with amplified pop music. By compensation, his blonde wife and pair of teenage girls were a visual bonus in their bikinis. 'My husband much likes yellow,' said the wife, rather apologetically, as we admired their canary-coloured superstructure. *Brandaris* was a smart little craft, fitted with a massively powerful engine and handled with enviable expertise. The basin took on the appearance of a British canal rally.

SARREBOURG

Plaisir de la navigation

Pour les vacances, on peut aller à la mer, à la montagne ou très loin, sous les tropiques. Une autre forme de loisirs est de plus en plus à la mode dans le pays : la navigation de plaisance.

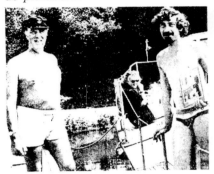

M. John Humphries et M. Hugh Mac Knight qui a écrit un livre sur toutes les voies navigables en France et qui sera bientôt traduit en français.

Les touristes qui voyagent sur les voies navigables de l'Est sont, chaque année, de plus en plus nombreux, le canal de la Marne au Rhin étant le parcours choisi de préférence. Dans la région, le plan incliné et ce sont les ports de Dutzelbourg en aval de celui-ci qui accueillent le plus souvent ces voyageurs. D'autres choisissent les ports de Xouaxange, Hesse, Lagarde et Mittersheim sur le canal des Houillères.

A Niderviller, chaque jour, plusieurs dizaines d'embarcations s'arrêtent dans les deux ports de la localité, dernièrement plus de quinze bateaux étaient arrêtés au port de plaisance du Vieux Moulin et une dizaine avait mouillé l'ancre au port commercial. Ces plaisanciers séjournent généralement deux ou trois jours sur place ce qui leur permet de visiter les curiosités touristiques de la région : Dabo, Abreschviller, Sarrebourg. Ainsi ces vacanciers de Fribourg qui ont remonté le Rhin jusqu'à Strasbourg, puis le canal de la Marne au Rhin en passant par le plan incliné, avant de rentrer en Allemagne et ces

Anglais, des Londoniens, M. Hugh Mac Knight qui a récemment écrit un livre sur les 8.000 km de voies navigables en France. M. John Humphries, fondateur, il y a 17 ans, de la «Blue Line», club proposant de merveilleuses vacances fluviales dans les quatre coins de l'hexagone, avec un service complet en «bateau bleu». Les plaisanciers viennent également de Suisse et de la vallée du Rhin ; s'ils s'arrêtent à Niderviller, c'est parce qu'ils aiment la région qu'il découvre à bicyclette, la verdure environnante et surtout l'accueil des habitants.

Le plan incliné en panne

Différents parcours s'offrent à eux : ceux qui viennent d'Alsace empruntent le plan incliné de deux tunnels, celui de Arzviller (2.800 m), celui de Niderviller (475 m) ; certains font un tour circulaire par le Rhin, la Moselle canalisée et le canal de la Marne au Rhin, d'autres sont simplement de passage sur le canal, d'autres encore viennent du Nord, par l'Angleterre et suivent la Seine et la Marne.

Quant au port de Niderviller, il est à même d'accueillir un certain nombre d'embarcations puisqu'il est en voie d'agrandissement ; deux pontons d'accostage ont été construits et une rampe de mise à l'eau est à la disposition des touristes venant avec leur voiture. Un détail, le permis n'est pas obligatoire pour les bâtiments de moins de 10 CV. L'endroit étant très prisé, les tentes fleurissent également ici et là.

On pourrait se poser la question d'une concentration exceptionnelle à Niderviller, c'est tout simplement une panne des machines du plan incliné qui bloquent tous ces gens dans leur parcours.

Le malheur des uns, faisant le bonheur des autres, tout cela contribue à l'animation de la région ; les résidents peuvent ainsi, de leurs jardins, voir se promener la barge tirée par un cheval, la Provence, la Lorraine, le Protecteur... Qui a dit que les vacances, c'était forcément partir ailleurs ?

When a local reporter arrived to get a story, we lost no time in selling him the English angle. *Le Républicain* subsequently devoted half a page of text and photographs to the *ancien fondateur de Blue Line* (John) and the *écrivain anglais* (me), whose fine vessel *Avonbay* had come all the way from *Londres* only to be held up by the Arzviller stoppage.

Early evening, Thursday, found most of the crews downing schnapps on deck. An official had announced there would be no movement until morning. Suddenly, a *péniche* engine started up with a cough and a puff of smoke, followed by all the others. The traffic light changed to green. *Avonbay* was running towards the head of the queue within fifteen seconds, *Brandaris* close on her tail. The other Dutch and Germans looked on with benign amusement, calling out: 'No

Our enforced delay inspires 'copy' for the local newspaper

90

moving until tomorrow'. Perhaps they had not reckoned with our blue ensign. We smiled, ignored their advice and shot past the traffic light as it turned back to red. This very nearly legitimate action gave us a fifteen-boat advantage, probably saving as much as a day's delay at the locks. Taking the 475m Niderviller and 2,306m Arzviller tunnels very slowly behind the barges, we were ready to work down the inclined plane next morning.

This section of the Canal de la Marne au Rhin is easily one of the most delightful in all France. Thick pinewoods cover the steep-sided valley of the River Zorn. Buildings of timber or pink sandstone are decidedly German in style. In 1908, Henry Rowland commented:

> The whole effect of the place reminded me very much of Japan . . . where a little mountain rivulet will be led successively into a series of diminutive rice paddies, each terraced against the hillside and receiving the overflow from the one above, and so descending to the valley beneath.

It is easy to understand what he means, even if the seventeen locks described were closed to traffic in 1969 and are slowly disappearing under vegetation. A new canal channel clings to the upper slopes of a ravine, leading to a space-age barge lift, operating over 108m of track set at a 41° angle. It is remarkably similar to the long defunct steam-powered Foxton lift in Leicestershire, except that the French version employs a single water-filled tank, rather than two. When built, Arzvillers was regarded as a small-scale model for much larger lifts elsewhere; current engineering practice seems to favour either deep locks or vertical lifts. We travelled in the *caisson* smugly knowing we were doing so toll-free, unlike the hundreds of sightseers who had paid to enter the complex! In an effort to clear traffic jams top and bottom, as many pleasure craft as possible were being packed in, herring-bone fashion. *Avonbay* was the largest in our batch of seven.

Throughout the forests, a constant whine of chain-saws provided a clue to one local industry. The whole region is extremely picturesque and attracts holiday-makers who come for walking trips or to catch the trout which rightly take pride of place on many restaurant menus. This time, we were unable to stop in Lutzelbourg, an enchanting Hansel and Gretel village spread around Écluse 21. Ruined castles crown the hilltops: one is said to have served as a finishing school for witches! A few days earlier, we had taken the car to another, the Château de Haut-Bar, from whose restaurant you can see the canal far below and, on clear days, the distant spire of Strasbourg cathedral. There was much manoeuvring while automatic locks set themselves. The day was roastingly hot, most of the other boaters remained good tempered and by evening we had reached the important town of Saverne, where we moored immediately before the abnormally deep Écluse 30/31. With a rise of 5.43m, this curiosity appeared in 1880, when two chambers were combined. A concealed side pond enables one-third of the water consumed to be used in the next operation. Unique in Alsace, similar examples can be seen on England's Grand Union Canal as well as on the modern Rhein-Main-Donau waterway near Nuremberg.

Saverne is a very likeable town, centred around a long pedestrianised shopping street, sloping away from the canal. Oddments of genuine Roman columns are cemented into a wall at the waterside, while there are several wooden-framed buildings of great antiquity, decorated with painted carvings. Two cottage industries are making cut glass crystal and pictures in marquetry. Monsieur Straub runs a workshop, where framed scenes are produced from slivers of natural wood veneer. Most depict nearby villages; our enquiry for one featuring a barge on the canal provoked little reaction. While quite expensive, we were fascinated by the laborious process whereby the designs are initially prepared on paper patterns, rather like painting by numbers. Would Monsieur Straub take on the commission of a portrait of *Avonbay?* We put the suggestion to him; being a man of few words, it was difficult to detect much enthusiasm. But in due course, a magnificent view of the boat arrived in England, meticulously complete and even indicating the guard wires around the deck. The border comprised an arrangement of roses, curiously similar to the painted flowers of the narrow boats. An antique of the future, it now hangs alongside a blue-and-white framed Delft tile, made for us in Amsterdam and showing *Avonbay* moored before a Dutch windmill.

Landscaped quays in a large basin face a neo-classical *château*, built in the eighteenth century as the summer residence of Cardinal Louis de Rohan. Impressive rather than beautiful, this Alsatian version of Buckingham Palace is now administered by the town council.

Locks were constantly busy during our day-long run to Strasbourg; looking at the map, it was necessary to remind ourselves that we were still in France, passing such villages as Schaffouse-sur-Zorn, Schwindratzheim and Brumath. Completed in 1853, the canal is now an established feature of the countryside. While still new enough to be regarded as a wonder of the age, it was used by Hungarian Count Edmond Széchenyi (1839–1922) in his steam launch *Hableany*, bound for the 1867 Universal Exhibition in Paris. Almost certainly, he was the first man to travel by inland waterway from Budapest to the French capital, making use of Bavaria's romantic Ludwigskanal, which had linked the Danube to the Main since 1846. The 1,600km expedition was completed in just thirty-two days. Much favourable publicity was generated, resulting shortly afterwards in seventy Dutch and German barges making a reverse trip to Hungary to load cargoes of wheat and flour.

Shortly after the Écluse de la Frontière and our turning onto the River Ill, we were thrilled to see a stork strutting along a gable end. Virtually adopted as the provincial emblem of Alsace, this bird is a highly regarded symbol of good fortune. Wooden rooftop platforms are erected in the hope that a pair will make their home there. Numbers have so declined that when storks do raise a family in Strasbourg, they achieve front page coverage. The omens were fair for our forthcoming excursion on the Rhine.

Past the Palace of Europe and up the fast-flowing Ill, brought us to a splendidly central overnight mooring at the Quai des Pêcheurs, less than five minutes from Strasbourg's ornate Gothic cathedral spire. *Avonbay*'s 1.30m draught is seldom a problem. The Ill proved to be an exception and we were intensely irritated to notice a signboard indicating a 0.70m maximum draught, had we attempted to travel a further kilometre up river to photograph the boat against the superb backdrop of medieval half-timbered buildings at La Petite France. It was also doubtful if we could have cleared a footbridge spanning the single small lock on this enchanting route. Arrival here in a hire cruiser some years earlier, had been quite by chance; the city waterways and docks offer a complex of alternative routes.

A large-scale map in the *Carte Guide* explains all. Rather than drop immediately into the mighty Rhine, we retreated to the barge-filled Bassin d'Austerlitz, braved the attentions of a highly conscientious guard dog at a fuelling station and continued through the city docks to

A smooth descent on the Arzvillers inclined plane boat lift. Note counterweights between the rails at the top

join 36km of *péniche*-sized Canal du Rhône au Rhin that duplicates the canalised Rhine (or Grand Canal d'Alsace) to Rhinau. This way, all doubts were removed about finding a safe halt for the night, for the Rhine has few wash-free pleasure craft moorings. Our chosen waterway had poorly maintained radar-controlled locks; we were warned to expect problems when the first keeper volunteered details of a VHF radio channel with which we could call up help.

Alsace was sizzling in the heat of a Sunday afternoon. Diana, on the outside steering station, failed to notice an old fisherman asleep in the shadows of a bridge hole. He had two lines right across the navigation; we caught each on our stern gear. Waking with a start, the angler's immediate reaction was that he had caught the canal carp of the century. A second later, one expensive rod was wrenched from his grasp while the other was hauled from its support and began to follow *Avonbay*. None of this was our fault, but canal anglers do not universally understand that the channel is for boats and can turn quite nasty. The shiny-looking fishing gear doubtless represented several weeks pension. Attack was our best defence. 'Oh, monsieur,' John called out 'You have fouled both our propellors. My friend must now dive under the vessel to free them!' At this, I leaped into the blissfully warm water. The old man was less agitated than we might have expected, but direct communication was difficult, for he appeared only to speak Alsatian. Quite rapidly, I removed the tackle from our shafts, recovered the still moderately intact rods, and the crew of *Avonbay* cried 'Bravo!' as if we had done him a great service.

An overworked young man in a swimming costume repeatedly responded to our radio calls when the locks were being sulky. All the while, he was dividing his attention between us and some barges further down the line. We swam often to cool off; so did he. Numerous ice-cold drinks, taken from the fridge, were shared with the keeper. This friendliness paid dividends, for he stayed on duty half an hour after the regulation closing time, seeing us through to the junction with the Rhine.

In a deserted wasteland of pebbles and willow scrub, the mighty river poured by, extensively remodelled between the thirties and seventies; now there are vast canal cuts, hydro-electric stations and a series of deep locks in these upper reaches of the navigation. The Rhine remains Europe's busiest and most powerful waterway. Here, nearly 800km above its Dutch estuary, it commanded respect. We ate dinner on deck. Then, as a thick darkness descended, I went down among the engines, carefully checking oil levels, filters and water pumps. Tomorrow would be a testing time for the machinery: upwards of twelve hours pushing against the stream. We planned to reach Switzerland by nightfall.

11

Rhine to Switzerland

SIGNIFICANTLY, there are no hire cruisers on the Rhine – 2,000-tonne ships, huge floating hotels, little barges, tugs, high-speed private cruisers and even canoes are all controlled by rather fearsome police launches. On this watery motorway, everyone is carefully watched. With a displacement craft like *Avonbay*, tackling the uppermost 100km of navigation would be slow but not impossible. The downstream return was dramatically faster.

At 6.30am precisely, we entered the Ecluse du Rhin, waved goodbye to the friendly Canal du Rhône au Rhin and headed out into the current of the great river. Ahead, the first of the giant locks presented a barrier of concrete, shore to shore. Closer investigation revealed two chambers, both closed against us. Using a greeting in well-rehearsed French, I radioed to the keeper, surprisingly receiving a reply in German. Few French-speaking pleasure craft venture into these waters, where German is the normal language of communication. Coaxing the unseen voice into his native French, I received an assurance that we would be kept waiting for fifteen minutes. Traffic lights glowed red and green; then a gate opened, signals changed to green alone and we surged into the vast dripping cavern. We, the only boat, hooked onto a floating bollard and smoothly floated to the upper level.

An earlier British explorer of the upper Rhine was Donald Maxwell (The Log of the Griffin, 1905). His little sailing vessel was constructed in an Alpine village and successfully ran downriver to the North Sea, eventually reaching the Thames at Teddington four weeks after departure from Rheinfelden

At first, everything was quiet on the broad expanse of river beyond the lock cut. Oily black water gurgled past, undisturbed by other traffic. But as the morning wore on, barges began to appear – giant bluff-bowed monsters – throwing out a plume of wash which rocked us violently, fore and aft. Five minutes later waves, bouncing off the distant stone banks, returned to centre channel where we now rolled from side to side. Emerging from Marckolsheim lock, *Avonbay* received enthusiastic waves from pampered passengers on the high deck of Köln-Düsseldorfer hotel ship *Britannia*. We considered dipping our ensign in salute but made do instead with a long blast on the horn. Apart from occasional yacht harbours on the German side, there were few mooring possibilities. Just twice we noted lengths of vertical quay instead of sloping concrete; these were lashed by waves and would have provided a very uncomfortable berth for a small boat, so we kept on the move, regularly checking the engine room to make certain all was well. Scenic interest is very limited. Towns sensibly avoid the flood plain, so the navigator must spend hours contemplating a vista of poplars, willows and shingle.

Below Vogelgrün lock, the entrance to Colmar's branch canal slipped past. Several hours and two locks after that came a junction with the main line of the Canal du Rhône au Rhin, which would lead us back into Burgundy in due course. Now, there was considerable industrial development, sited to benefit from the superb transport facilities: factories; warehouses; cranes and wharves; all packed with commercial craft.

Close encounter in Augst, one of two locks on the Swiss Rhine. Astern of Avonbay *are our Dutch friends aboard* Brandaris

Kembs, final lock of the day, was the first to be built on the Grand Canal d'Alsace, in 1932. Here, lines of fixed bollards necessitated our progressively shifting the ropes as the level rose. Our ascent was accompanied by a deafening whistle when water gushed through a series of ports the length of the chamber, leaving the surface pocked with huge bubbles. This experience was heightened by a violent thunderstorm. For much of the last 10km to Basle, we could hardly see where we were heading in the bad light and driving rain. Back in the Rhine proper, the flow increased to 3–4 knots. We lit the navigation lights and grew rather apprehensive. Our chart was of little help in pinpointing a suitable mooring for the night. Deciding to try our luck in the Kleinhüningen harbour at the downstream outskirts of the city, we were greatly relieved to find our Dutch friends on *Brandaris* made fast to a quay. Subsequently, this turned out to be the only safe place to lie. It was hardly convenient, being a long tram ride from the city centre; also, we were kept awake much of the night by ships coming in to take on fuel unpleasantly close by.

A posse of Swiss Customs officers boarded us at 7am; at this stage we were uncertain that we had crossed the border! A searching inquisition began. Ship's papers and passports were required as well as replies to a comprehensive questionnaire detailing our supplies of alcohol, tea, coffee, fuel, cameras (we declared nine), tape recorders (three), typewriters (none) and finally *feuerwaffen*. To be thus rudely plunged from French – which we had virtually mastered – to German (I had six weeks instruction more than twenty-five years earlier) when not properly awake was testing indeed. *Feuer*, I recognised as 'fire', so started counting our array of extinguishers, installed in quantity to satisfy Thames Water Authority regulations. As I reached six, the Customs officer became visibly agitated, drew a pistol from his holster and demanded, in German: 'You have six of these?' Interrogation over, there was no duty to pay. The harbour master waived an 8 Swiss franc mooring fee, we watered, found fresh food at a small shop by the road frontier round the corner and in bright sunshine we followed *Brandaris* upriver, our Swiss courtesy flag fluttering merrily.

Basle stands at a crossroads on the borders of France, Germany and Switzerland. Outside our harbour, a rocket-shaped structure acknowledges this: for an instant we could have justified flying all three flags at once. The waterfronts are most attractive, with numerous tall buildings rising sheer from the river. Small passenger ferries, more suited to Hong Kong harbour, scuttle from bank to bank on captive wires. The current tears through bridge arches and our progress declined to a crawl. A constant watch had to be kept for commercial traffic, for this is the most important freight corridor into Switzerland. Nowhere was there a suitable pleasure-craft mooring;

when we tried to tie up at a yacht-club pontoon, we were firmly told that we couldn't stop to explore the city. At this, we rather lost interest and pressed on to Birsfelden, first of the two Swiss locks. Not far beyond, all signs of earlier commercial wharves and barge traffic disappeared. Woods and meadows, vineyards and chalets made the last 13km of the Rhine a delight. Prompted by seeing locals swimming, we also bathed while waiting for the final lock at Augst, confident that we were beyond the reach of the notorious Rhine pollution. Three months afterwards, a disastrous chemical spillage in Basle resulted in 30 tonnes of mercury being washed into the river, virtually wiping out all life between there and Holland.

'The flow is now insignificant,' a local boater informed us. We measured a current of perhaps 4 knots and wondered what it would be like when the melting snows regularly raise levels by as much as 4m.

Augst, the Roman trading centre of Augusta Raurica, dates from 44 BC. Excavations since the sixteenth century have revealed an amphitheatre, forum with basilica, thermal baths, and extensive remains of temples and houses equipped with sophisticated plumbing. The lock, completed in the early twentieth century, is small by Rhine standards at 85x11.20m. It features particularly slippery, sloping sides. A genial keeper chatted away in fairly unintelligible German as he threw down ropes to which we made fast, just as a large passenger vessel entered, took up station in the centre and attached itself to a cable stretched from bank to bank. We felt small and rather vulnerable.

Rheinfelden, at the head of navigation, is part German, part Swiss. We planned to spend a day here, but hovering in the racing current below the rock-filled bridge arches, there seemed a total lack of safe moorings. Without expert knowledge, nothing was going to make us approach the stony sides. We dropped downstream for a kilometre and came to rest on a yacht-club pontoon. Getting ashore past a locked gate was a problem conveniently solved by a friendly boat-owner who offered to drive our Dutch friend and me to arrange a mooring on piles at the Café Graf, in a narrow channel just below the bridge. Two hours later, after a well-intentioned but unwanted tour of the Feldschlösschen brewery and its private steam-powered railway system, we returned to the boats where our respective crews had given us up for lost. *Brandaris*'s small dog had managed to jump ashore and then made suicidal attempts to return to the pontoon by leaping into the raging torrent. June, always resourceful with animals, suggested greasing the creature with butter so it could be slid through the locked railing gate. Our arrival with key holder was fortunately just in time to prevent this risky plan being put into operation. All the professional skill of the Dutch family was required in coming alongside the Graf mooring piles. We breasted up and went ashore for coffee and cream cakes. Throughout our stay, the Rhine drove *Avonbay*'s propellor shafts like turbines, a phenomenon never experienced before or since.

A better choice than Rheinfelden could hardly have been made for our brief contact with Switzerland. From the mooring, a long pedestrianised street was lined with Black Forest shops and houses encrusted with baroque painted decoration. Elaborate gilded wrought-iron signs projected over the cobbles, advertising a variety of trades. While the site was occupied by deer hunters 10,000 years ago, the present development can be traced to the early tenth century when a noble Burgundian family erected a castle stronghold on the rocky island. Fortification towers point to many centuries of conflict, as the town switched from France to the Austrian Empire. During the Thirty Years War, the seige of Rheinfelden began in 1634 and was to last for a quarter of a century. Incorporated into Switzerland in 1803, the town's future lay in its development as a spa, following discovery of salt springs in the 1850s. Most fashionable immediately before World War I, recent attempts have been successful in promoting the medicinal qualities of the area.

John and I were having a working Swiss breakfast in the Schiff Hotel. By appointment, we were guests of the dozen stolid burghers who comprised the town council. We were appalled at the lack of convenient moorings for visiting craft and had devised a cost-effective system of pontoons on the island connected to the bridge which leads into Germany. The mayor and his retinue listened with polite attention, but it was soon obvious they had no intention of spending a franc. The Schiff's owner, Frau Marie-Therèse Dörfler acted as interpreter: 'This is a matter for the regional canton, not our town.' And so, Rheinfelden seems destined to remain one of the most worthwhile ports of call on Europe's greatest river, inaccessible to all but the most intrepid boatman.

Rheinfelden, uppermost limit of navigation on Western Europe's greatest river. Mooring here was not without problems

To turn *Avonbay* in a 25m wide channel where the stream tore past like a mill race, was an exercise that had to be done right first time. On reflection, it would have been safer to warp her round. Instead, we spun on both engines, only just avoided jagged rocks at the water's edge and began our descent of the Rhine at an unaccustomed 13½ knots.

Reaching Basle, we again spent one disturbed night in the Kleinhüningen harbour. Within seconds of getting lines ashore, a young and over-keen Customs officer was on board and knocking back our alcohol. He was clearly annoyed to learn we had cleared Swiss Customs the previous day. A halting conversation, in English, turned to the UK price of whisky. He considered this absurdly low and wanted to buy a bottle. As he had now long outstayed his welcome, John tried to speed his departure by offering one as a gift. In whispers, he promised to return for it after dark and out of uniform.

The sixty-hour visit to Switzerland was at an end. Down came the short-lived courtesy flag, to be replaced by a French tricolour. It seemed unlikely that *Avonbay* would ever sail these waters again. 125km of rapid progress down the Grand Canal d'Alsace brought us back to Strasbourg by evening.

Our last day in France saw us through the most recently constructed of Rhine locks at Gambsheim and Iffezheim. Still, surroundings were featureless. Onwards from here, the river surges unbridled all the way to the North Sea. The current became stronger; we were relieved we were not fighting it. All the while, the well-buoyed channel swings from bank to bank, with ugly training walls projecting into the stream. Remaining alert to spot 'blue-flagging' ships was always necessary. A blue board with a white flashing light at the centre denotes that the craft is navigating on the 'wrong' side, taking advantage of reduced flow. The French town of Lauterbourg came 54km after Strasbourg: northwards, the Rhine is totally within Germany. Several anxious moments passed while *Avonbay* was turned into the current to stem a fierce surge by the harbour entrance. We tied to a floating pontoon for the night, thankful to be in tranquil water again. Downstream barges flashed by 50m away, while those working upriver clawed into the torrent, the chuffing of their hard-worked engines remaining audible for twenty minutes.

Insufficient research had been carried out to reveal the location of the French and German Customs posts. Not only did we well know that the Germans would want to investigate us; but we also required documentary evidence of our departure from French waters, so avoiding payment of Value Added Tax at some time in the future. I cycled to the road frontier to pass a fruitless half hour interrogating officials of each country. No one had the slightest idea of how to process a boat! We had taken the precaution of writing to the London office of the German Chamber of Industry and Commerce for an Opinion on regulations. This information came with a £50 invoice and the suggestion that British vessels could visit Germany for a specified period, provided (1) evidence is carried to prove a permanent mooring in the UK; (2) the boat is not lent or hired to German nationals; (3) that use is strictly limited to non-commercial pleasure cruising; (4) that those in charge hold a current Overseas Helmsman's Certificate of Competence (obtained from the Royal Yachting Association). A final paragraph gave some cause for concern: 'We must point out that the decision as to whether or not a temporary use exemption from VAT will in practice be granted will always be a matter for the discretion of the Customs Office at the border.'

That evening, a bright green launch like a gunboat, but bearing the large sign *Zoll*, appeared in our harbour. We hailed it enthusiastically, in the hope of being cleared then and there. Several very amiable officers, wives, girlfriends and children clambered on board. We dispensed alcohol, made friends despite the severe language barrier . . . and learned that a visit to the Neuburgweier Customs post, 5km downriver, would still have to be made in the morning.

The Germans were waiting as we punched into the current rushing past a basin on the east bank. *Avonbay* narrowly missed being swept onto rocks at the downstream end of the entrance. Passports were checked and found in order. And that was all. No searching questions about VAT, importation or ship's stores. The entertainment ploy the previous evening had paid off. A document in carefully composed German had already been prepared by us, stating the *Avonbay* had entered the *Vaterland* on 9 August 1986. We must obtain an official stamp. With smiles, the Germans assured us this was not necessary. Determined not to be caught with a demand for French VAT in due course, we used the formula devised in similar circumstances in Calais. '*Andenken, bitte*,' I said, using the word for 'souvenir'. '*Ach, Andenken!*' exclaimed the officer, and an impression in violet ink from the Zoll Hauptzollamt Baden-Baden was forcefully added to the ship's paperwork.

Twelve months later, *Avonbay* navigated the Moselle upstream of Koblenz and crossed the border into France. Our exploration of southern Germany had been a great success, cruising the lovely Neckar, Main and Lahn. Frankfurt friends had kindly kept an eye on the boat while she wintered in the city's Westhafen. Even the dreaded Rhine Gorge had just been possible. Five holidays in Bavaria and the Rhineland were immensely enjoyable: now we were ready to return to our first love – France.

12

Moselle

EXACTLY a year to the day after entering Germany, we found ourselves back in more familiar and easy-going French waters. The frontiers of Luxembourg and Germany touch France at Apach lock. Once the huge chamber had filled, we went ashore with ship's papers and passports to clear German Customs in a building at the lockside. Being a small country, Luxembourg appeared not to bother with such matters: both our entry to and exit from their territory went unrecorded. The Germans raised no problems, so we walked next door to the French post. Introductions had just been completed when the lock-keeper burst into panic-stricken announcements over the public address system. The gist of his raving was that *Avonbay* must immediately be removed from the pen as a passenger vessel was waiting to descend. By this stage, the French were indicating that they would like to subject us to an onboard inspection; but already I had gone, leaving June and the girls to negotiate. The boat was moved several hundred metres out of the lock, to a mooring beyond the upper gates. Meanwhile, unable to wait a second longer, the passenger ship actually passed me at full speed inside the chamber. Now a speck in the distance, *Avonbay* was well beyond convenient reach of the Customs officers. They grudgingly relented and the crew rejoined me leaving a dissatisfied group of officials in their stupidly sited office.

Moselle washer-women encountered by George Waring (The Bride of the Rhine, Two Hundred Miles in a Mosel Row-Boat, 1878)

The Moselle has a varied navigational history. Used with some difficulty by the Romans, its shallow draught made movement hazardous for the early steamers of the nineteenth century. Improvements began with the building of locks and side canals at the upper, French end, so that by 1876 300-tonners could use the length from near Nancy to Metz. But as Alsace-Lorraine had been seized by Prussia in the war of 1870–1, and Germany supported railway traffic rather than the river, little more was done until France regained her lost territory after World War I. A further section was canalised down to Thionville by 1932, chiefly to serve French steelworks in the region. At last, Germany saw the sense of creating a modern waterway from France down to the Rhine, but another war was to intervene; joint action by France, Luxembourg and Germany in 1956 resulted in a 2,000-tonne capacity route upstream to the French border by 1964. Subsequent works have upgraded the higher reaches to the same standard, so that Rhine ships can now reach Neuves-Maisons, beyond Nancy. It remains to be seen if an additional scheme is ever carried out, to continue the line southwards to the River Saône, thus providing a Europa-ship link with the Rhône and the Mediterranean.

Best of the Moselle scenery is to be found in the German section, comprising almost continuous vineyards and dozens of historic towns. Our journey over this length had in part been frustrating because of a chronic shortage of safe urban moorings. Now, in France, we could tie up almost everywhere we chose. At first, Sierck-les-Bains, a charming settlement squeezed between the river and hilltop fortifications, appeared to be poorly served: sounding with a boathook along the town quay revealed much rock in shallow water. However, some distance upstream, we spotted a most convenient concrete projection, directly opposite the K246 marker post.

Sierck boasts a ruinous castle, originally built in the eleventh century on the site of the Roman *Circum Castellum*. Destroyed during the Thirty Years War, in 1643, it was reconstructed by Vauban, unsuccessfully attacked by the Duke of Marlborough in 1705, and remained as a border defence until 1866. Close inspection showed that there was rather more to explore than is immediately obvious. Tunnels, vaulted chambers and spiral stairs are hidden in the grassy mounds, high above the town's narrow cobbled streets. The girls and I whiled away an hour 'designing' an exclusive hotel such as would leave the exterior of the structure unchanged.

On the opposite shore, the small town of Conz-les-Bains is surrounded by one of the few vineyards visible from a boat on the French river. Until the late nineteenth century, a curious and ancient rite was performed each midsummer, when bonfires were lit on the Stromberg hill, above the vines. Straw was used to bind a great wooden wheel, which was rolled ablaze towards the Moselle, guided by young men clutching flaming torches. If the wheel ran beyond a particular well, Sierck had to present Conz with a barrel of white wine; but if it were to stop short, Conz would give Sierck a large wicker basket filled with cherries. By reaching the river, where the flames would be extinguished, a notable vintage could be expected from that autumn's harvest. Derived from some form of heathen fire worship, this boisterous event was regarded as a highlight of the calendar.

At first, the river scenery was pleasant if unremarkable, punctuated by the modern concrete locks of Koenigsmacher, Thionville, Orne/Richmont and Talange, all with chambers 176x12m. At several of these towns alternative *péniche*-sized locks remained in use, reminders of the Canal des Mines de Fer de la Moselle ('Camifemo') scheme of 1932. Although generally the only craft working through, we were unexpectedly asked for no payment, having previously understood that the Moselle was one rare French waterway where a charge is levied. From Thionville (renamed Diedenhofen after the German occupation of 1870) dejected surroundings with iron foundries gave us little cause to linger. It was a Sunday afternoon; our sights were set on a rather special mooring for the evening. A large lake, entered at K288, is fringed by sailing clubs, boathouses and glimpses through trees of the villas of the most affluent inhabitants of Metz. While determined to run *Avonbay* to the heart of this one-time independent city state, we found that rearrangement of channels over the years resulted in much confusion as to which was the correct route. Some travellers give up the hunt for a way through the maze, moor near the commercial harbour and leave with a poor impression of the place. With chart in hand, I consulted the keeper of Metz lock: he explained that we must continue up a broad reach, pass beneath an *autoroute* bridge, turn left across the top of a weir and run downstream along a little channel, bordered by trees and parkland. The way ahead widened into an attractive pool with several dozen motor cruisers and a presumably disused small lock at the far corner. We continued under a bridge to find ourselves on a quay close to the great cathedral and directly opposite the Protestant Temple. There was some initial difficulty in tying up without unduly disturbing troughs of magnificent geraniums suspended on railings.

Sunday evening and the following Monday closure was an economical time to explore the enticing shops, St Étienne's vast cathedral (awarded three stars in the *Guide Michelin Alsace et Lorraine*) and some impressive fortifications known as the 'Porte des Allemands'. Metz is a very green city, where rivers and millstreams are admirably planted with flowers, trees and lawns. Understandably, some of the leading public buildings are more German than French in

Opposite: Our mooring in the heart of Metz was reached after some complicated navigation

character. We enjoyed our brief visit and certainly intend to return.

Hoping to buy gas at the Port Robert Schuman marina (K301.6), we found they had none and were directed to a supermarket *à 300m* in Longueville-lès-Metz. As is often the case, the distance was more like a kilometre up a rough track; the empty bottle was hauled thither on our shopping trolley and being of German manufacture was expensively discarded in favour of a new French one. A great drawback to long-distance European cruising is that gas companies are often strictly regional, their agents refusing to exchange one brand for another. This purchase thus cost 200 francs more than it should.

After two weeks of rainy weather, a heatwave had now arrived, so we had few objections to a long cruise past the Roman aqueduct arches of Jouy and Pont-à-Mousson with its appealing triangular 'square'. Plenty of 300-tonne barges were in evidence, mainly loaded with gravel, but none of the large ships for which the upper Moselle was so recently enlarged. I seriously wonder if all that expenditure was justified. In the fields below Blénod, seemingly derelict steelworks belched out thick black smoke and flames. Often, there were the remains of disused locks, all swept out of use in the great rebuilding programme.

Bound for the Meuse and Belgium, our obvious course would have been to stay on the Moselle as far as Toul. However, on reaching a junction in Frouard, we decided to make a detour up the Canal de la Marne au Rhin to Nancy, which we had missed visiting on several occasions. Although rather inefficient, the keeper of the Écluse de Jonction was a jolly young fellow, accepting our bowline with a boathook as we entered the deep chamber but unfortunately failing to make it fast ashore, with the result that it fell back on deck. Having seen us through there, he clambered into a small car, drove for a considerable distance at high speed in reverse down the narrow towpath, prepared the next lock and was sitting fishing with his girlfriend when we arrived with the air of one who hasn't moved all afternoon. There onwards, the run into Nancy is on a level, past busy railway tracks where locomotive drivers hooted at the girls sunbathing on deck. Below, the once navigable River Meurthe trickled grubbily through a *zone industrielle*. On the right, a somewhat severe building proclaimed in paint at least a quarter of century old that it had been a regional headquarters of the Cie Générale Française de Tramways, operators of a fleet of towpath engines, used to haul unpowered barges.

A good mooring was selected through a bascule bridge in the little Port de Malzéville, alongside a drydock and canal maintenance yard. Had we continued a little further, the Bassin Ste Catherine would have been somewhat closer to the city centre. Among our neighbours there would have been the Cowley family on their Sheffield barge *Danum*, last seen two years earlier on the Marne.

According to an old saying, there were just three really magnificent ceremonies in Europe: the crowning of an emperor at Frankfurt; the annointing of a French king in Reims and the burial of a duke of Lorraine in Nancy. Certainly, the city has a rich past, and reaches a peak of glory in the great Place Stanislas, perhaps the most elegant eighteenth century site in the whole of France. Stanislas had been removed as King of Poland and when his daughter married Louis XV, he was created a sort of Governor of Nancy. During the following thirty years, he improved and decorated the city, laying out the square which bears his name. Elaborate wrought-iron grilles, lanterns, a great fountain and other works of art are encrusted with gilding, while the enclosed area is bordered by classical buildings and arcades, including the *hôtel de ville*. Early in the morning, we set out across a beautiful park, known as La Pépinière, arrived at the Place Stanislas and spent the morning enjoyably shopping. Lunch – a shamefully expensive one – was taken in the Grand Hôtel Concorde, one of the best establishments in town. Our appetite for sightseeing now slightly diminished, we returned to the less salubrious surroundings of the canal, noting on the way numerous shop fronts and other buildings in a wonderful variety of *art nouveau* designs, for it was here that the taste for modern architecture flourished in the early years of the twentieth century.

While a welcome sun blazed on deck, the engines were treated to a well-deserved oil change and I managed to give *Avonbay* a layer of white gloss where the superstructure had been covered in undercoat for the previous three months. Then, it was back to the Moselle, travelling in company with *Danum*. Not many years before, the journey between Nancy and Toul would have been along the *péniche*-sized Canal de la Marne au Rhin. Canalisation of the upper Moselle involved demolition of an aqueduct carrying the old waterway over the river at Liverdun, a town sometimes called 'Little Switzerland'. A barge tunnel which I vividly recall alive with traffic is now dry and overgrown, 22km of the former line are derelict and from time to time we would see the remains of locks with rusting paddle gear.

A friendly towpath locomotive in retirement near the Foug Tunnel, Canal de la Marne au Rhin

Aingeray lock was shared with the Sheffield keel and three unladen *péniches;* showing that these 38m vessels have a good turn of speed when motoring in deep water, they easily overtook us in a wide, buoyed, reach beyond, throwing plumes of white spray high in the air from their barely submerged propellors. When the cathedral of Toul came into sight, we began to look for a short length of new canal that would lead us out of the Moselle so that we could rejoin the Marne au Rhin. By pulling a length of piping suspended from a bridge, we prepared Écluse 27 *bis* for ourselves, passed through an arch in the city walls, and shortly moored in the pleasantly landscaped Port de France to plan the next stage of the journey.

Some years before, June, John and I flew from London to Luxembourg to join the Harvingtons on their cruiser at the bottom of the Moselle in Koblenz. We were to travel via the Main as far as Nuremburg, while Flossie and Grant were to continue down the Danube to the Black Sea, conveying *Melitina* by low-loader across the gap created by the unfinished Rhein-Main-Donau Canal. The ship's dinghy had been carried away in a storm off the Channel Isles; at a late stage, we had been requested to collect a replacement inflatable from a Piccadilly chandlery. We landed in Luxembourg with this suspicious-looking large parcel, explaining to the Customs that we were in the habit of taking a liferaft with us when ever we flew over the sea! This pleasant attempt at humour fell on unreceptive ears: never before had a boat arrived at the little airport. We would have to pay duty on it. Explanations that we should be leaving the country within the hour by train were unheeded. The duty was exacted and a receipt given which I produced at the German border with a request for a full refund. The train was consequently delayed for ten minutes and our fellow travellers expressed their objections volubly.

Now it was time to return to Luxembourg airport. Auriole was flying back to England; John and Evelyn were coming out to join us on the boat. Train timetables appeared useless. A return taxi for the considerable distance involved would be ruinous. Our car was parked several hundred kilometres away in Koblenz where a German garage had perhaps finished fitting a new automatic gearbox. The only possible solution was to hire a self-drive car. This proved to be unexpectedly easy: we took the sporty little Renault on a food shopping trip and by the time I was ready to depart for Luxembourg, I had located reverse gear. When the new crew arrived, it was obvious that June had passed a very busy day alone on the boat, washing, cleaning and even painting. In 1983, our voyage down the Meuse to Verdun had been aboard a somewhat elderly hire cruiser with a heavily scarred plastic hull. Now we were keen to return and show the locals what a British boat should look like.

13

Meuse to Belgium

THIRTEEN mechanised locks spread through 18km of Canal de la Marne au Rhin, lifted us away from Toul towards a junction with the Canal de l'Est (Nord) at Troussey. The waterway was busy with barges and a variety of pleasure craft; nevertheless, we enjoyed a rapid passage, negotiated the 866m Foug tunnel and stopped in the Lay-St-Rémy basin at the far end for a welcome swim followed by lunch. Water quality in country canals, while churned to a cloudy consistency by passing traffic, is probably fairly good. We have swum regularly for many years and never experienced any ill-effects.

I have long considered that the River Meuse suffers a great injustice in being officially described, prosaically, as the Canal de l'Est (Branche Nord). True, artificial cuts do characterise the uppermost reaches as the infant stream chuckles along at the side, but soon the navigation joins some of the most glorious lengths of river in Europe. It winds through the dense forests of the Ardennes, crosses the frontier into Belgium and eventually loses its identify as the Dutch 'Maas' in the Rhine Delta.

Our plan was to travel for 353km through sixty-four locks all the way to the Belgian city of Namur. First sighting of the river was obtained just before we left the Marne au Rhin to work through five

Dinant on the Belgian Meuse. Detail from a lithograph by C. Stansfield (1793–1867)

109

descending locks to Euville. Briefly, we were introduced to the Meuse itself, before turning into another canal section upstream of Commercy: this pattern would continue for several days until we reached Charleville-Mézières. Situated in border country, the river has suffered repeated rape over the centuries. Intense fighting has come no fewer than three times in the last 120 years (Franco-Prussian War, World War I and World War II) and a feeling of melancholy hangs in the air. The Meuse has recovered her ravishing beauty, but memories of appalling slaughter are never far away. We moored beyond a lock in Vadonville for the night and watched several *péniches* run south through curls of mist early next day. It was going to be hot.

Combines were harvesting grain in vast golden fields as we passed a succession of small towns and villages. Churches in St-Mihiel contain examples of the work of locally born sixteenth-century sculptor Ligier Richier. A swooning Virgin Mary carved in wood and a vivid marble entombment of Christ are among his best known works. Unfortunately, there was little enthusiasm on *Avonbay* for viewing art treasures that day; we tied to a maintenance barge for lunch, then entered a long, locked canal cut through water meadows where creamy cattle grazed beneath pollarded willows. But for the French buildings and frequent meetings with freight barges, this could have been the highest reaches of the Thames.

During our waterway travels, we have met a fascinating assortment of people, but none were quite so curious as Mr Sniffle, encountered on the Meuse, four years earlier. It was early evening when we had moored for the night in a field somewhere above Verdun. On hearing the sound of an engine, we looked up to note a solid little steel cruiser heading upstream. As she passed, we were astonished to observe that the skipper was steering stark naked in his open stern cockpit. He turned to wave in our direction, smiled, and disappeared from view round the next bend. Even now, such an event would be a trifle unusual on the sun-drenched waterways of the south. In these northern French latitudes, in 1983, we thought it highly odd and wrote him off as a dangerous pervert!

Two days later, we caught up with the same cream-painted cruiser, named *Sniffle*, and inevitably found that we were sharing locks with her. The captain, alone on board, now wore a pair of shorts and replied to our French greeting with a flow of utterly unintelligible words. Noting his Dutch ensign, I tried German and then the few Dutch words I knew, all with the same result. Attempts at conversation were thus extremely difficult, although we did somehow extract the information that a 'Sniffle' was some form of hound. Eventually, we came to the conclusion that our friend hailed from Friesland. By restricting ourselves to the most basic Anglo Saxon words, a degree of understanding was established. White haired and probably nearing sixty, Mr Sniffle was undertaking a voyage from Groningen to Paris, without so much as a word of French, only the slightest knowledge of the route he must follow and nothing resembling a map. He remained with us for several days, stopping when we did, starting up again when we moved off in the morning, all the way to Vitry-le-François. Never did he bother to go shopping, relying for meals on the contents of a saucepan which ceaselessly boiled on a small stove at the cabin entrance. Within, was a scene of total chaos: clothes; fuel cans; odd pieces of timber and scraps of newspaper thrown onto the two bunks. He was splendidly uninhibited and would happily talk for minutes on end to uncomprehending canal staff.

Arriving at one lock, the upper gates failed to close completely, resulting in more water pouring into the chamber than was leaving by the lower paddles. Sizing up the situation, Mr Sniffle hauled a length of good-quality carpet from his cabin floor, used it to plug the gap and proceded to drag a bottom gate open against the head of water by attaching a rope and running his boat's engine hard astern. He was certainly resourceful. We could hardly believe our eyes when watching his night-time mooring procedure. Out would come two massive iron stakes, each as tall as their owner. Somehow, these were hammered into the towpath, followed by a heavy fisherman's anchor flung overboard. These precautions would have kept him safe in a hurricane.

For all his busy bravado, Mr Sniffle had us worried for his well-being. Rather in the way that you feel obliged to care for a wounded wild animal, we started feeding him, arranged a source of fuel when his diesel supplies were nearly exhausted and set him firmly on a course for Paris as our routes finally diverged. I often wonder if he made it to the capital; even more if he and the scruffy *Sniffle* ever arrived home in northern Holland. Probably to this day he regales a circle of boating friends with tales of the great voyage through France, that strange land where no one can understand a word you say.

Poor planning brought us to the heart of Verdun on Monday with most shops closed. The elegant quaysides were rebuilt with financial aid from England after terrifying bombardment in 1916. Seventy years on, it is difficult to reconcile the nineteenth-century buildings with old postcard views of shattered houses and piles of rubble. Now, there are excellent moorings with plenty to see ashore. Verdun is ancient Gallic for 'powerful fortress'. Onwards from Roman times, the city has been constantly attacked: its great preoccupation now is with the slaughter of World War I. The tourist office promotes visits to the battlefields, the Douaumont Ossuary, burial place for 100,000 unidentified troops and the 4km of underground passages in the Citadel, where the body of the Unknown Soldier was chosen on 10 November 1920 for burial at the Arc de Triomphe in Paris. It is all rather depressing.

We had explored Verdun thoroughly four years earlier, so moved on into open country for the night, expecting the spectre of death to be less overpowering. Near Écluse 22, we had a barbecue on the bank and afterwards strolled in the fading light to a tiny settlement on the main road. A church, *mairie* and two or three modern houses stood by a stone soldier reaching for his gas mask. Underneath, we read the inscription: *'Ici était Samogneux'*. Virtually everything in the little town had been blown into oblivion in 1916.

With plenty of time in hand, we ambled on, briefly halting to explore small villages. At Stenay, a *port de plaisance* has been created in a small basin. We moored opposite a navigation authority barge, fitted out as a travelling exhibition celebrating 150 years of the Canal des Ardennes. The French are becoming very aware of their waterway history and are making commendable efforts to introduce cruising facilities, especially on routes where commercial traffic is declining. The little manufacturing town, once heavily fortified, had been headquarters of the German Crown Prince for eighteen months during World War I. Dinner ashore at the Hotel du Commerce was a bargain at 408 francs for the five of us, a clear indication that eating out need not be expensive.

All the while, the Meuse was broadening, with sparkling weirs composed of wooden needle sluices. Apart from fishing punts there were very few local pleasure craft. When we stopped for lunch in meadows at Pouilly, not a single boat came into sight for two hours. A backwater, just above the lock at Mouzon is now equipped with jetties, so we moored to visit the Gallo-Roman town, still partly fortified and with an impressive abbey church, dating from the twelfth century.

Clear skies and a blazing sun brought us to a series of floating pontoons close to the centre of Sedan. Arranged at right angles to the stream, they were unexpectedly awkward to come alongside. Fortunately, our fenders absorbed the resulting impact.

Avonbay now required refuelling, so we worked through two locks of the Canal des Ardennes to a commercial boatyard at Pont-à-Bar. Here, little can have changed in fifty years: *péniches* were under repair on sideways slips, while an old wooden barge ashore had been turned into a workshop. Outside the boatmen's café, an open air bowling alley featured an ingenious chute for the return of the bowls, just like another we had discovered years earlier on the Canal de l'Est at Corre. Back at the junction, the keeper proudly showed us his 1932 vintage electric pump which lifts river water to supply the canal. Each lock is similarly equipped, progressively pumping pound by pound to the

Opposite: *A péniche heads slowly down the Meuse at Écluse 21, Champ, between Verdun and Mouzay* Overleaf: *Canal du Midi. Medieval fortified town of Argens-Minervois, at the western end of Le Grand Bief*

summit level, 21km and seven locks south-west. My expertise was tested by one barge skipper, who was navigating the Ardennes for the first time. With *Carte Guides* in hand, I was able to talk him through his route to the Aisne at Compiègne.

Back on the river, a selection of locks has been automated with radar sensors detecting approaching craft and preparing chambers accordingly. Most, however, had keepers, suggesting that the system is unreliable.

One of the highlights of a Meuse voyage is Charleville, a seventeenth-century 'new town', established by the Duke Charles de Gonzague as a manufacturing centre. Its great treasure is the huge Place Ducale, one of the finest urban squares in France, surrounded by classical buildings in pink brick and yellow stone. Recently restored, many still bear painted signs in elegant late nineteenth-century lettering. Shop fronts are protected from the weather by a long series of vaulted arcades. A market was in progress, including stalls of *brocante*. Among the items of collectable junk were decorative cast-iron wood-burning stoves, long made in the Ardennes, antiquated domestic and agricultural equipment, rusty upright bicycles and turn-of-the-century postcards. These are an excellent source of old waterways views: I passed an hour leafing through several thousand, while the girls made a raid on (to them) the equally irresistible clothes shops.

Our mooring on stages by a municipal camping site at Mont Olympe, up a backwater, was convenient both for the town centre and a restaurant offering, surprisingly, seafood specialities. John reduced our waitress to convulsions of helpless laughter by ordering *tortue* (tortoise) rather than *torteau* (crab). After that, nothing we said was taken very seriously. My third visit to Luxembourg Airport in as many weeks put Diana on a flight to stay with friends in Monte Carlo.

When we were ready to resume our cruise, the skies had clouded: much of the remainder of the journey to Belgium was in characterisically rainy Ardennes weather. Even so, the river looked superb, winding past dense forests with outcrops of limestone, reputedly inhabited by deer and wild boar. Traditionally, ironwork such as decorative railings is cast in small foundries in the bankside towns but these detract little from the magnificent surroundings.

High above the little town of Château-Regnault, whose castle was destroyed by Louis XIV, four bare rocks project from the forest. These are known locally as the Four Sons of Aymon. With the aid of a magical horse named Bayard, they repeatedly got the better of Charlemagne in a series of exploits that might have been inspired by a modern strip cartoon. Eventually, peace was made with the Emperor, who agreed that the brothers could return to their castle perched above

Opposite, above: *River Rhône. Twelfth-century fortress of Tarascon.* Below: *Canal du Midi. Spring snowflake* (Leocojum vernum) *growing wild at the waterside in Colombiers. This attractive and prolific March flower is extremely rare in Britain* the Meuse. One condition was that Bayard should be weighted with a millstone and cast into the river; easily breaking free with a well-aimed kick of his hooves, the horse swam to the distant bank and can still be sighted, grazing in a glade, by those who believe in legends of the Ardennes.

Monthermé is the gateway to the most beautiful reach of the waterway, with a great meander almost through 300°. In spite of a noisy fair encamped on the best moorings above the bridge, we halted there, eventually locating a drinking-water tap concealed in a group of caravans. Directly opposite, the town hall clock marked each quarter *twice* with a somewhat flat rendition of 'Three Blind Mice'. We liked the place for its friendly shops rather than a peaceful atmosphere. The map shows that a peninsula of France projects into Belgium for the final 40km of river. Earlier explorations by car had revealed that the French Customs are active well inside the border: we had been stopped for a search long after crossing over from Belgium. Our intention being to spend several days exploring the Belgian Meuse, we considered it wise to unload a store of alcohol accumulated in *Avonbay*'s bilges during the previous three years. Several months earlier, when driving to the boat in Germany, I had acquired a black mark on my passport for an alleged cigar smuggling offence: I maintain that my guilt was highly questionable, but now having a 'record', there was no point in taking risks. Accordingly, after dinner at Monthermé's Hôtel de la Paix, we prevailed on the owner to take care of several cases of spirits until our return.

Givet is a French frontier town where the Customs officers have long enjoyed a reputation for aggressive thoroughness. Admittedly, this postcard of 1908 must have been staged, but doubtless fierce dogs and loaded pistols were then normal practice (they are today!). Note the contraband strapped to the waist of the fraudeur

Scènes de Douane à la Frontière

8 — *Arrestation d'un Fraudeur - Signal d'attaque*

Further rock pinnacles, rising several hundred metres above the water are known as 'Les Dames de Meuse'. History relates that Hodierne, Berthe and Iges, beautiful daughters of the great and powerful Lord of Rethel, were left disconsolate in the *château* of Hierges, while their gallant husbands, Héribrand, Geoffroy and Vauthier were engaged in a crusade to Christianise the Infidels. Unfortunately, three highly attractive knights came trotting over the castle drawbridge one day. Things happened . . . and the ladies were turned to stone. Almost a thousand years later, the Dames de Meuse survey what is quite possibly the finest river reach in Europe. Not such a dreadful fate.

Tunnels at Revin, 224m, and Ham, 556m, cut through a pair of the most exaggerated loops. Beyond the first, we met a converted Dutch sailing barge, owned by a former British Airways pilot. Although well over normal retirement age, he still flew full time for an African airline whose standards are not so exacting. New to inland boating, he had duly checked in at the Belgian Customs and supposing all formalities were over, had chugged straight past the French post in Givet, where several cheerful characters on the shore appeared to be waving. Arriving at the next lock, our friend threw a rope up towards a group of bystanders with the request that one of them might like to make it fast to a bollard. 'Monsieur,' came back a reply 'it is of no interest whether your boat is secured or not. You failed to stop at our Customs office and have entered France illegally. We shall now be coming on board.' Then followed a meticulous search of the vessel, with the officials becoming more and more agitated as they failed to discover any hint of concealed contraband.

We tied up on the left bank, between a pair of bridges, presented ship's papers and passports and received an instant authorisation to proceed into Belgium. Re-entry, some days later, was rather different. A boiler-suited inspector was waiting for us on the quayside and lost no time in rummaging through lockers. Obviously prepared to get quite dirty, he was about to descend to the engine room when he changed his mind and headed for my cabin, in the stern. Several unopened packets of *Cruising French Waterways* caught his attention. On learning I was a canal author, his attitude suddenly became almost friendly. The search was rapidly concluded and we were invited to continue on our way. Clearly, if our store of alcohol had not been offloaded at Monthermé, real trouble would have resulted.

As befits a border town, Givet has a hilltop fortress, good shops and ample moorings on quays and floating stages. In 1964, this was the sixteenth busiest port in all France, handling 3.5 million tonnes annually. The extensive railway-served trans-shipment basins still seemed healthily active. To recount that I found a shop which replaced an inner tube on one of *Avonbay*'s bicycles conveys little indication of the wonder of this achievement. British and French tyres have subtle differences.

Now it was time for the Belgian Customs, several kilometres downriver at Heer bridge. They glanced at the ship's registration papers and dispensed a document, to be returned when we came back into France. Just before leaving England, a friend had fortunately reminded me of the absolute necessity of flying a *drapeau de navigation* on our bows. Without this red flag with white square at the centre, entry is refused to Belgian locks. The regulation applies equally to pleasure and commercial traffic and is designed to signify that a boat is under way and should be treated with prompt attention by navigation employees. Ours was made up by a London chandler, 30cm square, as we did not intend to discover they were unobtainable at the frontier. So, with *drapeau* fluttering from the pulpit staff and a Belgian courtesy flag at the masthead, we were primed for a brief sortie into our fourth country in twenty-eight days.

The French Meuse is superb but neglected by tourists, being in the north of a country that offers the more tempting Mediterranean. Cross into Belgium and a startling change is immediately obvious. This is the fashionable south: we found passenger boats, grand waterside villas and *châteaux*, smart hotels and an air of holiday gaiety. It was rather like Maidenhead in its thirties heyday with touches of the Rhine Gorge thrown in for good measure.

Locks were now at least 100m long and of an ancient but rugged design. At first, the heavy machinery for working gates and paddles was manual, requiring a pair of keepers dressed in orange overalls, one to each side. I foolishly started to wind a gate capstan and soon wished I had left it to the experts. Later, there was an expensive rebuilding and electrification programme in progress, clear proof that the Belgians take water transport seriously – 60 Belgian francs (90p) was charged for a return journey down to the Dutch frontier. Any notion of paying for a lunchtime mooring in the delightfully situated marina at Waulsort was discarded when we explained we should soon be heading downriver again. Repeatedly, the locals showed great kindness: we throughly approved of Belgium.

A long and leisurely cruise might easily be made on the Belgian Meuse, perhaps canoeing or rafting down the fast-flowing River Lesse, visiting one of several *châteaux*, exploring various extensive underground caverns in small boats or rock climbing. Aboard *Avonbay*, we were content to move slowly from one mooring to the next, happy to have found such a pleasant part of Belgium – a country not widely appreciated by foreign holiday-makers.

Dinant was our favourite discovery: a little town of grey slate roofs, crammed between the river and a range of cliffs. A cable car took us to the citadel for a close-up view of the bulbous belfry of the collegiate church. Far below, central moorings had been found on a crowded jetty with 'parking' tickets issued by a machine that served cars as well. Local souvenirs, vigorously promoted, consist of macabre stuffed wild creatures from the Ardennes forests, a huge variety of objects in pressed copper and giant honey-flavoured biscuits known as *couques*. We purchased several for the decorative value rather than their tooth-shattering qualities.

Six widely spaced locks were shared with a flotilla of Belgian motor cruisers, whose crews appeared to derive much pleasure talking to each other via VHF radio, even when within shouting distance. Finally, Namur came into view, a large and pleasant fortified city on a site first occupied in Neolithic times. Ignoring a cluster of pontoons on the Meuse, we nosed into the River Sambre, to tie up by *Le President*, an eighty-year-old Dutch passenger ferry, now offering agreeable seafood menus.

It was time to head back to France. A succession of barges trundled through the arch of a bridge decorated with the flags of the European community. Bound for the Ronquières inclined plane and Brussels, or perhaps the Pas de Calais via the Canal du Centre, they would continue their purposeful journeys as *Avonbay* lay quietly on winter moorings near Strasbourg.

Dinant, seen in an early twentieth-century poster advertising steamboat services on the Belgian Meuse; and today, with Avonbay *cruising past the collegiate church and citadel*

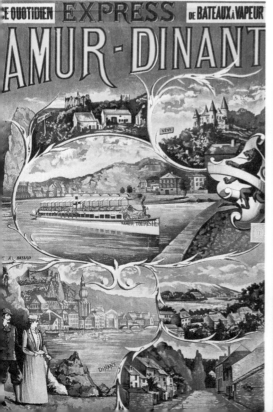

14

Doubs in Flood

RECALLING the problems of the flood-ridden Upper Saône twenty-four months earlier, I suspected we might experience similar difficulties at Easter 1988. The plan was to move *Avonbay* through Strasbourg, up the Grand Canal d'Alsace, and down the River Doubs (Canal du Rhône au Rhin) and through Franche-Comté to St Jean-de-Losne. Here, she would be ready for a two-stage journey in search of Mediterranean sunshine, later in the year. Study of French weather in the English press indicated that the north-east had been through a very wet March. British television news had shown dramatic pictures of German Rhine towns where flooded streets were awash with wine barrels. Driving to Alsace proved depressing, as every river crossed seemed to have burst its banks, converting large expanses of the surrounding countryside into impromptu lakes. But, having spent every Easter afloat for the previous twenty-eight years, we were determined to make an attempt.

When Blue Line established their hire base at Hesse in 1985, prompting an influx of forty or fifty boating parties each week of the season, commerce in the little village soared to undreamed of levels of prosperity. After a long drive from the Channel coast, we naturally headed for the nearby restaurant only to find a cheerless place of bare floors, noisy football machine contestants and decidedly tough steak. In an effort to obtain better value for what remained of our meal, I introduced John as the *ancien fondateur* of Blue Line, that fine enterprise which brings much trade to the district. Madame was startlingly unimpressed, observing: 'Oh yes, we get people off the barges in here too!' We lost no time in leaving the chilly atmosphere and returning to the centrally heated comfort of our boat.

June and John's third and fourth daughters, Amanda and Diana, made up the crew together with Amanda's fiancé Charles, looking forward to his first French boating holiday. The two of us spent a tiring day, using a pair of cars to deposit transport at St Jean-de-Losne, ready for the homeward drive. En route, we diverted to Strasbourg, to view conditions on the Rhine. Watching barges hurtling downstream it was debateable if *Avonbay* could safely manage the long upriver struggle, necessary to reach the Canal du Rhône au Rhin near Mulhouse. Next, an inspection was made of the River Doubs, a notoriously tricky navigation, even in peaceful summer conditions. Unguarded weirs were transformed into angry cataracts, while sections of towpath were completely submerged, conditions where sudden engine failure might result in fatal consequences. I reluctantly decided to abandon plans to take this route; instead, we would travel by the familiar and rather less hazardous Marne-Rhin, Est and Saône.

Back at base, the others had been taking advice from the Blue Line staff Philippe and Alain. They convinced John that the Doubs was now safe, emphasising that *Avonbay* was quite equal to any dangers. Having wanted to go this way from the start, I was pleased but had severe misgivings. However, water levels might fall considerably during the next day or two.

We glided through a winter landscape of brown reeds and leafless trees, working down the valley of the Zorn towards Strasbourg. Negotiating the lock in Lutzelbourg, we were delighted to be hailed by our travel agent friend Freddy Soler, out for a boating weekend with girlfriend and one of only two hundred British bulldogs in Switzerland, by the name of Indiana. All three clambered on board, Indiana mopping up crumbs and cocktail biscuits from the saloon carpet like a demented vacuum cleaner. She was a fierce creature, equipped with an array of rotting teeth. These were menacingly demonstrated to John as he searched the drinks locker for the last bottle of Mareuil-sur-Ay champagne. Not quite the behaviour expected of guests!

Delaying entry to the Rhine for as long as possible, we followed the little Canal du Rhône au Rhin between Strasbourg and Rhinau, reaching the Grand Canal d'Alsace junction late on a Wednesday evening. Notice boards nailed to nearby trees warned of rabid dogs.

John, Amanda and Charles, as previously arranged, departed by taxi next morning, leaving June, Diana and me to brave the problems that lay ahead. Last time, the greater distance to Basle had been covered from here in a long summer's day, so I had every expectation of being off the unfriendly Rhine by nightfall. The broad river was cold, slightly misty and deserted. Averaging a mere 6kph against the current, we edged painfully upstream, finding the going harder in artificial cuts. Commercial traffic built up as the day wore on, powerful barges wearing white moustaches of wash around their bows. Darkness arrived, chilly rain lashed down and we were still one lock and several kilometres short of safety at Niffer. Barges poured past in the gloom, relying on local knowledge and radar. We had neither, so pulled in to a quay at the Mulhouse/Ottmarsheim freight port for the night, making fast to a mobile crane. This situation was akin to parking on the hard shoulder of a motorway. We had no other choice. Fortunately, the constant wash from passing ships subsided in the early hours.

'Av-on-bay!' yelled a voice close to my cabin window. I jumped from a deep sleep, rushed outside and saw an agitated but not unfriendly German crane driver on the quay – 4,000 tonnes of freight in two close-coupled barges was inching along the wall towards us, less than a boat's length away. Few further words were necessary. Never have our engines been fired so rapidly. Ten seconds after we had cast off, the barges lay where we had been, ready to unload. Ahead, the Ottmarsheim lock showed a green signal. Any idea of a leisurely breakfast evaporated. Our sole option was to continue, immediately. It was 6.45am, still dark and extremely cold. Preferring to obtain maximum visibility, I made for the rooftop steering station, wearing only a towelling bathrobe. Dressing was achieved item by item as the girls brought clothes out to me at the wheel. What a way to start the day!

Inside the lock, beneath a glare of sodium lamps, we exchanged greetings with the crews of a Euroship bound for Switzerland and a French-registered *péniche*. At such an hour on a cold morning in early April, we were treated on equal terms, just like real Rhine mariners. I drank my second cup of warming coffee and reflected on the experiences missed by fair-weather summer pleasure boaters.

Enjoying the unusual sensation of overtaking the laden *péniche* as it crept upstream, hugging a bank where the current was less powerful, we eventually reached the Canal du Rhône au Rhin at Écluse Kembs-Niffer. Our relief at joining still water was considerable. Enquiries of the keeper, installed in a futuristic concrete watchtower designed by Le Corbusier, produced the information that the Doubs 'is open at present, but if it continues to rain, the situation will be anyone's guess!' Rain duly fell steadily as we navigated an enlarged channel to

Mulhouse, fringed by the Harth-Sud forest.

Development of this waterway, joining the Rhine to the Saône, is a complicated saga, starting with completion of a line in 1833. Numerous locks climbed to a summit at Montreux-Château, then came a descent to L'Isle-sur-le-Doubs and thereafter, navigation mainly followed the course of the river as far as Dole. A final canal section eventually reached the Saône near St Jean-de-Losne. Originally, locks were 30m long. Those at the western end were lengthened to 38m by 1882, but it was not until France regained the eastern length (beyond Montreux-Château) from Germany that 38m *péniches* were able to navigate the entire line, in 1921.

Following enlargement schemes on the Rhône and Saône, a plan emerged in 1965 to upgrade the Canal du Rhône au Rhin. This will allow the use of 4,000-tonne Rhine convoys through to the Mediterranean. The present 114 locks are to be replaced by a mere 24, each 185x12m together with a pair of boat lifts. More than half the 229km distance will consist of artificial canals with the remainder in the course of the River Doubs, flooded to create a series of lakes. Comparable to the Rhein-Main-Donau scheme, the huge enterprise involves 2.6 million cubic metres of concrete, 74 million cubic metres of earthworks and a 1,100m tunnel under the city of Besançon. Environmental opposition throughout the Doubs valley was vociferous when we travelled through in 1979 shortly after the necessary legal permits had been granted. Every village was plastered with posters screaming '*Non au Grand Canal*'. Such tactics generally achieve little success in France, although a decade later only the most preliminary excavations had started, under the aegis of the Compagnie National du Rhône, whose work elsewhere was finished some years before. I would not wish to underestimate any transport benefits, but the new waterway will undoubtedly change this lovely area beyond recognition. The protesters have a strong, if futile, case. We were anxious to explore the present navigation once more, knowing this could be our last chance.

Once a free city, Mulhouse was not incorporated into France until 1798. Now at the heart of a flourishing manufacturing area, we found elegant and fashionable shops, but sadly could spare no time for any of the outstanding museums of cars, railways and fabric printing. The Musée de l'Automobile contains upwards of five hundred classic cars including an unrivalled collection of Buggattis acquired from their owner in distinctly dubious circumstances. Another worthwhile expedition can be made to the Alsatian Open Air Museum, 15km north, near Ungersheim. Here, fifty traditional timber-framed farm buildings have been gathered from the region and carefully re-erected.

Arrangements were made for a keeper, the first of several, to speed

Avonbay through a long series of locks. Surroundings soon became deeply rural, the canal passing little smallholdings with red-tiled barns. By evening, we had negotiated thirteen of the thirty-eight steps to the summit. Barge traffic, lately delayed by the floods, was light. Next day began with a thick mist. After three locks, we were abandoned by our keeper, who had turned his attention to a descending *péniche*. An hour passed before he rejoined us. This system of travelling canal staff must play havoc with the keepers' domestic arrangements as they are suddenly required to leave home for several hours to work a boat into the next section. Once in the system there were no opportunities for exploring ashore, all efforts being directed to moving us uphill.

'*Profitez du soleil!*' called out the man at Valdieu top lock as the sun finally appeared, shining over the flight up which we had toiled. Improvements in the twenties resulted in several chambers being removed on the summit as well as further on, where the River Allan is crossed by an aqueduct. Here, a little-used branch to Belfort was once intended to form a link with the Saône; only 14km was built towards the end of the nineteenth century before the project was abandoned.

We were now in the charge of an unruly family, comprising father, mother and numerous lively children. They raced off down the towpath in a battered car, several menacing dogs bringing up the rear. The previous summer a long *chômage* had enabled construction of 4km of new waterway past Montbéliard. Variously explained as works connected with the proposed Grand Canal, but more likely designed to facilitate expansion of a Peugot car factory, a brand new electric Freycinet lock was worked by a pleasant woman with three children. The youngest offered a bouquet of wild flowers, receiving a handful of sweets in return. This prompted similar gifts from her brother and sister who plied me with a string of uninhibited questions relating to my age, how many children we had and whether we were very wealthy.

The echo-sounder registered more than 9m of water under the boat. Raw banks of gravel bordered the channel, reminding us that canals are singularly ugly in their infancy. Soon afterwards, these slopes would be planted with no fewer than 700 semi-mature trees, conveyed from a Lyon nursery aboard two *péniches*. Thirty lorries would have been required, had the consignment travelled by road.

Next day, a bright and sunny Sunday morning, brought a sense of foreboding. Willows were showing a hint of green alongside the narrow rock-lined cutting leading to Voujeaucourt lock: beyond, our first sighting of the Doubs revealed a river in spate. Between this lock and the guard lock 18 *bis*, the angry stream cut across the navigation on the level. We studied the *Carte Guide* carefully, pouring over a detailed map showing how boats should head for a specified towpath bridge arch to avoid being swept over a pair of weirs to starboard. Tree trunks, branches and other debris careered across our path. Here was one rare instance where maximum engine power must be engaged. The torrent slammed sideways onto our hull, causing *Avonbay* to lurch briefly at an angle of 40°. We reached the safety of the guard lock 50m ahead whose bottom gates were closed to prevent floodwater entering the next reach of canal.

In these conditions, all thoughts were directed towards safe navigation of the boat. Even in summer, the river channel must be strictly adhered to; wandering only a short distance off course means contact with submerged rocks. Each page of the *Carte Guide* details precise instructions as to how close craft must keep to the towpath. Our chief concern now lay not with possible grounding, rather, it was vital to make a clean entry into the locks, most of which lay directly alongside raging and totally unprotected weirs. Sudden engine failure would result in certain loss of the boat, for it was impossible to envisage *Avonbay* remaining upright if dragged into these 10 knot waterfalls! Everything depended on lock-keepers getting the top gates

Péniches *on the Doubs near Baume-les-Dames*

open in plenty of time to receive us.

Joining the river at L'Isle-sur-le-Doubs was just like travelling on a runaway escalator. June stood next to the wheel, checking the chart as I steered. We made remarkable progress, spinning past woodland, meadows and limestone cliffs under a clear blue sky. Unknown villages came and went, each having a small church whose tower was topped with an inverted harebell roof. Keepers appeared on cue, did all we expected of them and congratulated us on being the first downhill vessel in more than two weeks. Considering almost constant recent rain, precisely how long we might continue was debateable. The best plan would be to race through to Dole, end of the river sections, praying that levels would not rise further, thus closing the navigation once more.

We were agreed on one point: our first night on the Doubs could only be spent in the safety of a canal cut. Breaking free from moorings at 3am and being flung over a weir was not worth contemplating. Accordingly, we drove in mooring stakes at Écluse 33, Branne, knowing we could never reach the next canal section at Baume-les-Dames. A low sun cast deep shadows on an undulating field in front of the clifftop village of Roche-lès-Clerval. Preparations for dinner were interrupted by the arrival of a rather surly keeper who tried to insist that we continued for two further locks that evening. I produced the chart, showing him that such action would place us within dangerously close proximity to a weir for the night. He retreated, mumbling hard, only to return with another young man. This one was in his late twenties, had long blonde hair and the clothes and bearing of a superior gamekeeper. Firmly, he explained that by moving down to his lock, Écluse l'Ermite, we could make an early start next day. If we refused, he could not guarantee our passage until the afternoon, as he had a series of laden barges coming upriver. Objections were discarded with an assurance that we could tie in complete safety on a length of steel campshedding by his upper gates. Reluctantly, we complied. He was there to catch our lines as we hovered above the weir and promised to see us through the lock at 6.30am.

As good as his word, the keeper tapped on the cabinside at the appointed hour. We noted that levels had risen appreciably; barely light, there was a dense fog. Nervously sitting in the chamber for an hour, we waited for the keeper's next move. Suddenly, he announced that we must leave, for the first of the barge convoy would be arriving within five minutes. By the time *Avonbay* had recovered a straight course after tackling the weir outfall below the lock, a headlight appeared in the mist, followed by another. Boats travelling with a 10 knot current have little control compared with those fighting it; sensibly, the leading *pénichier* indicated that we might pass him on the 'wrong' side; probably he knew only too well that there was little option.

Once the sun had burned through the mist we enjoyed a glorious hot day. Confidence grew as it became clear that *Avonbay* was revelling in her flight down the Doubs gorges. Often, we have shown appreciation to lock-keepers by buying garden produce or eggs from their miniature farms. A novel purchase, in Douvot, was a 100 franc bottle of home-distilled *eau de vie des mirabelles;* this colourless plum brandy, supplied in a Martini container, proved to have the strength of virtually pure alcohol. A teaspoonful did wonders in a cup of coffee. More than half remained, a year later.

During a previous ascent of the Doubs, John had placed the blame for an unfortunate mishap squarely on me. I was seated on the bows, engaged in extracting the meat from a freshly bought giant crab with a pair of pliers. Fascinated, the helmsman's attention was diverted; he failed to notice the entrance to a lock cut and so steered us up the adjacent weir stream. Diana suddenly shouted with delight that big

Even greater floods than ours have affected the Doubs in the past. This log jam was photographed in Besançon, January 1910

fishes could be seen on the pebbly bottom of the river. We ran hard aground. Rather than risk propellor damage, John and I lowered ourselves into the water, wading about for sufficient depth to reverse in safety. As the boat eventually floated free, I clambered back to take control but John said he felt less athletic. Instead, he would make for the bank to rejoin us somewhere downstream. He was to reappear five minutes later, visibly shaken. Out of sight of the crew, he had reached the shore and grasped a barbed wire fence to haul himself out. With his legs still in the water, he instantly discovered the fence to be electrified and received quite a nasty shock. Trust the French to use both barbed wire *and* electricity!

Keeping religiously to the correct channel at Chalezeule, where the chart warned of a 'dangerous bend', we encountered a particularly vile group of bankside anglers who were obviously quite ignorant about matters navigational. Judging from their shouted abuse, we were expected to jeopardise the safety of a valuable motor cruiser by avoiding their inconsiderately placed lines. There was no time to explain that it was vital to remain exactly 10m from the bank or risk ripping the bottom out of the boat. Instead, we returned their abuse with friendly waves, being secretly relieved that they did not leap into their *Deux Chevaux* and continue the argument at the next lock.

Besançon, sited within a great loop of the river, has many claims to fame: Roman town of Vesontio, now capital of Franche-Comté; centre of clock-making; birthplace of Victor Hugo and the Lumière brothers and university city. Since 1882, barges have passed directly under the citadel through a 394m tunnel, equipped with a lock at the downstream entrance to the vault. When the keeper asked questions about our point of departure and destination we provided answers willingly, knowing of a French liking for such statistics. However, the probing continued in greater detail than I felt was good for us; the man was behaving like a Customs officer and clearly had no authority to quiz us in this manner. We fell back on the useful pretence that we couldn't understand what he wanted to know. Whether this exchange had any bearing on our arrival at the next lock, Velotte, to see the top gates closed against us, is uncertain. It appeared that the customary telephone call had not been made to organise matters. We hooted long and hard, slackened speed as much as possible and were relieved to note two distant figures rushing to the gate capstans. The adjoining weir was too close for comfort by the time there was enough space to slip into the chamber.

Regardless of any conflicting instructions, we determined to stop that evening in a lock cut by the twin towns of Avanne and Aveney. Not having eaten ashore since Strasbourg, we felt that dinner at the Restaurant des Pêcheurs was well deserved.

Back into the Doubs at the two-rise lock of Rancenay, it was evident that the river had risen slightly in the night. Yet again rain was falling so we pressed on expecting to reach Dole by evening. Most of that miserable day we steered inside, something I would not have considered earlier on this flooded stream when greatest possible visibility had seemed prudent. But now we had become almost nonchalant about the conditions. One cheerful lady keeper accompanied us through ten widely spaced locks, reappearing again and again when we thought we had offered our final thanks and farewells. She drove a navigation authority van fitted with VHF radio, enabling her to remain in touch with central control. Her sterling efforts were suitably rewarded with several bottles of wine.

A slight delay at the Orchamps guard lock was caused by freight barge *Entreprise*, working upstream with a red-bearded skipper who surprised us with a greeting in fluent English. Early evening found us in Dole, birthplace of Louis Pasteur and a lovely old town, grouped around a canal basin. Anxious to put the Doubs behind us before dusk, it was frustrating to discover no keeper on duty at the first of two locks. Furtively, we ignored the regulations, putting ourselves through after a reasonable wait and arrived at the following lock fully expecting a reprimand. Here, the keeper was engrossed with fishing until we had done most of his work, seemed quite untroubled and phoned ahead to get us back into the system. Shortly, we entered the final canal, leading calmly to the River Saône at St Symphorien. After the beauties of the Doubs these last 17km are an anticlimax with a disagreeable patch of industrial development at a chemical works in Tavaux-Cité. By contrast, our last night's mooring in woods near Samerey was alongside carpets of yellow cowslips. Spring had arrived at last.

In the two days since leaving Montbéliard, *Avonbay* had covered a very creditable 99km with thirty-eight locks. Not once had she given us the slightest cause for concern on a river where engine failure would have been bad news. Three more locks lowered us to the surprisingly placid Saône: a short distance downriver we left the boat with our friends in St Jean-de-Losne. I was looking forward to a slightly more peaceful journey when I returned in late May to continue the long voyage south.

15

Saône

ST JEAN-DE-LOSNE is a good place at which to introduce Philip Gilbert Hamerton (1834–94). Born in England, he married a French girl, set up house in Scotland on an island in Loch Awe and four years later moved to France where for much of the remainder of his life he indulged in a passion for travelling in small boats. Two books resulted: *The Unknown River* (1866) in which he explored a Loire tributary in a paper (!) canoe and *The Saône: A Summer Voyage* (1887). Decorated with exquisite etchings by a talented young American artist named Joseph Pennell, this volume provides a detailed record of a journey throughout the waterway, starting in Corre and finishing above Lyon. Hamerton was mildly eccentric and probably a rather tiresome companion. Robert Louis Stevenson made excuses for not accompanying him. Yet, more than a century later, his account remains relevant to any modern cruise on the river. The most remarkable feature is how little the bankside towns have changed in the intervening hundred years. Apart from the design of barges, rebuilding of bridges and recent replacement of nineteenth-century locks by much enlarged chambers, most remains exactly as in Hamerton's day.

Excursion by paddle steamer on the lower Saône at Beauregard, early twentieth century

He regarded the Saône as an incomparable sailing river but as there was no suitable overnight accommodation to be found on the upper waterway, he hired a *berrichon* barge, complete with captain, boy and donkey, for the run down to Chalon. This vessel, built for the narrow locks of the Canal de Berry, was fitted with tents for the voyage. Thereafter, Hamerton's own steel sailing catamaran, *L'Arar*, was used; Pennell declined to stay for the second stage and the remaining illustrations, provided by P. G. H. himself are of an inferior quality. We shall return to this pioneering voyage of 1886 from time to time: a journey that produced one of the classics of waterways literature.

My first memory of the Saône dates from 1957, when my sister and I spent several weeks staying with a French family in the heart of Lyon. We also visited their country house in what was still a deeply rural village called Francheville-le-Haut, now absorbed into suburbs to the east. This was my first excursion outside Britain. I was fourteen, had recently discovered canals in England and regretted that among treats on offer, a boat trip on the Saône was not included. But we walked by the river, swam in it from a sandy beach somewhere upstream of the city and saw numerous purposeful *péniches* at work. Surprisingly, I failed to ask that we should be taken to see the nearest lock. I do, however, recall thinking that French waterways might be worthy of exploration in the future.

Long before the Saône was equipped with locks or weirs, it formed a vital transportation corridor up the centre of France, providing a link between Burgundy and down the Rhône to the Mediterranean. Under Roman rule, Cabillonium (Chalon) boasted a river traffic superintendent, the *Praefectus Navium Araricarum*. At the time of my first voyage, in 1975, most of the late nineteenth-century locks remained in service. These were large, manually worked structures, 150m in length. By 1988, all eleven between St Jean-de-Losne and the Rhône had been superseded by a mere five, larger, mechanised replacements. Water levels had changed, resulting in rows of dead trees where one reach had been flooded, or former quays left high and dry by the receding stream. The object of these improvements is part of the great scheme to create a 4,000-tonne capacity navigation from the Rhine to the Rhône delta, via the Doubs and the Saône.

The journey between Burgundy and Lyon is along a river that is unmistakably French, past expansive fields of cattle, lines of white poplars and several historic towns. Nowhere is the grandeur of the Doubs or Rhine gorges to be found. The Saône's gentle gradient produces only the slightest of summer flows – in a normal season. Arriving to set out in *Avonbay* at the end of May, I was surprised to find a 4 knot current. Another rapid trip lay ahead.

Today, the little town of St Jean-de-Losne prospers as a centre of

Above: *A tempting sign at a waterside restaurant in Seurre. Prices have since increased considerably!*

commercial barge activity with all the attendant fuelling and repair facilities. Increasingly its future is being directed to catering for pleasure craft. Small-scale moorings and a floating chandlery, developed in the early 1970s, have since been joined in the *gare d'eau* by Blue Line's extensive hire cruiser base; drydocks off the Canal de Bourgogne are busy building or converting *péniches* for holiday use. Floating jetties are occupied by craft in transit and those seeking vessels to buy could do no better than start at Charles Gérard's H_2O Company, a name readily understood by boaters from several European nations who congregate here. Close to the great basin, a new supermarket made easy work of obtaining supplies for *Avonbay*'s galley.

Modern waterway engineering rarely enhances a river. This is especially true of a long, straight and intensively dull channel leading from several kilometres below St Jean to the new lock at Seurre. We were pleased to escape from this broad canal, lined with sheet piling and concrete, to sail past a quay, where a huge seventeenth-century building with rear courtyard was built as a salt warehouse, later serving as hospital and now partly converted to tenements. Earlier visits to Seurre had resulted in discovery of many half-timbered houses and a restaurant specialising in a range of dishes composed of a variety of freshwater fish.

With just my mother on board as crew, I would effectively be working the boat single-handed down to Lyon and beyond via the Rhône to Valence. While locks en route are vast, they are few in number, mechanically operated by keepers and could all be negotiated by the simple expedient of attaching a single line from our centre cleat to bollards set in the lock wall.

Passing through a second lock, Écuelles, late in the afternoon, provided an opportunity to spend the night at a favourite mooring in Verdun-sur-le-Doubs. This was my fifth journey along these reaches and the first time I had been able to ignore the former Verdun lock, navigating instead where a weir had until recently blocked the channel. We turned left out of the Saône to head up the River Doubs, tying alongside a flotilla of brand new hire cruisers being fitted out for the season. Shortly after, two British sailing boats arrived; I suggested they should make fast to us.

Verdun spreads beyond an island site, formed by the Doubs, the Saône and a barely navigable backwater. Houses rise sheer from one-time fortifications planted in the river bed, combining to create perhaps the most attractive waterfront in Burgundy. Elements include a single-arched bridge, ancient stone walls and red-tiled rooftops. Three years before I had spent an unforgettable February night here with June and John shortly after France had experienced the worst

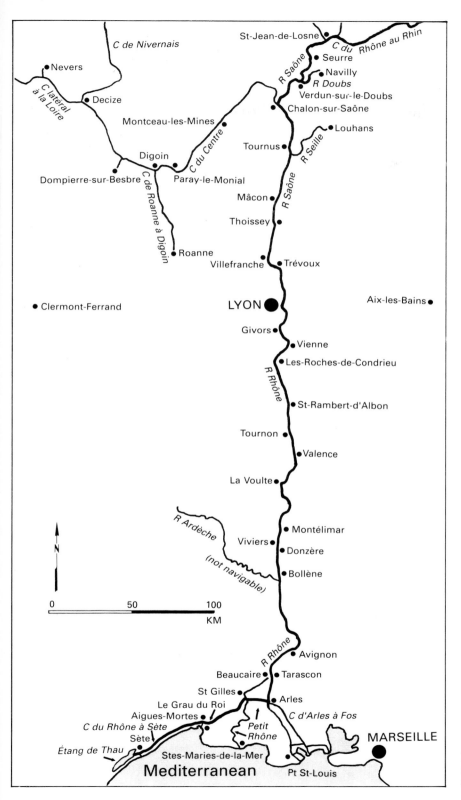

The route south to
the sea via the Saône
and Rhône

blizzard for many winters. Everything lay deep under a mantle of snow and floodwater prevented us getting ashore off the hire boat we were delivering from the Camargue to St Jean-de-Losne. An eerie silence descended on the darkened town. During the hours before dawn, June woke to hear the sound of children wailing and sobbing; she was convinced that events of extreme sadness must have occurred long ago. While far removed from the supernatural status of Borley Rectory, the Humphries' home in Wimbledon is not without its share of inexplicable happenings, so these manifestations were, I felt, to be treated with due seriousness. Just what disasters had befallen Verdun were to remain a mystery until the present voyage. But where could I make enquiries? You can hardly walk into a shop, accosting the owner in imperfect French with: 'Tell me about Verdun's tragedies over the last few hundred years!' However, the *Maison de la Presse* produced a small paper-covered history of the place, compiled by members of the local antiquarian society. Its erudite language, uncut pages and a publication date of twenty-two years earlier, suggested that few tourists seek out the secrets of Verdun's past.

As I suspected much has happened here from the days of a Gaulish camp in the time of Julius Caesar to a fierce siege in 1592. Later, came the dreadful cholera epidemic of 1854, followed the next year by a catastrophic flood. In more recent times, a hospital camp, equipped to receive ten thousand wounded Americans, operated in nearby Allerey towards the end of World War I. Atrocities carried out by the Nazis preceded Verdun's liberation from German rule in September 1944; widespread destruction reduced some houses to ruins, while of four bridges only one escaped intact. Similar tales could be found in many other French towns, recalling a turbulent past. Watching fishermen motionless in their punts, women shopping in the open market above the river wall and visitors wandering through the ancient streets, these events seem both improbable and remote. I am still little closer to knowing the truth about those crying children who returned on a snowy night in February 1985.

Next to the church we took our seats in the Restaurant des Trois Maures, an old-fashioned family concern, ultra-respectable without being at all pretentious. The tall-ceilinged, square room was comfortably furnished in the style of a slightly faded bourgeois drawing-room. As long ago as the 1890s, this hotel was famous for *pôchouse*, a superb stew made from river fish and the subject of a sonnet by Burgundian poet François Fertiault.

Freshwater fish stew sounds singularly unappetising until you have tasted *pôchouse de Verdun*, similar to a *matelote de la Loire* or the celebrated *bouillabaisse* seafish soup of Provence. We naturally included some in our 85 franc menu, also enjoying an entrée of *pâté* and salad; *roses de baie* (a mushroom-like *psalliote* fungus in cream); *poulet de Bresse*; cheese and dessert. There Bresse chicken, highly prized in the region, is free-range, fattened on buck wheat and maize and always sold with a certificate of authenticity. It bears little resemblance to the cotton-wool flavoured fowl available elsewhere. In spite of bones and pieces of fin, we so much enjoyed our *pôchouse* that I sought out the old Verdunoise receipe which I recommend wholeheartedly especially to readers who reach Verdun-sur-le-Doubs, only to find the Trois Maures closed for the day:

> Ingredients (for six persons): *2.3kg of river fish, including pike, carp, perch, trout, especially eel and for best results, crayfish.*
> Place in a saucepan six cloves of garlic (preferably crushed), some shallots, onions, thyme, bay leaves, parsley, bacon fat, a bottle of dry white wine, a litre of consommé or fish stock, pepper and salt. Boil and simmer for about 30 minutes. Cut the fish into small portions, adding these to the bouillon and poach for 15-20 minutes until tender. Shortly before serving, drop in some balls of butter, rolled in flour. Strain the liquid, having placed the fish in a deep hot serving dish. Thicken with a cupful of double cream adding a generous measure of Cognac. Fry some *croûtons* in a garlic-butter mixture, putting some on each plate, then add pieces of fish and pour on the soup. The *pôchouse* is now ready to serve.

Saône boatmen, 1897. From L'Illustration *magazine*

I would suggest that everyone on board chooses this dish or at the very least those who have eaten it are well supplied with breath-fresheners!

There were few commercial craft moving on the Saône. Just a handful of 300-tonne *péniches* running short hauls with gravel. Never was there a hint of 4,000-tonne convoys, made possible by recent lock-building. Not for the first time, I was reluctantly forced to conclude that waterway enlargement has come too late to this part of France. We reached Chalon well before lunch, tied to a jetty in the *port de plaisance* behind the Île St Laurent and walked into town. Little now remains of Roman and medieval fortifications but a wealth of old timber-framed houses can still be seen, some projecting over the narrow streets. A museum and bronze statue commemmorate Nicéphore Niépce who preserved the first photographic image with a *camera obscura* in 1822. As an insatiable collector of all objects concerning inland waterways, I was delighted to discover a small *faïence* dish, depicting Eiffel's celebrated Briare aqueduct on the Canal latéral à la Loire. Opened to barges in 1896, this item of pottery seems likely to have been produced for the inauguration.

Sometimes the river broadened to lake-like proportions; off Chalon's commercial harbour it was over a kilometre wide. Arriving at the Écluse d'Ormes, we notice a board composed of vertical green-and-white stripes indicating we should pass directly over the weir, a procedure I would normally have attempted only when the river was truly in flood. As slowly as the current allowed, *Avonbay* headed for the sluices. Our progress was watched with keen interest through binoculars by the lock-keeper. When we failed to ground, I consulted the *Carte Guide* and calculated that our present reach extended for more than 100km making it almost certainly the longest level on a locked navigation in the whole of France.

That night, we pulled into a quay at Tournus, now looking rather different from the last time I was here on a bleak February morning in 1985, when cars could barely drive through the drifting snow. Another change: the suspension road bridge had been removed and a new structure was half completed in its place.

A Tournus *ruelle, from Philip Hamerton's* The Saône *(1887)*

Something about the angle of the roofs of Tournus conveys a faint suspicion of southern France, even though the Mediterranean lies far off down the distant Rhône. Tiny dark alleys, known as *ruelles*, are lined with towering buildings and connect one main street with the next. The town is best known for its eleventh/twelfth century abbey of St Philibert, a massive Romanesque structure with twin towers. Over-priced antique shops abound, one of them installed inside an ancient church.

Less than two days had elapsed since the present cruise had begun. While we were making splendid progress, I was keen to reach Valence in good time, where, all being well, some boat maintenance could be carried out. Yet no sooner had we passed the entrance to the River Seille, than I started to regret not making a diversion up this enchanting stream to the head of navigation in Louhans: 30km long with just four locks, the deserted waterway ranks with the Charente for sustained peace and beauty. Hardly touched by a main road, it winds through lush pastures with scarcely a building other than the occasional crumbling watermill. The Seille is a gem among French rivers.

As the only safe mooring in Mâcon is at a *port de plaisance* 3km upstream of the centre, we restricted our investigation of the city to what could be seen from the deck of *Avonbay*. A 2,000m rowing course was marked out with buoys. Eights, fours and single scullers were practising for what seemed likely to be an important regatta. Recalling my own oarsmanship on the Thames Tideway between Putney and Mortlake a quarter of a century before, I throttled back so that our wake produced hardly a ripple. Not so the selfish skipper of a French cruiser who overtook us at high speed, nearly swamping the frail rowing boats with his wash. I shook a fist at him, but as the oarsmen seemed quite unconcerned, I concluded that different standards of navigational behaviour prevail in France compared with what is expected in England.

By this stage of his journey, Hamerton had shed his paid hands and transferred to the uncomfortable sailing catamaran of which he was inordinately proud. With a son and nephew as crew, he had them hauling from the bank until well after sunset as what breeze existed was unfavourable. The party had eaten nothing since lunchtime so devoured a cold supper before climbing into their hammocks. Next morning, the insufferable Hamerton was awake at dawn, almost allowing a touch of humour to intervene as he noted: 'those young men had dined so heartily that there was nothing in the provision-box for breakfast. Stephen found a piece of dry bread for me and a pear. He had not even a glass of ale to bestow on his aged parent.'

My aged parent, by contrast, never lacked sustenance aboard *Avonbay*. Although widely travelled during the twenties and thirties, her knowledge of France was restricted to a brief visit to Paris and recent boating excursions to Brittany and Alsace. Through each day she compiled copious notes, filled numerous pages with pencil sketches and observed the passing scene with an interested but independent Anglo-Saxon detachment. Almost an exact copy, in fact, of the activities for which Hamerton had been arrested and threatened with imprisonment on the upper Saône! In his day, memories of the Franco-Prussian War were fresh in the minds of the authorities.

Hamerton commented that:

> . . . the unique distinction of Mâcon amongst the cities of the world is, that a Council of the Church was held here in the year 585, during which learned ecclesiastics argued solemnly on the question whether a woman ought, or ought not, to be considered a human creature.

A navigational bypass is planned, enabling 4,000-tonne capacity barge tows to avoid the confined arches of the St Laurent bridge. This new channel will effectively convert about 5km of river through Mâcon into a navigable backwater, leaving the historic bridge unscathed.

We dropped through Dracé lock, first change in level since Écuelles, and gradually the river started to narrow past Belleville, Montmerle and Villefranche. Wooded hills now accompanied us for most of the remaining distance to Lyon. As we rounded a great bend, the town of Trévoux reared up to port, a tight cluster of buildings topped with the ruins of an ancient castle. On impulse, we decided to moor for a short exploration. Already, I knew of a suitable length of deepwater quay, upstream of the road bridge. To turn *Avonbay* into the current was not difficult but I was alarmed at the speed of the stream where we planned to come alongside. The single-handed manoeuvre was made just possible by leaping ashore, attaching a short centre line to a bollard and then rapidly getting ropes fixed fore and aft before the river had a chance to fling us back into the torrent again.

Philip Hamerton's live-aboard donkey, Zoulou

For the first time in this journey, the afternoon was hot with the sunshine of early summer. Trévoux, until 1771 independent capital of the Principality of Dombes, retains its seventeenth-century parliament building. Unseen by any caretaker we let ourselves into the curious council chamber whose ceiling is supported by wooden beams, decorated with bright painted designs. Beyond the tall windows, the Saône could be seen rushing towards its confluence with the Rhône.

Lyon lay just 31km downstream, an easily attainable objective by evening. Not without difficulty, I cast off and backed out into the flow, grateful for my ability to turn the boat by running hard in forward gear on one engine, while reversing on the other. Soon, we were alongside the range of Mont d'Or hills and dropping for the last time on the Saône at Couzon lock, beyond Neuville.

Now, bankside interest was increasing as we penetrated the suburbs of Lyon, second city of France. Nineteenth-century bourgeois villas facing the water were dotted among trees. One of the most attractive had a tower planted on rocks at the upstream end of the Île Barbe, a 600m long island, connected to the shore by suspension bridges. Part is reserved as a public park, while elsewhere are remains of a once powerful abbey, disbanded in the sixteenth century when the monks petitioned the Pope with a request that the establishment should be closed down. They saw this as the only solution to ending their life of vice and good living!

To approach any great city by water is exciting: thirty-one years after my childhood visit to Lyon, the austerity of the fifties had been replaced by obvious affluence. Many bridges were destroyed in World War II; new structures now introduced an unfamiliar element. Tall buildings in the Italian Renaissance style crowded in on each side, providing an impression of navigating through a deep gorge. Beyond, streets rose steeply to the Fourvière hill, crowned by the Byzantine basilica of Notre Dame, erected in thanksgiving after Lyon was spared invasion during the Franco-Prussian War of 1870–1. Although plans had been formulated to create a *port de plaisance* on the Rhône, upstream of its confluence, latest information suggested that nothing had yet materialised. We therefore proposed to lie on a quay where the Saône flows past St Jean's cathedral, a splendidly central spot even though it lacks any facilities for pleasure craft in transit.

Already, a group of cruisers was moored either side of an elegantly modern pedestrian suspension bridge a little above the Pont Bonaparte. With its course narrowed by embankments and a series of oddly flood-prone car parks, the river runs swiftly here and craft are controlled by one-way working when the current is fast. I turned *Avonbay* to face into the flow, edged carefully towards the shore and several boat-owners gathered to take my lines. This seemingly kind gesture was prompted in part by a resolve that I should not career into their own vessels. Great satisfaction can be derived from skilful handling of a boat under the critical gaze of an audience. Judging the speed of the stream with care, I had *Avonbay* neatly alongside, threw a stern rope to a willing bystander and then found to my horror that we were unexpectedly starting to race upriver, caught in a powerful back eddy created by the bridge pier. Within seconds we would be slamming hard into a plastic-hulled sailing cruiser, so I sprang back to the controls to engage reverse. An unintelligible shout came from the Frenchman on the other end of our rope; unable to hold on, he let the line slip from his grasp. Inevitably, the starboard engine stopped dead as its propellor became fouled. Furious at such elementary incompetence, I backed off for another attempt, narrowly avoiding collision with the bank, now that handling was impaired by the loss of one engine. A sympathetic crowd gathered to watch the evening's entertainment while I stripped off, rigged the swimming ladder and lowered myself into the deep, murky and uncomfortably chilly river. Lacking diving gear, it was just possible to locate the festooned propellor with my feet. Twenty minutes in the water was all I could tolerate. A length of rope was freed; what remained seemed solidly wound round the shaft. I emerged for a hot coffee laced with whisky. The crowd melted away, leaving me to ponder on our situation.

An 1896 view of the Lyon-Vaise gare d'eau, *a little upstream of the city centre*

Two possibilities were available. Craneage facilities existed several kilometres down the Rhône. Here, the stern could be lifted clear of the water. But next day was a Saturday and we did not particularly want to wait for attention until the Monday morning. Further, I was unhappy at the prospect of limping down the speeding Rhône with only half our normal power. Lord Harvington, no stranger to navigational excitements, had once wound a mass of fishing nets round his propellors in Avignon. According to his account of the episode, the local fire brigade had positively welcomed use of their divers in a purposeful exercise. Moreover, this service had been performed free of charge. In retrospect, I suspect that being the Baron Harvington and former Deputy Speaker of the House of Commons, might have helped Grant in his predicament. Although a mere Monsieur, I decided to seek help next day from the *sapeurs-pompiers*.

Any chance of vandalism, always a possibility in large French towns, dictated that we should not leave the boat unattended. Consequently, rather than seek out a restaurant in this world capital of gastronomy, we ate on board that night. Just before dusk, when floodlighting was making a fairyland of the Bibliothèque Municipal, cathedral and basilica of Notre Dame de Fourvière outside our windows, torrential rain, accompanied by thunder and lightening, obliterated the view for ten minutes. Snug inside our boat, further unwelcome rain could only produce an adverse effect on river levels. By morning, the water was lapping at the top of the stone quay, while the current had increased to an unfriendly 6 knots. The mooring lines were stretched taut, like piano wires, with a wide gap between our deck and the bank. A small cruiser painfully inched her way upstream, came to a standstill under 'our' bridge, and sensibly decided to tie up until conditions improved.

My knowledge of Lyon was three decades out of date; even in 1957, it had not extended to the location of fire stations. After breakfast, I braved steady rain, dressed in green wellingtons and matching wet suit and thus attired as an impersonation of a French fisherman, I climbed the quayside steps to find a taxi. 'Please drive me to the nearest fire station,' uttered with a degree of urgency, prompted my driver to tear off at high speed through the city streets. Past the Place Bellecour, over the green, glacier-fed waters of the Rhône and I was in unexplored territory. Eventually, we pulled up outside a building marked *sapeurs-pompiers*. I rang a bell and a window by the pavement was thrust open.

The duty officer listened patiently as I explained the problem: '. . . so I would be most obliged if you could spare a frogman.' *Hommes-grenouilles*, it appeared, were in short supply that day. Pending further enquiries, I was left standing in the street in streaming rain until my eventual rescue by the station chief, a cheerful man in his early forties. 'And what part of Lyon do you live in?' was his first question after I had once more told of *Avonbay*'s troubles. Probably, he hoped that responsibility for my rescue lay with another station. 'I'm not sure whether we can help,' he continued, 'after all, no one seems to be in danger of drowning!' That I was not even a French resident provoked much thought until a hint of *entente cordiale* and the notion of assisting fellow members of the European Community began to surface. Prospects improved still further when I admired a visual display unit on which were shown the whereabouts of Lyon's numerous fire appliances. I had struck a sympathetic chord and was subsequently treated to a thorough explanation of the department's workings, taken for an extended tour of the premises and expected to admire the length of rescue ladders and the ingenious design of resuscitation equipment. This station occupied the buildings of a former convent, with the chapel fitted out as a gymnasium. In the kitchens, I was introduced to a man whose turn it was to cook for the week. Dozens of firemen were employed there, repeatedly shaking hands as they came and went. Fire-fighting was clearly a flourishing trade.

Eventually, two hours and several cups of coffee after my arrival, a thin little man in a grubby white pullover and his young assistant were presented as the *hommes-grenouilles*. Masks, flippers and gas bottles were packed into a shabby saloon car parked on the kerb and we raced back to the Saône. It was a matter of three minutes' work to cut the propellor free. Our rescuers came into the saloon for a hot drink, where I raised the question of payment, half expecting to hear that the service was free. '200 francs, please,' said the senior of our flipper-footed friends. Relieved to be restored to full mobility, I doubled the amount. There was the customary moment of polite hesitation; then the hand closed over the four one hundred franc notes.

Guests were due on board for dinner so we turned our attention to buying supplies. With an open air market in progress in the street immediately above, we returned laden with the first of the new season's melons, a joint of pork, fresh vegetables and a suitably impressive apple tart. Halfway through lunch a series of violent crashes suggested that we were being bombarded with bricks. Dashing up the steps to street level, I was just too late to apprehend a gang of council workmen clearing market refuse from the roadway. Rather than load a cart with wooden cases, vegetable refuse and other rubbish, they had thrown it over the balustrade where some had fallen, as intended, in the river. *Avonbay*'s wheelhouse roof was littered with half a sackful of carrot tops, several dozen over-ripe tomatoes and a quantity of plastic sheeting. I resolved to complain to the city authorities: somebody might have been seriously hurt or even killed. Sadly, I have to report that my protest was never made: composing a well-argued letter in French is not a task I undertake lightly and other more pressing matters intervened.

In the afternoon, we took turns to explore nearby streets. Thirty-one years had somehow shrunk the now pedestrianised Rue de la République to half its remembered width. The fashionable shops appeared lively and flourishing. Greatest change of all (in common with much of France) was a lack of continental smells. Back in the fifties, the French drainage system had seemed rudimentary, while to travel on public transport involved face-to-face confrontation with blasts of garlic-laden breath. Now, all was sweetness, or had the passing of time obliterated my sensibility?

Within five minutes walk across the Saône, extensive restoration has revealed a complex of superb fifteenth to seventeenth century buildings along the Rue Saint Jean. This was the core of medieval Lyon, centre of the world-famous silk trade. Ancient stone-faced houses with spiral stairways installed in courtyard towers have been painstakingly refurbished. Climbing steep streets towards Fourvière provides a magnificent panorama over the city, a sea of red rooftops, spreading out from the two great rivers.

Many days might have been passed in visiting Lyon's museums of fine art, local history, fabrics and the Résistance et de la Déportation. From long before, I recalled the magnificence of formal flower beds in the Parc de la Tête d'Or. As a keen horticulturist, it would have been interesting to see how well this combination of park and zoo had stood the test of time. Perhaps another year . . . Earlier research had not met with spectacular success in identifying any of the allegedly world-class restaurants said to abound in the city. That evening, however, was reserved for on board entertainment. Our guests were my hosts of 1957, the Marcet family, paying a visit from their apartment not 500m away.

Father, once a shadowy figure too deeply involved with his business affairs to pay much attention to visiting foreign children, was a charming old gentleman aged eighty-six. His wife of seventy-seven had taught English, a distinct disadvantage when the purpose of my visit to them had been to improve my French. Considerable mental adjustment was required with their daughter Agnes, transformed from a thoughtful, dark-haired fourteen year old into a mother in her mid-forties. She was accompanied by husband Paul, a boating enthusiast with a small sailing vessel at their Corsican holiday base. To have arrived on their doorstep all the way from the Thames was considered to be a notable achievement. That the journey, by way of Switzerland, Germany, Luxembourg and Belgium had taken three years of spasmodic travel was a feature I played down: the main object of cruising to Lyon was seen as arranging a *rendez-vous* with the Marcets! They piled praise on *Avonbay*, decorated in a *véritable style anglais*; and consumed our food *vraiment Britannique*, seemingly oblivious of the fact that the ingredients had been purchased within sight of the mooring. The evening ended in an aura of conviviality.

Early next morning, the river had risen still further. The wash of each passing boat threatened to deposit us on the submerged quay; it was time to head off down the Rhône. Releasing a cat's cradle of mooring lines and springs, I engaged the help of a Belgian boat-owner to cast off our final rope, so maintaining full control under engine power before we were whirled downriver. The normally placid Saône had played too many tricks for me to take any further chances.

Ample space on the tiller for the boatman and his family. From L'Illustration, *1895*

16
Rhône

NOT very long ago, the Rhône had a fully justified reputation as a vicious river, careering unbridled for 323km between Lyon and the Mediterranean. As the only north–south navigation through this part of France, commercial and pleasure traffic had no option but to confront the strong glacier-fed flow, using teams of horses, steam tugs of various designs including those with revolving underwater grabs to claw their way over the rocks, and, more recently, extremely powerful diesel barges. Fierce currents were generally worst whilst Alpine snow was melting in the spring. By late summer, levels would fall, exposing treacherous reefs and the greatest danger then would be one of grounding. Within recent times, all pleasure craft were strongly advised to employ local pilots for a downstream journey; all but the fastest craft faced the expense of a barge tow for their upriver return. Wrecks were frequent and pilots seemed to derive positive pleasure from pointing out the remains of the latest unfortunate casualty, holed and frequently beyond repair, while of course stressing that here was a yachtsman who was too mean to pay for professional services.

Early nineteenth-century view of Lyon

Taming the flood was a long-held dream that took thirty-two years to achieve from the construction of the earliest of twelve locks and barrages just after World War II. My first upstream voyage, in 1975, aboard the powerful motor yacht *Melita*, predated building of the final three locks by five years. Formidable difficulties still remained, but with a decline in demand for pilots (resulting in a corresponding increase in their charges), we selected a Lyon-bound barge at Arles, grimly followed him at a safe distance and arrived on the Saône little more than forty-eight hours later without parting with a single franc. But this was not enjoyable cruising: we generally halted only while locks were made ready – indeed there were then few reliable moorings. Only since 1980 has civilised Rhône cruising been possible, pausing to explore bankside towns and expanding the journey time to five or six days for the present distance of 310km. Even now, careful planning is necessary to be certain of reaching a good overnight stop before the advent of darkness. Summer flows are such that moderately powered craft can usually make upstream progress with a margin of safety.

Generation of hydro-electricity, conservation of water for agricultural use and improved navigation were all factors that prompted the French government to invest in the great canalisation scheme. Considerable lengths of artificial channel now provide somewhat tedious surroundings in parts; elsewhere, the natural river is embanked, raising water levels and so providing splendid views of the rugged countryside. By the halfway point of Valence, a strong hint ot Provence prevails in the rocky cliffs, gorges and arid vineyards. Only canoeists will regret the passing of the wild, untamed river.

But the Rhône still commands respect. Shortly after my 1985 ascent in a hire cruiser, the former Rhine hotel ship *Fleur du Rhône* went into service between Arles and Mâcon. 110m long, with a 250 passenger capacity, she was one of Europe's most luxurious inland waterway craft. Her second voyage, downstream in mid-May, coincided with flood conditions producing a 15 knot current. When a lookout on the bows signalled that there appeared to be insufficient clearance under a bridge at La Voulte, the skipper desperately engaged full power astern but was unable to prevent her crashing broadside into the bridge piers. Fortunately, passengers were enjoying a shore excursion; on attempting to pull *Fleur du Rhône* clear with a tug, she was holed and promptly began to sink. The twenty-five crew members were rescued by rigging ladders between the upper deck and the road bridge. Badly under-insured and completely blocking the navigation for a long period, there was eventually no solution other than to cut her up with underwater oxy-acetylene gear. These events were very much in my mind as *Avonbay* whirled down the last of the Saône and was picked up by the icy waters of the Rhône at the Lyon confluence.

Running at a gentle speed of 2,000rpm on each engine, timing tests using the kilometre posts proved we were making a speed of 25kph (13.5 knots). These conditions are quite satisfactory until either you wish to stop or, rather worse, the engines decide to take an unscheduled rest. While the anchor was rigged for instant use, I doubted its holding power under such circumstances. Oil depots and commercial wharves whistled past. There was time for one last glance astern at the increasingly distant Fourvière basilica, before our first lock, Pierre Bénite, loomed up. We entered a protected pool above the gates and immediately slowed as if grasped by some giant unseen hand. Now there was only a strong wind to contend with during the twenty-minute wait that ensued.

One slight worry was that when inside the chamber (this first example would drop us 11.8m and others were considerably deeper) and *Avonbay* was secured to a floating bollard with a single centre rope, the distant keeper would summon me to his office with ship's papers, leaving the descending boat in the sole charge of my far from expert mother. On my return (assuming the rope had not jammed or become detached) I would face a vertigo-producing return to the boat down a slimy ladder set inside the lock wall. I resolved to keep all keeper communication to what could be achieved by radio telephone, while concealing the undeniable fact that the vessel was undermanned according to any reasonable interpretation of the official regulations. In fact, this situation never arose, either here or at any of the other locks to Valence; a cheerful wave in the direction of the keeper high above in his concrete cabin was our only contact.

Now followed an 11km artificial cut, long, boring and fringed with unfriendly loose boulders. We pressed on with all speed, emerging in the natural river upstream of Givors, where adequate moorings had previously been identified on the right bank. These upper reaches of the navigation are among the most pleasant, with green banks, orchards and considerable interest in the waterside town of Vienne, where there are extensive Roman remains. Already, I had planned a halt in the excellent sheltered marina at Condrieu (K41), 7km below the Écluse de Vaugris. A loop remaining from realignment of the waterway provides pontoon moorings for 350 craft, claimed to be the largest inland marina in the country. Just above a suspension bridge, whose single pier is planted in the river's centre, we turned to stem the current, heeled over as the flow caught our hull and crawled at full power into calm water. This well-executed manoeuvre was watched by a crowd of boat-owners. Several came running to take *Avonbay*'s lines: hopefully, I expressed sufficient gratitude for this well-intentioned but unnecessary assistance and then spent the next ten minutes retying warps to my own liking.

After a late lunch on board, we explored the twin towns each side of

Opposite: *The Mediterranean at last! One of our crew tries out her new French bikini* Overleaf: *Canal du Midi.* Bacchus, *last of the long line of Midi freight craft, laden with wine at Trèbes, Easter 1989*

the Rhône, sheltering from heavy rain in a covered courtyard. Beyond an earth dam, a portion of the former navigation channel, with rusting marker posts still in position, has been adapted into a landlocked water sports lake with swimming beach, dinghy sailing and windsurfing. The weather was unexpectedly cold for early June with a fierce wind funnelling down the valley. The whole of the Rhône is not infrequently subjected to this mistral, roaring ceaselessly for days at a time, numbing the senses and encouraging unusually violent displays of bad temper. There was a time when murderers could successfully plead mitigating circumstances if able to prove that the mistral was blowing and was thus responsible for the crime. Looking out from our reasonably placid mooring to the swirling eddies and sizeable Rhône waves, I decided to remain in Condrieu until morning, rather than risk putting in several more cruising hours, only to find that there was no safe haven for the night.

Departure from Condrieu provided several anxious moments as we were thrown about in whirlpools by the bridge: ahead, a dredger was anchored with wires extending across the fairway. Signals displayed suggested we must follow a seemingly narrow passage close to the rocky shore. Some years before we had only just avoided running into just such a mooring cable on the Saône at Seurre. However, on rounding a slight bend, it became obvious that we had ample space.

For a great river navigation, commercial traffic was pathetically light, especially when compared with the massive tonnages found on the Rhine. During our time on the Rhône we encountered fewer than twenty barges, all but two of them being 'small' 350-tonne capacity *péniches*. We were, however, joined in the locks by an increasing number of pleasure boats, including one single-handed German sailing cruiser, the skipper of which appeared quite incapable of bringing her alongside the chamber bollards; eventually, the Sablons keeper angrily descended from his control tower to offer a brusque lesson on locking procedure. Upstream of this point, the natural river is bypassed by an artificial channel, leaving the former barge town of Serrières on an unnavigable backwater. I had rather wanted to visit the town's museum where relics of Rhône shipping are displayed but lack of a suitable mooring on the canal coupled with a 4km journey overland suggested that investigation by car at some future date might be preferable.

Navigation markers, either buoys or poles planted in the river, were becoming more frequent. As a result, there was never the slightest doubt as to where our correct course lay, even though the Table du Roi rock at K89 was fully submerged. Here Louis IX (St Louis) is said to have paused for a meal in 1248, when bound for one of his crusades. Recent engineering works have respected the historical site. Water

Étang de Thau. Sunrise over the distant Mediterranean, seen from the harbour at Marseillan

depths in mid-channel averaged 10m on the echo-sounder, clearly indicating how much the banks have been raised.

Beyond the Écluse de Gervans, I had hoped to stop for the night in a small harbour by the centre of Tournon. The ancient town offers good shops, a market, a two-hour trip on the narrow gauge Vivarais steam railway and impressive views, opposite, of the celebrated Hermitage vineyards where some of the most powerful red wines in France are produced. I recalled how, years before, one crew member was nearly left ashore as *Melita* was dragged from the port into the swirling river. 'Find a taxi and meet us at the next lock!' shouted our host to his not unimportant guest, stranded on the bank and seemingly likely to be pulled into the Rhône as he struggled to control a rapidly shortening length of mooring line. With great difficulty, we eventually returned to the shore, collected our friend and resolved to avoid further sightseeing halts. This time, Tournon's little marina seemed equally unapproachable. *Avonbay* tore past the entrance: I decided to keep going until Valence, one more lock and a further 21km.

A two-month mooring had already been reserved in the Port de Plaisance de l'Épervière, an admirable marina established a decade earlier in a basin off the river downstream of Valence. Total security, repair facilities, chandlery, fuel point, vast nearby supermarket and year-round restaurant in the club house, seemed to ensure that we would be well looked after. Always content to buy peace of mind when abandoning *Avonbay* abroad, I paid a not insignificant 1,930 francs.

Equidistant from Lyon and the French Alps at Grenoble, our view over the river terminated in a series of massive grey crags, part of the Corniche du Rhône. Downstream, a rusting hulk attracted my attention: this was the *Ardèche*, a surviving Rhône steam-driven chain tug, with tall funnel, comically exposed steering wheel and distinctly hogged hull. Efforts had been in progress for several years to restore this magnificent monster to her former glory but vandalism seemed to be getting the upper hand.

Once the car had been recovered from St Jean-de-Losne, our remaining days in France could benefit from greater mobility. One morning was passed driving switchback roads through the gorges of the Ardèche between St Martin and the natural stone bridge at Pont d'Arc. It has long been my ambition to hire a canoe at the upper end of this dramatic (but otherwise unnavigable) tributory of the Rhône, float downstream for several hours and return to the start by road. To date, no one has volunteered to accompany me. We travelled southwards to marvel early one morning at the cave houses in Les Baux-de-Provence, set high in a barren landscape of white rock pinnacles, and then moved down to the Rhône delta for an investigation of coastal ports along the Mediterranean fringe of the

Camargue. After a particularly enjoyable seafood dinner in Stes Maries-de-la-Mer, and having at last found some sun-filled beach-lazing weather, we spent a night sleeping in the car on the Plage de Faraman. This vast stretch of sand near the mouth of the Rhône must be one of the most remote corners of southern France. Watching the sun rise over the sea made the inevitable discomfort of the night well worthwhile.

Much hard work was accomplished on the drive to rejoin *Avonbay* in early August. June and I were accompanied by A-Level History of Art and Classical Studies students, Diana and Auriole. We worked hard in the museums of Paris and then moved on to the Hospice de Beaune in Burgundy, for further culture and lunch. Here, we encountered perhaps the most ill-mannered waiter in all France. He showered us with fragments of wet glass when he lost control of his drinks tray and offered neither apology nor made any attempt to clear up. We continued the meal surrounded by debris. Next stop: Lyon. In truth it was not the Roman remains that delayed us here until early evening, although the amphitheatres were afforded due consideration; the girls discovered some uniquely interesting clothing boutiques. With difficulty they were persuaded, complaining, back into the car, reason at last prevailing when we explained that in spite of hard driving there was now every prospect of reaching *Avonbay* too late for dinner in the marina restaurant. Emerging from the city on the A7 *autoroute*, we headed into a torrential thunderstorm with consequent nightmare driving conditions. Our reserved table waited at the Port de l'Épervière, reached soon after 9pm.

Inside the Bollène Lock, whose rise and fall of 26m is achieved in about seven minutes. Grooves in the chamber walls house the vital floating bollards

Next day brought astonishingly heavy rain that gushed through the edges of the sliding wheelhouse doors in a manner never experienced before or since. Then the sun arrived to bring a Mediterranean glow to our lives which was to last without a break for over three weeks. Before a final car-based day of antiquity searching and the continuation of *Avonbay*'s journey south, there was a pressing problem to sort. One of the boat's two vacuum loos was due for replacement by a superb example of marine sanitary engineering known as a Blake Baby. Conveyed from England, lovingly wrapped in clean bedding sheets, it featured polished brass fittings and a ruggedness suggestive of having been designed back in the twenties. Already, I had created a plinth of varnished mahogany but lacked the courage to attempt removal of the old model and securely fix this newcomer to the fibreglass floor of the compartment reserved for such equipment.

The harbourmaster provided us with a skilled handyman who struggled intelligently for four and a half hours and seemed close to tears when the triumphal first flushing failed to introduce water into the bowl. I suggested priming the pump. This produced the desired effect and Mr Blake has subsequently assumed a role as one of the most valued members of the ship's complement. Our fitter demanded an unrealistically low 250 francs for his labours. I doubled this and both parties were well satisfied.

Amanda and Charles arrived by air from London to join us for the first part of a voyage to the Canal du Midi. Now, there were no fierce currents to contend with: had we chosen we could have drifted downstream with engines silenced and come to no harm. A final foray to the supermarket, purchase of 200 litres of diesel and we were ready to go by midday on Saturday, 6 August. Conditions were dreamlike: roastingly hot with a clear azure sky. The boat was performing splendidly and our freezer manfully churned out ice cubes for a continual succession of cold drinks.

That day, and many that were to follow, was gloriously free from any hint of anxiety: this was the kind of river cruising we had always longed for. Cicadas chirped on each herb-scented bank and dressed in swimming costumes we soon developed the makings of respectable Mediterranean suntans. Seated at the rooftop steering station, I stood up after several hours to find my stomach bizarrely striped. We radioed ahead to the Écluse de Beauchastel, rapidly working through in company with several other cruisers. Then came La Voulte with its fifteenth-century *château*, Italianate church and a sea of brown pan-tiled roofs. Another lock at Logis-Neuf and the nuclear power station of Cruas appeared to starboard. This is one of several sited by the lower Rhône to benefit from the abundant supplies of cooling water.

The river had now achieved an exceptional width, passing rocky islets covered with young willows. The shores seemed remote in the heat haze as we followed a channel through black and red posts. In the distance, a well-laden *péniche* came gliding upstream towards us. To our surprise, the young captain stood stark naked on deck, sluicing his hatch covers with a hose. The wheelhouse roof and sides had been folded open to reveal his pretty wife at the helm, also *au nature*. Out here, in the great expanse of river, they were in a world of their own: under these conditions, there had to be many worse ways of earning a living.

The Écluse de Châteauneuf (K164) dropped us a massive 18.5m; next day, there was a still deeper lock to come. Five and a half hours after leaving Valence, we reached our chosen overnight mooring, the Viviers quay, a short way up the old river, opposite the lower end of the Châteauneuf cut. Already knowing that space on the wall was limited, we saw with dismay that all possible places were taken by craft in transit. We hovered in midstream until invited to breast up with a charming Dutch couple aboard a home-built cruiser. Notwithstanding reports about its contaminated state, we lost no time in plunging into the Rhône for a welcome swim. It was surprisingly warm for a glacier-fed stream.

Drying off, I noticed a catamaran flying a red ensign and obviously searching for a berth, followed by an American motor boat. These were duly motioned to make fast to us, so creating a miniature United Nations, extending far out into the river. The British vessel was crewed by a middle-aged couple. As I took a rope from her, I was struck by the wife's impeccable Chelsea accent. 'We've been boating with McKnight,' she remarked suddenly, 'and it's just full of mistakes!' As my *Cruising French Waterways* had won the Thomas Cook Guide Book Award four years earlier, and I generally receive several appreciative letters from readers each week, I was a little startled. 'That's interesting,' I replied, 'can you remember what mistakes you found?' Husband, now joining in the conversation, was quick off the mark. 'You're not Hugh McKnight, are you?' I agreed that I was and thought it kind to disappear. Within two minutes the skipper was tapping on our cabinside: 'I must apologise for my wife's rudeness. She was confusing your excellent book with the *Carte Guides!*' This represented rapid thinking, was nearly believable and strongly suggested that Mr Catamaran was in the Diplomatic Service. The Americans now approached bearing a United States edition of the same work. 'We recognised your boat, Hugh,' they cried with typical transatlantic familiarity. 'Please could you sign our copy?' Several minutes passed and Mrs Catamaran emerged, amazingly also in quest of an autograph. Even as I wrote 'With the Author's best wishes', I was wondering what more appropriate inscription I might have added.

The little city of Viviers lies well back from the river, approached from the port up an avenue of plane trees. Capital of the Vivarias and an ecclesiastical settlement since the fifth century, it comprises a tangle of ancient cobbled streets, grouped around the soaring twelfth-century cathedral of St Vincent. Medieval buildings stand side by side with Renaissance houses of which the most beautiful is the Maison des Chevaliers, with a richly decorated stone façade. During our exploration in the lengthening shadows of a summer evening, it was impossible not to sense a strong feeling of unease. Black enshrouded dark-skinned women – gipsies or perhaps immigrants from the former North African colonies – lurked in the gloom of doorways. I felt our presence was just tolerated, provided we quickly went on our way. Centuries before, the Fête des Fous (Mad Carnival) would begin on Christmas Eve, inhabitants dressing irreverently as bishops and clergy and indulging in three debauched days and nights of street revelry. Similar to the pre-Lenten Festival of Venice, the *fête* has recently been revived. We dined well at a restaurant on the edge of town. The weather was to remain too hot to cook much on board, so evening meals were either towpath barbecues or taken in bankside *auberges*. For once, June enjoyed a real holiday from the galley.

The Pont d'Avignon, although much reduced in length, is an impressive structure. Excellent pontoon moorings are situated immediately upstream

Next day passed so peacefully as we negotiated three locks in the 60km to Avignon, that it was difficult to appreciate we were travelling a river with a long history of ship-wrecking. The Rhône was positively placid as we were funnelled into the Donzère gorge, bordered to the

east by sheer cliffs, and then turned into 28km of man-made channel, cut through the Plain of Tricastin. At the far end was the Écluse de Bollène, first of the Rhône locks to be built. When opened in 1952 it was the deepest such structure in Europe, dropping 26m. Six other cruisers joined us for the descent completed in a mere seven minutes. Sightseers on top shrank to doll-like proportions, the dripping chamber grew cold and with some relief we glided beneath the guillotine gate at the lower end. Above us the keeper's cabin, in its austere post-war *art deco* design, was a reminder that complete management of the waterway had taken three decades.

Earlier rich vegetation was now replaced by sun-bleached rocks. To starboard, Roquemaure lay at the centre of the Côte du Rhône vineyards, opposite the ancient Château de l'Hers. Not far off to the north-east was Châteauneuf-du-Pape. There was much we might have explored in these fringes of Provence but by now our goal was the Mediterranean shore. Late afternoon saw us turning back on our tracks, upriver to Avignon, a city today bypassed by the through navigation.

Making up a flotilla of five boats, we drew level with the impressive walls of Avignon and its huge Palais des Papes planning to find a mooring (none too secure in this busy tourist centre, I feared) on the quayside. Just upstream of what remains of the original twenty-three arches of the famous twelfth-century bridge, we were delighted to see extensive floating stages at a newly created *port de plaisance*. Arriving in unexplored territory it is comforting to be made welcome. But we had not expected the laudable efficiency of the harbourmaster, who came out by motor launch to meet us, directing his visitors to various pontoons, according to their size. Our berth alongside a sailing cruiser adorned, like *Avonbay*, with an undefaced blue ensign, commanded a splendid view of the bridge and its little chapel dedicated to St Nicholas. As patron of river travellers he must have been hard worked until recent times, looking after the barge people of the Rhône. Having paid a very reasonable fee, we passed an evening exploring this one-time centre of the French papacy, enjoying the bustle of the Place de l'Horloge where street entertainers were attracting sizeable crowds. Our hastily selected restaurant dinner was sadly typical of many tourist traps: overpriced and uninspired. Determined not to allow the experience to spoil our brief intrusion into this hectic urban setting, all six of us discarded any pretence of adulthood and leaped aboard a gaudy carrousel set up in the town centre.

Long ago, when Diana was not quite two, we had endured a tour of the sparsely furnished Palais des Papes. Vainly, I tried to persuade our culture-conscious A-level students that what couldn't be seen from outside was barely worth investigation. Gamely, June assumed her rightful role of responsible parent and took the crew next morning. I sensibly remained on board catching up with engine maintenance. We had decided to meet for lunch in a tree-shaded courtyard restaurant, recalled from a visit some years earlier. Memory established its location near a watergate, close to the river but we could remember neither exact position nor the name. The rest of the party, as anticipated, were foot-sore and slightly fractious. 'How can I help you, monsieur,' complained a gentleman we had stopped to ask directions, 'if you do not know what it is called?' I suggested it was a very expensive establishment. '*Bien sûr*,' he replied unhesitatingly, 'you mean the Hôtel d'Europe!' and accompanied us on a short walk to make certain we did not get lost. Costing little more than the disaster of the previous evening at 150 francs each, the meal fully lived up to expectations. We returned to *Avonbay* well satisfied: it was time to move downstream again.

A final lock, Vallabrègues, lies 2km upriver of the Rhône's most impressive fortress at Tarascon. Rising square from rocks washed by the river, the *château* was started in the twelfth century and completed in the fifteenth by King René le Bon. Eventually converted into a prison where inmates included English sailors in Napoléonic times, it was restored and opened to the public in 1926. We had made an enjoyable tour in 1982: this was just as well, for there is currently no possible mooring anywhere within walking range. Here lurked the Tarasque, a singularly ill-tempered, child-eating, fish-like dragon, tamed by St Martha in the first century AD. The monster reappears during an annual carnival on the last Sunday of June, propelled through the streets by a team of eight men.

Beaucaire, on the starboard shore, has recently experienced new prosperity at the terminus of the Canal du Rhône à Sète. During the late eighties, 18 million francs were spent on pleasure craft moorings and facilities and *Fluvial* magazine claimed that the long-stay rates charged were perhaps the best value in the entire country. Until advent of the railway, Beaucaire hosted one of Europe's greatest fairs each summer, ships arriving with goods from all corners of the Continent. A lock provided a way into the Rhône until 1970 when changed river levels severed the connection. Now a hire cruiser centre, effectively in a navigational *cul de sac*, we would have had to make a detour of 61km via the Petit Rhône and St Gilles to visit the town. A replacement lock is, however, planned, offering direct access to the Rhône and so creating a very worthwhile cruising circuit with only three locks.

Although our inland route to the Canal du Midi would at last soon take us away from the mighty Rhône, one more riverside town remained to be explored: Arles, 3km below a junction with the Petit Rhône. We intended to spend a night, even though I recalled that the sloping quays did not provide the best of berths. The ancient Roman city lies on the east bank, a huddle of brown-tiled rooftops above a pair of road bridges. Opposite, we were heartened to see that a floating stage had been installed since our last visit; a space was soon found between several other pleasure craft.

Within two minutes walk, a modern supermarket was able to cater for all immediate galley requirements. But first, we crossed the bridge in the early morning, heading for the Roman amphitheatre. Dating from 40 BC, this remarkable structure could hold 21,000 spectators and measures 136x107m. During the Middle Ages, it was filled with 200 houses and a church. As much of the original building remained intact, a full restoration programme was slowly carried out from 1828. We climbed to roof level, to be rewarded by a view of the Rhône and, far beyond, the wetlands of the Camargue.

Vincent Van Gogh arrived at Arles station from Paris on 20 February 1888. It was snowing. He was to die two and a half years later in Auvers-sur-Oise. During his fifteen months in Arles, he produced a frenzy of 185 paintings and 125 sketches which have fashioned the whole way we now look at this part of Provence. Until I visited the region, I was inclined to regard his pictures as the outpourings of a tortured mind. Only when confronted by lines of contorted cypress trees, a field of gaudy sunflowers or the brilliance of houses baking in the southern sun, does his genius suddenly become obvious. One masterpiece, 'The Starry Night', shows the Arles waterfront with glowing orange reflections of gaslights in the darkness of the river. We went to find his bascule bridge spanning the little-used Canal d'Arles à Fos, south of the town. Vincent's original was demolished in 1932, but an identical wooden replacement was erected in 1961 at the Écluse de Montcalde. After the unfortunate episode of Van Gogh's ear, which he cut off and presented to a brothel keeper, neatly wrapped in an envelope, a body of townsfolk petitioned the mayor to have him removed to a place of safety. Little did they realise that this genius among modern artists would soon bring fame and prosperity to their locality.

In the early afternoon, we cast off, steered *Avonbay* into the middle of the river for the last time and headed upstream to the Petit Rhône junction, gateway to the lost and mournful land of the Camargue.

17

Camargue

SILT carried from the Swiss Alps towards the sea during thousands of years has created a wilderness of swamps and shallow lakes in the Rhône delta. One-time seaports have retreated inland over the centuries and the actual confluence of the river with the Mediterranean is an unnavigable chaos of sand-banks. Craft instead turn to the east, locking into a basin at Port-St-Louis and so make their way to the coast on the Golfe de Fos. Westwards, we were to penetrate the edges of one of Europe's most remote wildlife reserves: the Camargue Regional Park.

Taking its name from Annius Camars, a Roman imperial governor whose estate encompassed the delta marshes, the Camargue extends to 86,000 hectares (212,500 acres). Sea-salt production, where evaporation ponds are regularly emptied to form small mountains of the material around Salin-de-Giraud, and cultivation of rice in paddy fields are two unusual industries that threatened the unique wildlife until rigorous controls were established in 1970. This is a place of stunning sunsets; warm, brackish lakes teeming with fish; elegant flamingoes by the thousand; white egrets, bee-eaters and various rare examples of water fowl; sand lilies, narcissus, purple iris and orchids; and the legendary wild white horses and black bulls. *Gardians*

Europe's most important flamingo reserve is to be found in the Camargue

162

(cowboys) have origins far older here than their United States counterparts, even if the saddles, hats, jackets and boots available for tourist purchase are most likely to be American imports. Often the only practicable access to huge tracts of countryside is on horseback. While large areas are strictly closed to all but landowners and accredited naturalists, the holiday-maker has numerous opportunities for hiring horses by the hour. More than once, we considered such an excursion into the interior, but were so saddened by the fly-blown, undernourished state of the animals that we felt it was kinder to desist. Nearly twenty years earlier we had, however, formed an equine crocodile under the leadership of a young man whose bare feet displayed big toe nails painted bright pink. We ambled down sandy tracks known so well to the horses that little work was necessary on the reins. '*Vous allez faire le galop?*' our guide suggested to the more confident among this equestrian rabble. We agreed and our mounts broke into a dejected trot, obviously their maximum speed. '*Formidable,*' exclaimed the young man, totally without conviction.

Close association with England's water industry was later to result in John accepting an invitation for us to visit the Camargue preserves of the Tour de Valet Ornithological Research Station, founded by industrialist Dr Luc Hoffman. Warden John Walmsley introduced himself, wearing a camouflage jacket and was clearly alarmed by June's brilliant yellow trouser suit. He looked extremely dubious when she explained she would be filming the wildlife we expected him to produce for us. Whether the flamingoes have since overcome a one-time shyness or have greatly increased in numbers, I cannot tell. We saw few that day compared with the massed flocks sighted as *Avonbay* cruised gently down the Canal du Rhône à Sète. If ever again invited on an official birdwatching expedition, June will know better than to dress in fashionable bright yellow.

Apart from four bridges in the 20km of Petit Rhône to St Gilles lock, there are few signs of civilisation. Isolated *mas* (Camargue farmsteads) could sometimes be glimpsed if we stood on the highest part of the boat. Vineyards extended northwestwards towards Nîmes, with a maze of small drainage canals and lakes between us and the distant sea at Stes Maries-de-la-Mer. Although rather narrower than the main course of the river we had just left, this is a broad waterway, dredged for large barges but occupying its natural course past sandy banks clothed with willow and tamarisk. Tethered buoys and long avenues of tall black or red steel posts clearly showed where the channel lay as we weaved our way past untrodden sand-banks.

An impression that we were boating through an enchanted Garden of Eden was heightened by a group of young people bathing nude from a beach – in much the same way that the French regularly use the more deserted parts of their coastline. Later, a couple, similarly enjoying the hot sun, passed by on their sailing cruiser. Not another living person interrupted our peace for the rest of that day.

It was all too beautiful to be rushed, so, on reaching an extensive spit of near white sand in midriver, we lowered the anchor, carefully positioning the boat clear of the fairway but remaining in deep water. I had heard that levels can drop quickly overnight: we did not want to wake up hard aground next morning. The dinghy was launched and a shore party scoured our 'desert island' for kindling for the evening's barbeque. Rather than fight the considerable current, we plunged into the warm water well upstream of *Avonbay*, floating down towards her. Hair-washing and hull-scrubbing finished, we lay back on the sand, watching black kites wheeling in the clear blue sky above. In the remoteness and utter silence, I realised that this was why we had made our second home in France. The English Channel crossing seemed a long way off.

Next morning brought us to a junction: we continued ahead through the large concrete lock chamber of St Gilles. To our left, the Petit Rhône followed a now unbuoyed course towards the sea at Stes Maries-de-la-Mer. *Avonbay* is both too deep and too high to take this route, which is almost exclusively used by outboard powered fishing punts. Shortly, we might have turned right again, to reach St Gilles and the canal terminus in Beaucaire. Knowing the Canal du Midi offered much greater interest, we headed westwards, little realising that exceptional events would prompt an unplanned visit to the town the following Easter.

We were now on the Canal de Beaucaire, long absorbed into a succession of channels through the *étangs*, collectively known as the Canal du Rhône à Sète. Frankly, there is little to admire in these initial reaches. Long straights past desolate scrubland offered only brief interest at the villages of Franqueraux and Gallician. Once, we caught sight of a man harvesting thatching reeds; elsewhere, a gang was occupied burning mature trees at the waterside. This part of the Camargue boasts so few attractions that we felt positively sorry for those holiday-makers who had started their hire cruiser trips nearby and would have to travel considerable distances before discovering surroundings that would make their journeys seem worthwhile.

Everything was to change when, 10km after St Gilles lock, a series of magnificent parasol pines framed the lofty Tour de Constance, rising from the walled city of Aigues-Mortes. We recalled how, twenty years earlier, this remarkably intact survival from the Middle Ages enjoyed a lost and undiscovered existence in the marshes. Barges were in regular use; a comic little train clattered several times each day over the canal swing bridge, carrying holiday-makers between Nîmes and the sleepy little fishing port of Grau du Roi. Within the square formed by its massive grey walls, life continued for the people of Aigues-Mortes much as it had for more than eight centuries. Tourists would descend in droves on the better known and more flambuoyant hilltop city of Carcassonne, leaving Aigues-Mortes with its memories of more prosperous days. Much has since altered. Now, when we took our place on the quayside among several dozen other cruisers, a local authority employee arrived to charge a fee. Inside, boutiques and souvenir shops carry out a flourishing trade, as do the many restaurants.

However, for all that, it remains a genuine town, where people live and work. Spreading little beyond the original 500x300m boundaries, buildings hide behind the surrounding walls. With the coming of night, road traffic vanishes, tourists melt away and it is easy to imagine oneself back in the thirteenth century, gazing up at the towers and crenellations that rise from the swamps of the Camargue.

Wishing to establish a port on the Mediterranean, Louis IX (St Louis) acquired the site of an abbey in 1240 and ordered the building of the 32m high Tour de Constance. Stone was brought in shallow-draught boats from near Beaucaire. Special exemption from taxes encouraged citizens to colonise this inhospitable place. Louis was to

The massive Tour de Constance at St Louis' crusader city of Aigues-Mortes

set sail on two crusades to the Holy Land, assembling his fleet at the new town. He died of typhus, contracted on the second expedition in 1270. Aigues-Morte's walls were not finally completed until the end of the century. Within less than a hundred years a receding sea and silting channels had rendered the port useless. Its name of 'Dead Waters' became increasingly appropriate. The Tour de Constance was eventually turned into a highly effective prison, with a fire burning on top after dark to act as a lighthouse. We climbed a series of stairways to a conical cage at the summit and gazed out over the rooftops to the distant sea. The town remembers its founder with a rather fine bronze statue, erected during the middle of the nineteenth century in the square which bears his name.

Our car had previously been moved to St Gilles and was now fetched so that we could spend one day by the Mediterranean. Amanda, Charles and Auriole would be flying back to England from Marseille the following afternoon. Driving via Le Grau-du-Roi and the attractive new marina at Port Camargue, we discovered a huge tract of sand beyond the Espiguette lighthouse. Many of our companions on this family beach were perfecting their all-over suntans; we tried hard not to stare and soon came to the conclusion that we would be less conspicuous if we followed their example.

Altogether, we stayed three nights in Aigues-Mortes, dining each evening at the very agreeable Restaurant des Voyageurs on a corner of the Place St Louis, just two minutes walk from our mooring. Tables under the plane trees almost filled the square, causing great confusion as to which belonged to any chosen restaurant until we noticed that each could be identified by the colour of its cloths. John and Evelyn were collected from Marseille airport, the car moved one jump ahead to Marseillan and it was time to set sail again.

Always keen to navigate backwaters, I would have liked to run down to the coast at Le Grau-du-Roi, pass through the swing bridge and turn into the River Vidoule which leads back to the Canal du Rhône à Sète. We had come this way six years before in a hire boat. But with a published water depth of only 1.1m on the final side of the triangle, the route was clearly impracticable for *Avonbay*. Instead, we left Aigues-Mortes astern, passed under a pair of guillotine gates which can be lowered to keep the flood waters of the Vidoule out of the canal and found ourselves in a strange waterway built across a series of lakes. Stone banks were pierced at intervals by openings enabling shallow-draught fishing craft to penetrate the rich waters on each side. Soon, we were within a kilometre of the coast. Until the sixties, much of this Languedoc seashore was a desolate area, plagued by mosquitoes. Huge government investment has since created a series of resorts, extending all the way to the Spanish border. The result is mainly very successful in establishing an increasingly popular holiday area, while detracting only a little from the wild beauty of this part of the Mediterranean.

Away to our left, La Grande Motte appeared as a cluster of ultra-modern concrete pyramids. Had we moored to a quay, the town could have been reached in a fifteen-minute walk. However, we chose to continue past Carnon and Palavas, two pleasant little holiday centres linked by navigable channels to the sea and our canal. Previous voyages had included diversions to these colourful towns of seafood restaurants packed with traditional fishing boats. In both cases, headroom under towpath bridges at the entry points was less than required by *Avonbay*. For us, a more interesting diversion awaited at the Island of Maguelone, a sandy mound covered with pine trees, bordered by the canal on one side and the sea on another. Rising over the lake is a pale-cream stone church, accorded the status of cathedral. We had often passed by boat but never attempted to explore. Moorings, recently improved, are not ideal; some work was necessary suspending fenders along our waterline to protect the paintwork from a submerged ledge.

Entry would have been most convenient through a triumphal stone archway on the canal bank. The gates were, however, secured and decorated with intimidating notices forbidding access. A succession of holiday-makers, returning in the late afternoon from the beach, were making their way along the estate's perimeter, before crossing the canal on a floating pontoon bridge. Taking a bicycle, I followed this same route, passing close to a flock of flamingoes feeding in the shallows of the Étang de Pierre Blanche. Within several minutes I was by the seashore, where several hundred naturists were browning themselves. Small breakers endlessly crashed on the pale sand, littered with thousands of shells. Now taking a lane that rose sharply towards the cathedral, I was soon inside the vast, empty building, dimly lit by narrow windows piercing the thick walls.

Erected on the Insula Magolona between the eleventh and thirteenth centuries, the ancient church of St Pierre was the earliest of the fortified religious foundations of the Languedoc coast. The site could be approached only by sea or in boats crossing the lake and was ringed with defensive walls against possible Saracen attack. Urbain II was one of several popes who stayed at Maguelone, declaring during his visit in 1096 that it was 'second only to my church in Rome'! Its very isolation was eventually to make it an anachronism; by the early seventeenth century, the bishop transferred his seat to nearby Montpellier. The fortifications were pulled down, some of the stone being used to construct the banks of the Canal de Rhône à Sète as it crossed the *étangs*. After the French Revolution, the great church passed through various secular hands, becoming ever more ruined. Acquired by Fréderic Fabrèges in 1852, restoration was started and pines planted on the denuded island site. Returned to the church authorities in 1949, the estate now serves as a training centre for the mentally handicapped, housed in nineteenth-century agricultural buildings. There are carefully tended vines, a mixed farm and fishery.

A suitable mooring for the night was selected on piling at Les Aresquiers bridge, opposite a picturesque row of canalside fishermen's cottages. At sunset, we walked a few hundred metres to the seashore for a late evening swim.

Morning came dreadfully early as *Avonbay* rolled in the wash of a series of high-speed fishing punts. This industry clearly flourishes and appears to provide an easy livelihood. Long cylindical nets suspended from poles are one method; elsewhere, winches control nets stretched across the waterway from bank to bank. These are wound below the surface for the passage of boats. As we had a deeper draught than most pleasure craft, it seemed prudent to glide by with both engines in neutral. Once, we spotted with horror a corpse floating face down in the water. While we considered what action should be taken, the 'body' suddenly rose up out of the canal, revealing itself to be a frogman searching for mussels. His considerable haul filled an inflated lorry inner tube, adapted into a raft.

Our next town, Frontignan, is famous for its sweet, rich muscat wine; and the recalcitrant lifting road bridge which opens to allow boats to pass at widely spaced intervals. English text in the *Carte Guide* informed us that 'because of machinery problems, bridge opening hours will be weedly'. Reference to the original French '*le mauvais état du méchanisme de ce pont nécessite un minimum de manoeuvre*' confirmed that there were three operations each weekday; but when our time arrived, at 3pm, there was no hint of weedliness. A dozen cruisers approaching from each direction raced for the gap and briefly it seemed like we should all pile up on a 900-tonne barge similarly bored with the enforced wait. A previous visit had coincided with a major breakdown in the mechanism, resulting in a twenty-four hour delay. Now, a broad channel was being dug to join the coast east of Sète, enabling large commercial craft to avoid the obstacle. Wine barges no longer serve the busy town, a place of some antiquity, much noisy road traffic and a shortage of charm. Too much of the immediate surroundings are devoted to petrol refineries. These did not seem to trouble a mass of flamingoes gathered in a lake whose fringes were being invaded by mountains of wrecked cars and other refuse. It appeared that we were now beyond the jurisdiction of the environmentally sensitive Camargue. Also left behind was the mistral, replaced by a no less insistent wind called the tramontane.

Conditions were near perfect as *Avonbay* prepared to enjoy her first taste of the sea in four years. Probably wrongly, we decided not to enter Sète, a sizeable port astride a channel that leads from the *étang* to the sea. But we were just too high to pass beneath a road swing bridge (opened twice daily) blocking access to the town centre; nor was there any guarantee that we would find a suitable mooring on the congested quays. Nevertheless, I regretted not visiting this seventeenth-century terminus of Pierre Paul Riquet's coast to coast Canal du Midi. Rather like a Gallic Venice, with elegant waterside buildings, it is a bustling place of wine merchants and fish markets. The site was a curious choice, demanding that horse-drawn canal barges must carry sails or be laboriously poled the length of the *étang* until steam tugs or diesel engines made light of the problem. How much easier life would have been for the early canal boatmen if nearby Agde on the River Hérault had instead been developed as the major trans-shipment point between the canal and the Mediterranean.

Three ports lie on the northern, inland shore of the lake. Unhurried by any pressing schedule, we enjoyed time visiting each. First call was to Bouzigues, a little village of white-washed houses surrounded by vineyards and overlooking a huge spread of oyster beds for which the region is famous. These sought-after products of the warm, salty water are cultivated by suspending the immature molluscs on a grid of wooden poles in the *étang*. We easily found our way up a shallow channel past these obstructions and entered Bouzigues' tiny harbour where there was just enough depth for our 1.3m draught. Local children were swimming from a jetty; disregarding the prolific jellyfish, we joined them for a while, had a lazy lunch and then set out for Mèze.

Étang de Thau. Links with the Mediterranean are available at Sète and downstream of Agde on the River Hérault

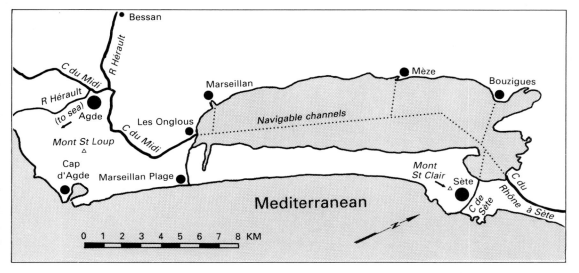

Here, a sizeable town spreads around three sides of a rectangular harbour whose entry is marked by lighthouses. Traditional open fishing boats with upturned bows jostled for available space with small pleasure cruisers. A mooring was found on the quay near the entrance, conveniently placed for a popular swimming beach. Eventually, we sought greater solitude by moving a kilometre out into the lake, dropped anchor and spent the remainder of the afternoon sunbathing and swimming from the boat. It had been a relaxing day and all rather different from our normal energetic progress through locks.

On returning to Mèze for the night, we were hailed by the crew of a hire boat, lying at anchor well offshore. The German holiday-makers on board explained in broken English that they had run out of diesel. Knowing that every British vessel is pleased to come to the aid of fellow mariners in distress, we agreed to take them in tow to the most convenient waterside fuel point at Marseillan, 7km along the *étang*. Our rescued friends seemed to be a singularly inept crowd, helping little with making fast a long towline. Once under way, they disappeared within, amid shrieks of ribald mirth. During the journey, another party of Germans appeared in a similar hire cruiser and exchanged a few words with our tow, resulting in more uncontrolled laughter. Forty-five minutes after the start of the operation, we cast the Germans off alongside the fuel pump. Probably, we might legally have claimed a substantial salvage fee although nothing could have been further from our thoughts. On the other hand, it was not unreasonable to expect some form of token payment: perhaps a few bottles of wine. To our amazement, the rescued crew all assembled on deck and one of them volunteered the information that 'we have been playing a game!' Not a word of thanks or any further explanation was forthcoming. True, they started to refuel, but it was quite clear that they had not been disabled in any way. We turned our backs on them in disgust and walked into town for a restaurant dinner.

Marseillan is a sleepy little town, doubtless founded as a sea port when the *étang* was still a coastal inlet. Great prosperity came during the nineteenth century when wine merchants erected large houses bordering the stone-sided harbour. Until the sixties, Canal du Midi wine barges regularly called to take on cargoes. Now they have all gone and even the once prolific fishing boats are outnumbered by pleasure craft. We first knew the town in the early seventies when Blue Line opened their second French hire cruiser base outside the elegant Château du Port. Then, this former vintner's residence was owned by a Dutchman as a genial hôtel and restaurant. Demand for additional moorings prompted installation of an array of pontoons outside the main harbour, protected from the *étang* by groynes of loose boulders. Today, a harbourmaster will call to collect mooring fees and

Marseillan seems certain to develop as an unpretentious little resort.

Two features were especially noticeable on the present visit: the quantity of large waterside buildings for sale at prices where conversion to holiday apartments would seem to offer a certain prospect of considerable wealth; and swarms of near-wild cats, lazing in the sunshine or lurking in the dark barns which are a feature of many mansions.

Once, in 1977, we had brought a boat here from Castelnaudary on the Canal du Midi, accompanied by another craft crewed by a party including the Earl of Snowdon and his children Sarah and David. There were frequent halts while Tony made beautiful sketches, worthy of his artist great-grandfather, Linley Sambourne. An invention, designed and crafted on the Canal du Midi was the 'Snowdon Patent

Cap d'Agde, part of which constitutes Europe's largest naturist resort

Flower Picker'. This consisted of a wooden pole (borrowed from a lockside garden) with a razor blade attached to one end. A system of strings and rubber bands enabled the operator to collect waterside flora as the boat was actually in motion, without any need to endure the tedious business of mooring up. At the end of their holiday, we drove his Lordship and crew to Agde station to catch a connection for their return by train to London. As they waited, a non-stop express rushed past the platform and Tony leaped up and down, shouting to his bewildered children: 'You fools. You've missed it!'

Use of the car enabled several of us to make a day-long excursion to the nearby resort of Cap d'Agde, created on sand-dunes by the Mediterranean. Two decades after the development began, the mixture of modern concrete apartments and traditional Languedoc architecture has mellowed. Sweet-scented shrubs and pines provide shade in the one-time mosquito-filled swamps. A pair of harbours offer shelter for hundreds of pleasure craft: it was these havens we wanted to investigate in advance of a possible coastal cruise on *Avonbay*. Another aspect was not without interest. One part of the complex is devoted to naturism – a complete town where upwards of 20,000 nudists enjoy the sun in peak season. There are banks, supermarkets, boutiques (some oddly selling swimming wear), restaurants and cafés, where clothed customers are decidedly in the minority. Average age of devotees would appear to be the mid-thirties but with a representative selection from all other groups from tiny children to septuagenarians. In August, the majority of visitors were French, augmented mainly by Germans who, together with the Scandinavians, lost their prudery long before such things were contemplated in the rest of Europe.

Entry is available to all – for a fee. Having parked the car, John drew our attention to a sign saying: 'The wearing of clothes beyond this point is absolutely forbidden.' In France, all manner of activities are *interdit;* but we had never expected this to be one of them. Heading for the beach, we chose an enclosure with sun loungers which offered (again for a fee) an element of selectivity away from the massed bodies on each side. By way of uniform, the young man in charge wore a coloured scarf on his thigh, although his pretty girlfriend/assistant had no need of any adornment.

It must be admitted that while such an opportunity to study the human form at close quarters revealed certain people who added little to the landscape, most of our fellow sunbathers were an attractive collection. In the few hours spent by the sea, there was little prospect of our emulating the magnificent tans of these dedicated lotus-eaters, so after an al fresco lunch of steak and salad we returned to the boat to begin the final part of our summer cruise.

18

Canal du Midi

A SHORT run across the western end of the Étang de Thau brought us to a pair of lighthouses in the marshes of Les Onglous. Almost twenty years after we had first explored the Canal du Midi we were returning in our own boat and planned to climb towards the summit level, leaving *Avonbay* for the winter at Castelnaudary. It was six years since we had visited these waters and were slightly apprehensive that relentless development would have changed the canal, bringing queues of hire cruisers at the locks and an aura of commercialism to what we recalled as one of Europe's most historic and beautiful waterways. But we need not have worried. Even now, in peak season, the Midi retained all its well-remembered charm; hard-worked lock-keepers were rarely disagreeable and there was never any difficulty in finding peaceful overnight moorings.

When we had inaugurated Blue Line Cruisers at Toulouse in 1969, the original seven craft (shortly transferred to a new base at Castelnaudary) were the sole inland hire boats in southern France. Other people were not slow to appreciate the potential of this holiday industry and by 1984 the number had grown to over 300 with further

Pierre-Paul Riquet, Baron de Bonrepos, the seventeeth-century genius responsible for the Canal du Midi

expansion since then. A mere 93 pleasure boats of all types were logged passing through Agde in 1964; two decades later, the figure had exploded to 6,115, representing a greater traffic density than at any time since the canal was opened in 1681.

Credit for realising a long-held dream to link Atlantic and Mediterranean, lies with Pierre-Paul Riquet. Having achieved considerable financial success as a gatherer of salt tax throughout Languedoc, this extraordinary Béziers-born entrepreneur had already passed the age of sixty when work began on the huge enterprise in 1667. He was virtually to bankrupt himself and his family in the effort and sadly died some months before the first boat from Toulouse reached the Mediterranean shore. Gradually, the canal was to meet with considerable success, bringing wealth to the Riquet descendants and widespread prosperity to the area it served. Louis XIV and his minister Colbert provided support for the scheme, an undertaking without parallel at that time.

Compared with many waterways constructed in Britain more than a century later, the Midi was a grandiose feat of engineering, running for 240km between the Garonne in Toulouse and the Étang de Thau, with over 100 locks capable of accommodating 30m vessels. The key to its triumphant conclusion was the provision of extensive water supplies in the Montagne Noire, where the St Férréol reservoir had a capacity of 7 million cubic m. Summer rainfall being insignificant, it was little short of genius on the part of Riquet and his engineer Francois Andreossy that traffic could continue for a large proportion of each year. Admittedly, throughout the eighteenth century lack of water would prompt closure for up to an annual eight weeks, this time being used to carry out required repair works. Addition of a branch line serving Narbonne in 1776 prompted the building of a further large reservoir, Lampy, and thereafter closures were reduced, on average, to a mere two weeks each year.

Early failure of a conventional lock of rectangular design prompted the decision to provide the canal with its characteristic oval chambers. Although not as convenient to use and more wasteful of water than the pattern normally adopted elsewhere, they have greater strength. The majority appear to be as originally built, more than 300 years ago. Rather than erect any exceptionally deep locks, multiples were installed where required; there are numerous such risers, comprising double, triple, quadruple and at Béziers, an eight-stepped staircase, overcoming a change in level of 30.6m.

In spite of being conceived as a link between the two seas, from the start the canal was used almost exclusively by inland vessels. Passenger and freight boats were hauled by men or horses until barges were converted to diesel propulsion in the thirties. It was effectively operated as a private company until the revolution and passed into railway control in 1858, some shares being returned to the Riquet family. Freight figures then fell sharply from 59 million tonne kilometres in 1859 to 28 million in 1896. A form of independence under state control was introduced in 1898, but cargoes increased only slowly, from 21 million tonne kilometres in 1921 to about 30 million during the sixties.

By the mid-eighteenth century, some 150 sailing barges regularly plied the waterway; this figure had grown to 273 craft by 1838, not counting occasional visitors from other navigations. At the turn of the century, on average the locks were passing just four boats each day. In 1965, a daily ten barges would work through the locks at Castelnaudary; at this time there were 166 freight vessels working on the Midi and the neighbouring Canal latéral à la Garonne, which since the mid-nineteenth century had bypassed the unreliable river reaches downstream of Toulouse.

Even though the Midi was considered fully completed by 1694, various improvements were later carried out including building a new line serving Carcassonne and bridging the River Orb at Béziers with a large aqueduct. Nothing was to come of a highly ambitious scheme to upgrade the waterway so that it would have rivalled the Suez Canal.

Canal du Midi, forming part of the Mediterranean-Atlantic link

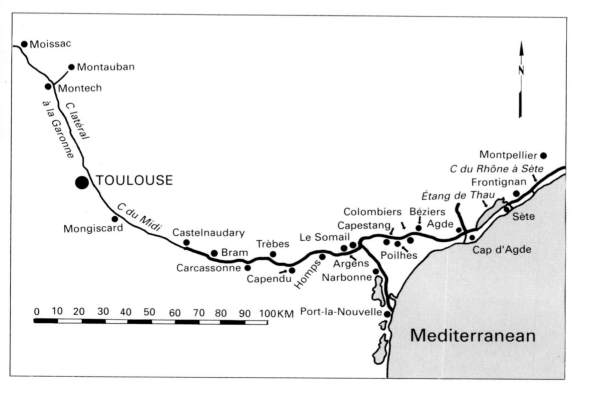

Advanced in 1884, the Maritime Canal plan proposed eighteen duplicated locks or staircases, each admitting ships up to 180x27m, over a distance of 490km.

Unlike many other French waterways, enlargement to the 38.5m Freycinet standard was not adopted in the 1880s. Necessary legislation was eventually passed in 1903, but it was not carried out on the latéral until the seventies. Unable to accept conventional *péniches* from elsewhere, Midi traffic spiralled into a decline. Year by year, tankers carrying wine and fuel and general cargo vessels were sold off for conversion to pleasure craft and houseboats. Discussions continued as to how locks might be lengthened without destroying the architectural heritage of this unique seventeenth-century monument. Finally, a portion was enlarged at the Toulouse end by 1979, followed by similar work from the eastern terminus and down the Narbonne branch. Single locks were increased in capacity by adding concrete extensions to the chambers and moving one set of gates. At the famous Fonserannes staircase in Béziers, this treatment was neither suitable nor environmentally desirable; instead, a 'water slope' device was installed alongside. This functioned for a short time after 1985, then suffered a spectactular failure. It was not reopened until the summer of 1989.

By the time *Avonbay* made her journey, the once great fleet of barges was reduced to just two: *Bacchus* and *Espérance*. All impetus to complete the modernisation seemed to have evaporated. More than three centuries after the first barges had appeared, they were now at the point of extinction. Saddened by this situation, I was nevertheless rather pleased that all those multiple risers in the canal's central section seemed likely to remain as in Riquet's day.

Arrival at Bagnas, first of our uphill locks, provided an opportunity to perfect a technique of getting lines ashore and making the boat secure before the keeper opened his gate paddles and a roar of water cascaded over the top sill towards us. It was helpful to put at least two people ashore before entering the chamber: one to take the ropes and another to help close the bottom gates. Climbing Midi locks is hard work; we would take some of the strain off the warps by careful use of the engines as the water surged in. Chambers were frequently shared with less experienced hire-boat crews, so it was useful to have five of us on board to share duties. Conversely, a west–east journey from the canal's summit near Toulouse to the Mediterranean is simplicity itself, for there is no turbulence at all inside an emptying lock. Anyone chartering a boat for a one-way cruise is always well advised to select the downhill option where possible.

Riquet's plan to bring his canal into the River Hérault, using it for 800m downstream and then branching off on the far bank a short distance above Agde weir works well enough during gentle summer flows. The Prades guard lock keeps floodwaters out of the canal when necessary but under these conditions passage of the river can be a hazardous undertaking. We decided to make a 5km detour up the Hérault to a fortified millhouse at the Bessan head of navigation. Deep, clear water is bordered by dense undergrowth, making this journey like a voyage through Amazonian jungles, enlivened by fat brown buzzards, roosting in the trees. Years before, we had met no other boats; now a hotel barge and several cruisers had similarly diverted into this wilderness. We dropped anchor in midstream for a long swim in the warm water.

Regaining the canal brought us to the famous Round Lock of Agde approached by a narrow channel fringed with massive plane trees. This short cut had been selected as the last resting place for one of the old timber-built Midi barges, originally belonging to the nationwide fleet of the Compagnie Général de la Navigation. By 1977, *Ville de Marseillan* had the look of a vessel whose working days were over. Stained canvas sheets were spread to keep the rain from wheelhouse

Canal du Midi. Springtime at the Round Lock, Agde. Avonbay is moored in a modern concrete-sided bay, built to increase the dimensions of craft able to navigate the waterway. Gates, top left, lead to the Mediterranean via the River Hérault

and cargo hold. Moss encroached on the once pristine decks. She had become a retirement home for an inland mariner. We wondered who would succumb first: *Ville de Marseillan* or her geriatric inhabitant. Returning in 1982, we found the barge half sunk and seemingly beyond recovery. Now, in 1988, the wreck had been removed and a fragment of Canal du Midi history had gone with her.

The Round Lock provided an elegant solution to a complicated problem. Not only did double sets of gates at 6 o'clock and 12 o'clock enable craft to continue down the canal regardless of whether levels in the Hérault were higher or lower, but a third pair of gates at 9 o'clock opened into a branch connecting with the river downstream of the town weir. Thus, it is possible to take a boat from the canal and past the city's fishing boat quays to the Mediterranean, 5 km downstream at Le Grau d'Agde. The unfortunate modernisation scheme involved excavating a concrete bay in the 3 o'clock wall, destroying its symmetry in the interest of admitting full length *péniches*. Soon after we had arrived, a *mêlée* of craft was jostling for positions. One passenger-carrying barge tried to jump the queue; we remained resolutely in mid-channel, ignoring their bullying tactics and entered the lock ahead of her.

For the next two days, guests would be travelling on *Avonbay*. We would have liked to descend to the Hérault, spend the night on the town wharves and welcome them aboard there, before returning to the canal via the Round Lock. For some reason, this scheme did not suit the overstressed lady-keeper. Even though her duties were restricted to pushing buttons — for this is one of several mechanised Midi locks — she insisted that entry to the river was possible only according to a strict timetable, twice a day. Now was not one of those times. Instead, we followed the direction of the other traffic and found a mooring among a clutch of houseboats outside a splendid eighteenth-century mansion. This had once served as an administration centre for the waterway and is perhaps the most impressive building on the whole canal.

That evening, we dined at La Galiote, a restaurant overlooking the river, housed in what appeared to have been an ecclesiastical establishment connected to the city's severe fortified cathedral. In the morning, food supplies were fetched by bicycle from a supermarket reached through hilly pedestrianised streets. Ripe melons, a selection of meat for the barbeque and a magnificent strawberry tart were to comprise our al fresco luncheon. The four guests arrived by taxi from their Béziers hotel and embarked for an introduction to inland boating. Some years earlier, they had sold up in Wimbledon and gone to live with the *glitterati* of Monaco. Knowing that their idea of cruising normally involves high-speed day launches on the Riviera, I feared that the pace of canal travel might seem rather tame. But by arranging diversions with dinghy and bikes, the visit was a great success. Mother and daughter lost no time in changing into their bikinis and were content to soak up the sunshine as we set off through a Camargue-like landscape of tall reeds, several times coming within walking distance of the coast.

Reaching a point where the little Libron River crosses at canal level, we were intrigued by a complicated system of stone arches fitted with overhead winding gear. Normally a placid stream, the river is subject to flash floods. Entry of such surplus water into the navigation would quickly have breached the banks. Initially, a special vessel, or floating aqueduct, was kept in readiness to be scuttled in the river bed, its raised ends protecting the waterway from flooding. When the water subsided, the barge would be pumped dry, removed and through traffic could resume. These delays would have been very inconvenient, so the present arrangement was substituted. This enables craft to work past the obstacle in stages, using guillotines to divert the Libron ahead and then astern of the boat.

In 1973, June had gone ashore here to film our boat passing beneath the arches. Standing on a narrow ledge, she had stepped backwards into deep water, totally disappearing from sight. Reluctant to release her grip on the heavy (and valuable) 16mm ciné equipment and not being a strong swimmer, she took a long while to surface. Fortunately, the accident happened in full view of Britain's Minister for Sport, Eldon Griffiths (now Sir Eldon), travelling in company with us in another boat. Unhesitatingly, he executed a magnificent dive, grabbed the very frightened June and hauled her out of the canal. The quality of Japanese ciné cameras is exemplified by the fact that the processed film clearly recorded the incident right up to the point of immersion. A quick drying out of camera and operator and they both continued to perform as if nothing untoward had taken place.

There was plenty of traffic about that day, with long delays at the three locks leading to Béziers. As our Monaco friend went ashore to fraternise, we were treated to a display of his delightful sense of humour. 'Beautiful weather, isn't it?' called out the British hirer of another boat. 'Oh, yes. But it's raining where we've come from and where you are heading!' replied our guest. When he was seen reading a copy of a pink French newspaper, assumed to be the *Financial Times*, he answered a holiday-maker's question of 'What's the market doing?' with 'If I were you, I'd contact England immediately and sell everything! I have.' The questioner visibly blanched and anxiously went in search of a telephone. Later, we passed a series of exhausted single scullers, competing in a 40km race. After more than a dozen had rowed by, our jolly friend shouted, in fluent French, to one tiring competitor: 'Well done! You're in the lead; all the others have dropped out!' At this the oarsman discovered new reserves of energy.

A disused arm, leading to the River Orb shortly before the 'new' basin of Béziers, was a reminder of Riquet's original route. Here, the navigation had once joined the river, leaving it well upstream at the foot of a great series of locks. Passage of craft was notoriously difficult especially if the river was in spate but it was not until 1857 that an aqueduct, designed by Jean Magues, removed the difficulty. At each end of a newly dug port pairs of two-rise locks lifted the canal to the required height over the Orb. The first of these locks was fitted with unusually tall bottom gates, enabling a barge to be deposited on a bankside drydock. Although destroyed in the lengthening scheme of the late seventies, when the four chambers were replaced by two deep ones, another example of this unusual docking arrangement survives on the Narbonne branch. Béziers, crowned by its medieval cathedral of St Nazaire, is seen to excellent advantage from the seven-span stone aqueduct, an elegant classical structure with Romanesque arches concealing walkways immediately alongside the navigation channel.

The *pièce de résistance* of this day was to be our ascent of Les Fonserannes locks, a multiple series of six (once eight) chambers, one leading directly into the next. By fortunate timing, our arrival coincided with an uphill hire cruiser convoy. Most of the crew went ashore to tend ropes. Mechanisation takes the form of little electric motors, operating individual paddles. Careful button-pushing by the keeper ensured that the tightly packed boats stayed clear of each other while the sluices released foaming chutes of water. But with several inexperienced craft it was a slow procedure as the flotilla gradually rose high above the valley of the Orb.

Alongside, the only water-slope in France available to pleasure craft, lay disused. I had expected *Avonbay* to add passage of this extraordinary structure to her catalogue of achievements. Modifications following a frightening malfunction several years earlier were not due to be completed until the next summer. The principle of the *pente d'eau* is well tried: another example had been in use by barges on the Canal latéral à la Garonne at Montech since 1973. It consists of a concrete ramp in which a wedge-shaped pool of water containing boats is pushed up or down the incline by a pair of engines attached to a mobile gate. Water consumption is negligible, for supplies used on downhill runs are replenished by the following uphill operation. Now, reeds sprouted in the approach channels. I suspected that a degree of embarrassment could still be detected in the canal's engineering department. We had to wait until the summer of 1989 for *Avonbay*'s first ride.

With the guests despatched by taxi to their hotel, we enjoyed a

In summer 1989, Avonbay was able to use the Béziers water slope after its return to service. Device, centre, is a moveable gate which proceeds up the slope, pushing a wedge-shaped 'puddle' of water in which the boats are moored. Here, we are travelling in a downstream direction. Note canal line, top left, leading to the Fonserannes staircase of six locks; these continue in service on certain days when the water slope is not used

peaceful evening cruise, setting out along the Grand Bief. This 54km pound is the longest lock-free canal level in France: a classic example of a contour cut. Winding through shallow excavations or perched on embankments overlooking vineyards, it features some astonishing bends, especially just west of Capestang. Rows of planes provide deep shade, arching over the water to create a canopy of greenery. Sometimes, you might see a following boat not far off across the fields. Stop to let it catch you up and a wait of fifteen minutes is likely. Little hump-backed stone bridges survive from the seventeenth century. This is the Midi at its most typical. Surprisingly, the ubiquitous planes, so effective at shielding boaters from the hot sun as well as stabilising the banks with their roots, were almost unknown here in the late eighteenth century. Of a total of 61,658 specimens recorded then on canal land, a mere 168 were planes; more than half were Lombardy poplars.

In the 167km between Agde and Castelnaudary, there are no fewer than twenty-four waterside towns and villages, almost all offering interest with sun-bleached houses, basic shops and restaurants. A very lazy cruise would be required to do justice to every one of them. Where possible, we stopped in places new to us, mooring elsewhere during our return by this route the next spring. At Colombiers, an extensive and still very raw basin had been created for hire cruisers. It contrasted unfavourably with the old bridge, red-roofed *lavoir* (wash-house) and mellow *château*, where meals can be taken in a gravelled courtyard. Changes are inevitable: we hoped that the planners fully appreciate what a priceless asset they are guarding.

Shortly afterwards, we arrived at the world's oldest navigation tunnel – Malpas. At 161m long and both wide and high compared with similar bores in England, it was built, according to a rather improbable legend, in a mere six days. Dogged by rumours that he would never complete the canal at an acceptable cost, Riquet ordered his labourers to dig through the Ensérune hill with all possible speed. When an inspection party of commissioners arrived on site, they were amazed to see the task finished. Riquet had confounded his critics. The eastern portal is decorated with a reasonably imposing stone arch, while the western entrance has nothing more than badly weathered natural rock. Drawings exist for a grandiose façade with columns, classical figures and an ornamental balustrade. Acute money shortages prevented this being added while the waterway remained unfinished and thereafter, the plan seems to have been quietly forgotten.

Either mouth of the tunnel offers a convenient approach to the site of an Iberian-Greek fortress, Oppidum d'Ensérune, founded in the sixth century BC. I accompanied Diana on an uphill bicycle expedition, the most enjoyable part of which was our high-speed return. En route, thirteenth-century drainage works at the Lake of Montady, have resulted in a fascinating series of triangular fields, spreading from a central point like the spokes of a huge wheel. Fragments of pottery artefacts, displayed in a two-storey exhibition centre, were judged by our A-Level expert in Classical Studies to be much inferior to those in the British Museum. The excursion is worth making for the broad views eastwards to the city of Béziers.

There are few more characteristic Languedoc towns than Capestang. Rising slightly from the bed of a lake, long ago drained, it is dominated by a soaring thirteenth-century church, designed by Deschamps, the architect of Narbonne cathedral. Outside, a plane-shaded square hosts a Sunday market. For the rest of the week the locals busy themselves with drinking in pavement bars or organising noisy boule contests on the gravel. It was all very charming in its old-fashioned sleepiness when June and I made our way there next morning for a catering expedition. Our guests had enjoyed themselves sufficiently to want to return for another day's boating. Whether Capestang's limited shopping facilities would provide as impressive a lunch as yesterday was very much open to question. Jokingly, I suggested we should start with pink champagne and canapés of *pâté de foie gras* and caviare. All the required ingredients were easily located in a tiny grocer's shop! After that, there was little difficulty in selecting several types of tinned fish in wine sauce, cold meats, salad and cheese.

The guests arrived, and once more under way, we headed for an unusually low arched bridge bearing the scars of numerous collisions. Fortunately, there was ample clearance; unlike some craft we had no need to flood the bilges or seek additional bodies to reduce air draught. Now followed an amazingly sinuous part of the Grand Bief where we covered perhaps four times the straight line distance, turning through all points of the compass.

On the outskirts of Argeliers, a lengthsman's cottage stands in isolation next to a bridge. Several tall pines shade its western elevation, with vineyards at the back reaching towards Montouliers and a range of rocky hills. Stopping to investigate in 1973, we found the pretty building was unoccupied: it would have made an idyllic holiday home, within easy driving distance of the coast. Eldon Griffiths was consumed by a passion to own it. While he never acted on the idea, we would refer to it as 'Eldon's House' on subsequent journeys. Each time we returned, the effects of vandalism had increased. Doors and windows were open to the weather; tiles fallen from the roof. Sadly, it appeared inevitable that it must suffer the fate of dozens of canal structures in England and be reduced to a pile of rubble. To our surprise and pleasure we now discovered that the little house had been beautifully restored and was operating as the restaurant *Au Chat Qui*

Pêche. For us, it will always remain *la maison d'Eldon*.

British companies were at the forefront of bringing pleasure cruising to the French waterways. They retain a strong presence and enclaves of English craft are numerous throughout the Midi. Some expatriates have selected an agreeable lifestyle in the southern sunshine, making homes on cruisers and barges. We noticed several at the Port de la Robine basin, where a junction is made with the branch line that proceeds via Narbonne to the Mediterranean at Port-la-Nouvelle. Continued settled weather influenced our decision to head for the coast where we could spend several days building on our sea-going experience before resuming the voyage up the Canal du Midi.

Easy work was made of seven descending locks through Sallèles d'Aude to the Écluse de Gailhousty. Here, a substantial late eighteenth-century keeper's house stands over a weir outfall. Designed in the form of a Grecian temple, it faces a lockside drydock in which a converted barge was under repair. The Narbonne line is reputedly shallow with an official draught of 1.4m. Recalling how laden barges had worked this route not many years before, we were surprised that *Avonbay*, 0.1m within the published limits, should ground badly on a gravel shoal as we headed for a pair of suspended poles, marking a channel across the River Aude. As no damage was sustained, everyone used this minor mishap as an excuse for a swim. Then it was time for the guests to call up a taxi and resume their journey home to Monaco. When they had left, we grounded again – rather more seriously above a weir – before regaining the safety of the southern part of the canal that leads to Narbonne.

Three further locks brought us to the city, where the most central moorings lie beyond the dangerously low arch of the 'Roman' bridge. Thought to date from the twelfth or thirteenth century, this river crossing originally comprised six or seven arches. All but one are now absorbed into the cellars of shops and houses. As you walk down the narrow street above, there is no hint that a navigation is concealed beneath. Two thousand years ago this was a busy port situated by an island-filled lagoon. It now lies well inland and is rich in mosaics and other ancient artefacts.

Since our last visit in 1975, the city quays had been landscaped with shrubs and a particularly dusty variety of pulverised gravel. Attempts to rewater ship were very tedious, requiring a spring-operated tap to be held in position. Later, we discovered a conventional water source, threaded for the hose, concealed behind a stone balustrade, just downstream of the public lavatory. In the adjacent tree-shaded square, a kiosk sold English newspapers. We ate at the nearby Brasucade Restaurant and most of one afternoon the girls enjoyed a frenzy of shopping. June and Evelyn are tapestry enthusiasts. An elaborate version of Renoirs's 'Jeune Filles au Piano' having been selected in a well-stocked needlework boutique, I asked (in my best French) a smartly dressed young man, presumed to be the owner, if the cross-stitch items were supplied painted on the fabric. Without a second's hesitation he replied: '*Tu est adorable . . . mais je ne suis pas le vendeur!*' Such startling familiarity left me speechless.

Visits were made to the Archbishop's Palace, the mighty cathedral of St Just and a superb late nineteenth-century indoor market hall where stalls were piled with a breathtaking array of fish, meat, fruit and vegetables. Rarely have I discovered a town so filled with interest.

The way to the sea lay through a marshy landscape, sometimes dotted with parasol pines. Considerably less frequented than the canal's main line, it reminded us of the best of the Camargue. Ruined farmhouses stood forlorn on the shores of several huge *étangs;* an unhealthy number of men armed with shotguns and numerous fishermen suggested that the abundant wildlife was in some peril. At the waterside, a sad little monument bore the inscription (in translation): 'A terrible accident. Drowned in the water was 26-year-old Louise Gautier and her young brother Maurice Berlan. 10 August 1841.' Had this pair been swimming in the canal in the heat of a summer afternoon? Perhaps the boy had fallen in and his sister made a vain rescue attempt. Whatever the truth, they had achieved an unexpected degree of immortality. We skirted the tree-covered slopes of the Île de Ste Lucie with its once proud *château* in overgrown grounds and now serving as some form of ecological research centre. It was a strange, lost area, totally devoid of any bankside facilities. One final lock lowered us into a mass of black mud-stained water. We were now at sea level and subject to the slight tidal influence of the Mediterranean.

Rounding a right-angled corner opened up a view of Port-la-Nouvelle's large harbour, packed with fishing trawlers and pleasure craft. Further on, ocean-going cargo ships were unloading in the commercial docks. Unable to find a suitable mooring, we returned to the canal. Nearby, a slightly dreary little town offered useful shops and the Restaurant du Port, where we enjoyed one of the best meals of the journey. Most of the other clients seemed to be French seaside holiday-makers.

By cycling towards a pair of lighthouses, we discovered a region of small family hotels, bucket and spade shops and seafood eating establishments. Vast sandy beaches stretched towards the Rhône delta on one side and the Spanish border to the west. A strong wind was blowing, making pedalling nearly impossible. The pilots' office provided a none too favourable forecast so plans to venture down the coast to the Costa Brava were discarded. Instead, a much shorter passage eastwards to Cap d'Agde was chosen. *Avonbay* set off early next morning, positively enjoying her first real taste of the sea for three years. Under a clear blue sky, visibility was excellent: we could almost see our intended destination through the binoculars. Five minutes out from Port-la-Nouvelle, the first patches of spray started to wet our decks. Breakables were hurriedly stowed. A quick conference indicated that not all on board were happy at the prospect of two hours of gentle pounding. Knowing that a sea trip was quite irrelevant to the successful completion of our voyage to Castelnaudary, we returned to the harbour. This was doubtless a wise, if disappointing, decision, for gusts up to force 7 were recorded that day. In a region bedevilled by the fickle tramontane wind, we would have to wait until the next summer before putting to sea again. Even then, repeated sorties into the Mediterranean would be of short duration: August seems not to offer reliable conditions along this part of the French coast.

The wine cave of Ventenac d'Aude, where locally-produced Minervois may be tasted (and purchased)

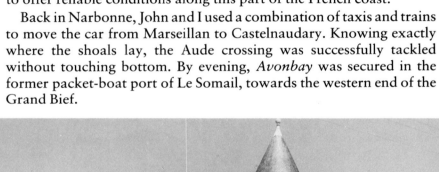

Back in Narbonne, John and I used a combination of taxis and trains to move the car from Marseillan to Castelnaudary. Knowing exactly where the shoals lay, the Aude crossing was successfully tackled without touching bottom. By evening, *Avonbay* was secured in the former packet-boat port of Le Somail, towards the western end of the Grand Bief.

One place here that never disappoints is a remarkable antiquarian bookshop, housed in the cavernous barn of a building near the bridge. My first visit in 1982 resulted in the purchase of 6,000 francs-worth of rare items, among them de la Lande's legendary *Des Canaux de Navigation et Spécialement du Canal du Languedoc* (1778): the definitive waterways handbook of its day. It weighs almost 5kg, runs to over 600 pages and contains a series of magnificent folding plates. This time, my haul included a leather-bound *Histoire du Canal du Midi* by Andreossy (1804); Bischambis' autographed work on the River Aude and associated navigations (1932); and an attractive biography of Riquet, published by Fernay in 1885. Added to that, three bound runs of the weekly *L'Illustration* for the 1890s each contained extensive pictorial features on French waterways.

The halt at Ventenac d'Aude was unscheduled. Stupidly (as I now realise) I had always assumed that a nineteenth-century building in pale-grey stone was a waterside church. This time, signs proclaimed it to be a wine cave, devoted to the preparation and sale of white and red Minervois. Quickly, we engaged reverse gears and came to rest alongside our own personal landing stage, complete with picnic table for lunch. Inside, huge barrels, shining pipework and a series of wooden stairways leading from floor to floor suggested that the ecclesiastical appearance was unusually apt for this was a veritable temple to Bacchus. A temporary exhibition of elderly carriages and other pre-motor car rural transport was on show. We toured the *fiacres*, dog carts and pony traps and then returned to a reception area to lay in supplies of ballast for *Avonbay*. Wooden cases were purchased as presents for friends at home in England. Several journeys were necessary to convey our booty to the boat. Fortunately, the management had the foresight to produce a two-wheeled trolley which accepted a sizeable load of boxes.

Of several small aqueducts dating from Riquet's time, that over the Répudre stream is the most impressive with a span of 9m. It was completed in 1676 and is approached by one of the most acute bends on the waterway. Not long after, Paraza comprises a terrace of houses perched above the navigation and commands a magnificent view over the vineyards of the Aude valley. Once again (and not for the last time) we assured ourselves that this was the most spectacularly attractive part of the Languedoc canal. Next comes Roubia, a third century AD staging post with the remains of a Roman signal tower.

The first of the unmodernised 30m locks was soon followed by a favourite village – Argens-Minervois. Crowned by a severe and almost windowless *château* with rectangular towers, we recalled how it had appeared to be an intact survival from the Middle Ages. Six years before, we discovered with delight a row of deserted medieval cottages on the edge of a precipice, close to the big house. Lacking all modern conveniences apart from slate sinks, they must once have been servants' quarters. A stunning view over the countryside to the north-west made them ideal for conversion to a holiday home (always assuming that one did not prefer a floating residence that would offer new scenery each day). But, since the previous visit, others had sought out the charms of Argens: 'our' cottages were fast approaching a state of ruin and a sea of not unpleasant but wholly inappropriate modern villas was spreading across meadowland between the *château* and the canal. No other Midi village would have so greatly benefitted from a total ban on new buildings.

Locking in company with a charming and conscientious German hire cruiser party, *Avonbay* worked through two-rise staircases at Pechlaurier and Ognon. We all moored up for the evening among a cluster of charter boats on the quayside at Homps.

When service that evening in the charming garden of La Guingette des Tonneliers became ever slower as our meal progressed, we were inclined to excuse the management whose customers included a party of fifteen Italians enjoying a last-night-of-the-cruise dinner. Finally, at 10.30pm, the bill was extracted; as it was less than half what we had expected, we questioned the proprietor. He hurriedly explained that we had been given someone else's *addition*, but he was far too busy to correct the mistake now. Perhaps we might return in the morning to settle up?

After visits to a captivating little grocery store, where the elderly owners complimented me on my French and we enjoyed a long discussion on the merits of the European Common Market; to the butcher's; and (abortively) to buy bottled gas from a firm operating British-built narrow boats, there was still no sign of last night's restauranteur. Repeated knocking at his door produced no response. By now it was 10.30am. Unable to delay our departure any longer, we decided we must deal with the outstanding account by correspondence. Predictably, as *Avonbay* was under way and passing the restaurant, a bleary-eyed figure appeared, frantically waving for us to stop. We re-moored, paid up and thought what a strange way to run a business. The food, however, had been most enjoyable.

Gas was finally located at an endearingly old-fashioned garage on the western fringes of Homps. In the cluttered workshop, the aged owner was appropriately repairing a pre-war car, amid mountains of automobile bric-à-brac. Had this curious survival been used as a film set, its antiquated nature would have scarcely been credible in the late eighties.

Laredorte proved to be well worth exploration, in spite of the derelict plastic water chute and minute swimming pool incongruously erected among houses on the quay. Opened in 1986, this was a highly unsuitable addition to the canal's tourist facilities. Presumably a commercial failure, it was now for sale. Remains of fortifications in the village and a huge deserted *château* mouldering in overgrown gardens suggested that the sleepy settlement had once enjoyed a more vibrant existence.

Locks steadily increased in frequency, for we were climbing up the valley of the Aude towards the distant summit level. One night moored in the wilds beyond Marseillette brought a break in the weather with the first rain since setting out down the Rhône from Valence. To raise morale, a snap decision was taken to lunch ashore at the Auberge du Moulin, alongside a triple lock staircase in the town of Trèbes. The

A pénichette hire cruiser ascends the triple lock staircase at Trèbes. Uphill journeys feature much turbulence when paddles in the intermediate gates are opened

flexibility of working these wide chambers was demonstrated by our passing a downhill boat as we moved from the bottom to the middle section. Riquet had constructed a level crossing of the River Orbiel, just beyond the town. Silt, washed into the canal in floodtime, created problems for some years so in 1687 Vauban designed a three-span aqueduct from which there was a fine view of Trèbes, situated on the banks of the Aude.

Carcassonne had originally been bypassed by the waterway; it was not until 1810 that a new 5km line was opened, with an aqueduct over the River Fresquel, approached by a new two-rise lock. We hurried on, for already glimpses of Europe's finest medieval city compelled us to reach a wide basin for the night. Several hotel boats and a dozen cruisers had similar ideas, so this urban halt by the railway station was not exactly peaceful.

Close at hand, shops and restaurants in the lower town are very convenient. Several of us took a taxi for an evening in La Cité, a fantasy of thirteenth-century hilltop turrets, surrounded by double rings of defence walls. Thanks to nineteenth-century architect Viollet le Duc, widespread (if slightly over-zealous) repair work ensured Carcassonne's place as a major tourist magnet. It is still a living town with houses, shops and numerous eating places. Even though many businesses are devoted to selling tawdry souvenirs, I refuse to subscribe to the view that it is ruined by over-commercialism. Fire-eaters, jugglers and equestrian troubadours greeted us at the entrance: all slightly theatrical, but who cared? As dusk fell we remembered being here on the night of 14 July 1971 when Bastille Day was celebrated with a stupendous firework display. The sky was filled

Espérance,
penultimate freight
péniche *to trade on
the Canal du Midi.*
Écluse de Béteille,
August 1988

with explosions of coloured light crashing over this fairytale Camelot.

Little more than a day's cruising would see *Avonbay* to her winter berth. With traffic mainly composed of private yachts and a large fleet of Blue Line cruisers from Castelnaudary, these higher reaches of the Midi are much quieter than the part nearer the coast. There are few villages, just a succession of locks. Waiting for the Écluse de Béteille to empty, we were thrilled to see the *péniche Espérence* emerge, eastward bound. With gleaming paintwork, she was one of just two Midi freight craft remaining in service, at the end of a line of proud vessels dating back 307 years. Two decades earlier, we would never have forecast the demise of this fleet. Within six months, the *Espérence* captain had sold her for pleasure use and bought a larger boat for trading on the Canal latéral à la Garonne.

The Écluse de la Criminelle posed all kinds of questions as to what dark deeds might have been committed long ago. The name was in use at least as far back as 1778 but its origins seem to have been lost. The present keeper had decorated his domain with brightly painted plaques extolling the virtues of Riquet and independence for Languedoc. There were also warnings about touching gates or paddles except when supervised.

This was the day when we nearly had quiche lorraine for lunch. A large portion, freshly baked, had been bought forty-eight hours earlier, double-wrapped in the shop and consigned to the boat's fridge. I arrived in the saloon, seconds after June had removed the dish from the oven and placed it on the table. Diana took one look and screamed: 'Don't eat it!' I was allowed a momentary glance before she flung the offending quiche into the canal, much to the amazement of John at the outside steering station. In that split second I had seen the surface was alive with wriggling white maggots, angrily aroused from their home by the heating process. 'Better wear my glasses when cooking in future,' was June's comment, adding: 'And I so nearly decorated the top with grated cheese!' We lunched on sardines.

Early in the morning of our final day we glided into the great basin of Castelnaudary created by flooding a little valley under the town walls. This provided a huge reservoir for the quadruple staircase of St Roch locks. Packing up for the winter is always a depressing affair. Most of all when water, gas and electricity are turned off and the ship is ready for hibernation. Arrangements were made with a Blue Line engineer to keep the batteries charged; mooring fees demanded by the Ponts et Chaussées were deposited with the local taxation office. Four weeks after starting a 500km voyage, we were at journey's end, exactly on schedule and with all systems functioning perfectly. It would be six and a half months before we returned to our faithful *Avonbay*.

Epilogue

SPRING 1989 was the twentieth anniversary of our epic voyage with the first seven Blue Line cruisers from Bordeaux docks, up the Garonne and along the *latéral* canal to Toulouse. What more appropriate way of celebrating the event than to repeat the journey in *Avonbay?* There would be a number of changes, not least the enlargement and mechanisation of locks. Since 1983, the Port de Lauragais, just west of the Midi's summit level, had provided a pleasure boat harbour where facilities are shared with a service station on the A61 *autoroute.* A strikingly modern island building in the basin, approached via a causeway, is the Centre Pierre Paul Riquet, with displays devoted to the canal's history. Diversions could be made: into the reopened Baïse navigation from Buzet to Vianne, where there was already talk of further restoration upstream to the lovely town of Nérac. On reaching Moissac, we would follow a branch into the Tarn reservoir. The following year, hire cruisers would be established on an isolated length of the River Lot in the rocky gorges near Cahors. All kinds of developments were starting to happen in the area. There was much worth investigating. This would be a fitting climax to our travels in the South of France before heading back to Burgundy. *Avonbay* had safely wintered in Castelnaudary, so we were happy to leave her there for several more months after her return trip to Bordeaux.

Blue Line's manager, John Riddel had serious news when we flew in from London, some days before the Easter weekend. Winter 1988–9 had been the driest in Languedoc for over forty years. Even the exceptionally low rainfall of 1948 had failed to close the Midi to traffic. But now water supplies at the summit were dangerously depleted. He advised us to move without delay to the Camargue, rather than risk being trapped by closures until the end of the year. His problems were even more serious, involving the likely relocation of scores of hire boats at alternative bases. 'I don't have a crystal ball,' he told us 'but prospects don't look at all good.'

Further persuasion being unnecessary, we quickly recovered from our disappointment and headed back down the Midi to St Gilles on the Canal du Rhône à Sète. Less than a month after this trip, all locks were closed in the 81km from Toulouse to Bram until further notice.

Avonbay was the first craft of the season to work down to Carcassonne on 21 March after the lifting of winter lock closures. Strong winds made boat handling tricky when entering the chambers but warm sunshine made us feel that summer had arrived early. At the beginning, trees showed no hint of leaves, providing an utterly different feel to the canal which we thought we knew so well. The banks were carpeted with thousands of pheasant's eye narcissi and masses of spring snowflake, a tall snowdrop-like flower, almost unknown in England. Both were so prolific that we suffered no scruples in collecting a vaseful for the saloon. A branch of sloe provided our Easter tree, its clusters of tiny white flowers contrasting well with the little painted eggs and rabbits, saved from earlier cruises to Bavaria.

As the week progressed, hire cruisers appeared in greater numbers, waterside restaurants were unusually welcoming after their winter break and we enjoyed seeking out villages where there had never previously been time to stop. On Easter Saturday, we were moored at Argeliers, when a familiar face appeared on the bank. It was our old friend Roger Pilkington whose series of inland cruising books had guided us through waterways from Sweden to southern Germany. Now retired from regular boating, he was living in his favourite part of Europe close to the Canal du Midi. He duly admired *Avonbay* and told us that the clocks would change to summer time that night.

Easter Sunday was a lazy day: with locks closed, a perfect opportunity for a slow cruise down the Grand Bief to Colombiers. Wishing to catch the first morning convoy down the Béziers staircase, we set the alarm but woke in such intense darkness that it might have been 4am. Had we miscalculated the time change? The hour's journey to Les Fonserannes was achieved with the help of navigation lights; dawn eventually arrived and the keeper was there to see us through.

Crossing the Étang de Thau was blessed with calm, warm weather, with dozens of little fishing boats scattered over the lake's surface. When we finally came near the sea beyond Frontigan, my ambition to swim in the Mediterranean in March was an exercise of very short duration. The water was extremely cold.

As I write, *Avonbay* waits in the Camargue for us to return, destination northern Germany and the Low Countries. There is so much left to discover.

Appendices

GETTING AFLOAT

The Network

About 8,000km of navigable rivers and canals serve many parts of France, with connections into the Belgian and German systems (not forgetting the short length of Swiss Rhine). Entry from the sea can be made at several English Channel ports: into the extensive (but isolated) Brittany waterways; at various points along the Mediterranean coast between the Rhône delta and Port-la-Nouvelle; and from the Bay of Biscay, north-west of Bordeaux.

Routes from Paris to the Mediterranean

It is possible to start either in Calais or Dunkerque and follow a series of quite heavily used commercial navigations to join the Seine near Paris. Alternatively boats that can be cruised with confidence on the sea will reach Paris more quickly via the Seine Estuary at Le Havre. Four different canal links from the Seine all converge on the middle Saône in Burgundy:

1 The Bourbonnais (Loing, Briare, latéral à la Loire and Centre Canals). From the Seine at St Mammès to the Saône in Chalon. Paris to Mediterranean: 979km with 168 locks. Pleasant scenery, offers the most generous of dimensions compared with other routes and is the quickest.
2 Canal de Bourgogne (Yonne, Bourgogne). From the Seine at Montereau to the Saône at St Jean-de-Losne. Paris to Mediterranean: 973km with 235 locks. Outstandingly beautiful but with many locks; air draught restricted through Pouilly-en-Auxois tunnel.
3 Via the Marne (Marne, latéral à la Marne, de la Marne à la Saône). From the Seine upstream of Paris to the Saône at Heuilley. Paris to Mediterranean: 1,056km with 167 locks. An enjoyable, well-maintained series of waterways.
4 Canal du Nivernais (Yonne, Nivernais, latéral à la Loire, and Centre Canals). From the Seine at Monterau to the Saône at Chalon. Paris to the Mediterranean: 1,033km with 245 locks. Very agreeable, but draught on the Nivernais is quite limited.

Route from Atlantic to the Mediterranean

Canaux du Midi (Gironde, Garonne, latéral à la Garonne, Midi, Étang de Thau). From the Bay of Biscay, via Bordeaux and Toulouse, reaching the Mediterranean at Sète: 360km with 144 individual lock chambers. Headroom is rather limited under certain Canal du Midi bridges.

Route Across Brittany
Using the Rance from St Malo, Canal d'Ille et Rance and River Vilaine, reaching the sea on the south coast of the Brittany Peninsula: 244km with 64 locks. Draught and headroom are somewhat restricted.

Route from the North Sea to the Mediterranean
Using the Rhine from the Hook of Holland, Grand Canal d'Alsace, Canal du Rhône au Rhin, Saône and Rhône: 1,619km with 139 locks. This should only be attempted by craft with sufficient power to ascend the Rhine and its fast-flowing gorge between Koblenz and Bingen. There are plans to upgrade the canal section from the Rhine to the Saône; when completed, this will reduce locks from 113 to 24.

Cruising Within France
Numerous circular routes make the country ideal for extended journeys without the need for putting to sea. Times taken will vary greatly, according to the number of locks, flow on river sections and personal preference. The minimum period for Paris to the Mediterranean would be about three weeks; infinitely more pleasure is derived by cruising much more slowly than this, enjoying the waterways and their scenery.

Maximum Dimensions
Most river navigations are large enough for all but the biggest pleasure craft. Restrictions apply to certain of the artificial canals. The majority conform to the Freycinet standard, providing Length: 38.5m; Beam: 5m; Draught: 1.8m; Height above water: 3.5m.
The most notable exceptions are:

Waterway	Length	Beam	Draught	Air Draught
Canal de Bourgogne	39m	5m	1.8m	3m (reduced at sides)
Canal d'Ille et Rance	27.1m	4.7m	1.35m	2.75m
Canal du Midi (central part)	30m	5.25m	1.6m	3.4m (reduced to 2m at bridge sides)
Canal du Nivernais (central part)	30.15m	5.1m	1.2m	2.7m
R. Vilaine	25.87m	4.52m	1.1m	3.2m

For fullest information consult *Inland Waterways of France* by David Edwards-May or the appropriate *Carte Guides* (see Bibliography).

Hire Cruisers
Blue Line, oldest and largest self-drive boat company in France was founded in 1969 when there was only one other firm on the entire network. Now, the industry is widespread with opportunities to explore most areas. Craft are mostly of modern design and well maintained, sleeping between two and ten people. Hire periods are normally in multiples of one week, although some concerns have boats

available for long weekends, especially outside the July/August peak season when prices are increased compared with March or October. Previous experience is not generally required. A recent trend is provision of one-way trips with arrangements for your car to be ferried to the finishing point if required. Optional extras normally include bicycle hire, much recommended for the traffic-free towpaths.

Among the leading agencies, with boats in all popular regions are:

Blakes Holidays Ltd, Wroxham, Norwich, Norfolk, NR12 8DH, England. Tel: (06053) 2911 or 2917 or 3221 or 3224.

Crown Blue Line, Le Grand Bassin, 11400 Castelnaudary, France. Tel: (68) 23 17 51. Or, 8, Ber Street, Norwich, Norfolk NR1 3EJ, England.

French County Cruises, Andrew Brock Travel Ltd, 10 Barley Mow Passage, Chiswick, London, W4 4PH, England. Tel: 081-995 3642.

Hoseasons Holidays, Sunway House, Lowestoft, Suffolk, NR32 3LT, England. Tel: (0502) 501010.

Addresses of operators may also be obtained from the **French Government Tourist Office,** 178 Piccadilly, London, W1V 0AL, England. Tel: 071-491 7622.

Hotel Barges

Operating on most scenic routes, these are either converted freight vessels or purpose built. Between twelve and twenty guests sleep aboard in private cabins and are provided with meals to a very high standard. All navigation and lock working is the responsibility of the professional captain and his crew. As might be expected, these cruises are expensive and many of the passengers are American. For addresses, contact the French Government Tourist Office, as above.

One much more reasonably priced alternative, self-catering or with meals, is the former grain barge *Pisgah*, travelling on different French navigations each year. Suitable for two families (up to twelve people), she is operated by her owner, a waterways enthusiast. Details from Enterprise Charter Cruises, 2a Southmoor, Buckleigh, Bideford, Devon, EX39 3PU, England. Tel: (02372) 75024 (winter) or (0271) 85561 (April–September).

Day-tripping Vessels

Mainly found on river navigations. Scheduled services offer outings ranging from an hour to all day (the Rhône between Lyon and Avignon takes two days). Details from the French Government Tourist Office or local tourist offices in the area.

Canoes and Inflatables

Lightweight, portable boats for camping expeditions and perhaps used with a small outboard motor, can be taken to a launching site by car. This is the cheapest and in good weather can be the most enjoyable way of getting afloat. Check importation regulations with the Royal Yachting Association or your motoring organisation. I have journeyed long distances in France using a motorised inflatable and tent; few difficulties of any kind were experienced.

Trailed Boats

The greatest advantage of a motor cruiser capable of being towed by a car of reasonable power is an ability to visit far flung or isolated canals and rivers. If parked ashore, at home, when not in use, mooring charges are eliminated. Conversely, overall length is unlikely to exceed 6m, with a resultant lack of living space aboard; ideal, however for two people.

Inland Cruisers

Boats designed specifically for river or canal use are widely used in Britain. If you already own one, there is every reason to have it transported to France, probably leaving it there for a number of holidays. Never be tempted to navigate the English Channel with unseaworthy vessels. Included in this category is the very popular flat-bottomed narrow boat, normally steel-hulled with a beam of about 2.07m, dictated by the width of many English locks. In 1989, road transport specialists were quoting from £750–£1,500 to move a 14m narrow boat from London to Calais, plus craneage charges at each end. To begin to be cost effective, the boat would need to remain for use in France for a considerable period. Alternatively, one firm with seagoing barges regularly running between London and Dunkerque will carry such a boat as deck cargo for about £350 plus craneage. Details from A & A Pratt, 770 Lower Rainham Road, Rainham, Kent, ME8 8AN England. Tel: (0634) 34147.

While boats like these are best not purchased specially for French travel, provided they are adequately powered to cope with Continental river currents, they can provide an economic alternative to hiring if the exercise is costed out over several long cruises.

Seagoing Cruisers and Motor Sailors

Almost certainly the most realistic solution, so long as dimensions are not too close to the limiting sizes of the waterways. Experience with *Avonbay* suggests that the ideal for use by up to six people would be between 11m and 14m overall, of steel or grp (plastic) and with an outside steering station for best helmsman visibility. We have seldom experienced problems through having twin engines, although the rudders/propellors are more vulnerable to damage when approaching shallow canal banks than are single screws. This is greatly outweighed by improved manoeuvrability and the ability to continue cruising if one engine should fail. Not only can suitable vessels cross to France from England under their own power, but sea passages to Spain and via the Baltic to Sweden are quite viable.

Motor sailors with fixed keels must not be so deep draughted that they are constantly hitting canal bottoms; in any event mooring would be a serious problem. Similarly, inability to give way to laden freight barges requiring the centre of a narrow channel could result in anxious encounters. Masts can be unstepped at most entry ports, as will be necessary to clear bridges. However, if the recumbent mast greatly projects beyond bow or stern, it constitutes a hazard, especially in locks.

Suitable boats in both categories are widely available, new and secondhand. If again buying a craft such as *Avonbay*, I would always go for a used bargain, subject it to a professional survey and be prepared to spend additional funds on adapting it to suit my personal taste. My own vessel, insured for £30,000, could not be replaced by a new equivalent for under £60,000. Various factors suggest purchase in England, enabling all required modifications to be made before the voyage to France. Equally, many suitable boats can be located on the Continent. Bear in mind the implications of French TVA (Value Added Tax), see below.

Advertisements in the British magazines *Motor Boat & Yachting* and *Boats and Planes for Sale* and the French waterways journal *Fluvial* should produce many suitable craft. *Avonbay* was designed by naval architects Robert Tucker Designs Ltd, 15 Wrensfield, Boxmoor, Hemel Hempstead, Hertfordshire, HP1 1RN, England. Tel: (0442) 53775. Plans may be purchased and something similar built to order. Among suitable new vessels are the Dutch-built range from Pedro Boats UK, 49 Victoria Road, Deal, Kent, CT14 7AY, England. Tel: (0304) 364950; and the Stevens cruisers, sold in England by Steelcraft Boat Showrooms, Shepperton Marina, Felix Lane, Shepperton, Middlesex, TW17 8NJ, Tel: (0932) 243722.

Converted Barges

Because they were designed for an inland environment, there is nothing better suited to canal and river use than a former freight barge. With hulls of iron or steel, they are rugged, offer capacious living space and in experienced hands can undertake sea passages. The most suitable examples are generally of Dutch origin and are offered for sale unconverted or ready for live-aboard cruising. In France, ubiquitous 38m *péniches*, lately retired from trade are often cheaper than more manageable examples 16–20m in length. Always remember the extra maintenance and mooring costs of the larger boat; also, except in the hands of professionals, anything much longer than 20m can be too much of a handful for a couple to navigate on their own. Notoriously long lasting, a canal barge of this type, launched before World War I, can often be a fully viable proposition. Again, a full survey is essential before purchase. Before getting too deeply involved, arrange to travel on such a boat to discover what will be entailed by ownership. Many Dutch barges, otherwise suitable for French waterways, have a beam slightly in excess of the permitted 5m maximum. If in doubt, this should be measured with care.

Barges are regularly advertised for sale in *Motor Boat & Yachting*, *Waterways World*, *Boats and Planes for Sale*, and the French *Fluvial* (64, rue J. J. Rousseau, 21000 Dijon, France. Tel: 80.73.39.39).

Recommended specialist firms selling converted and unconverted craft include:

Bowcrest Marine, The Marina at South Dock, Plough Lane, London, SE16 1AA. Tel: 071 231 0054.

The London Tideway Harbour Co Ltd, The Dove Pier, Upper Mall, Hammersmith, London, W6 9TA, England. Tel: 081-748 2715.

H₂O, Port de Plaisance, 21170 St Jean-de-Losne, France. Tel: 80.39.23.00 (English spoken).

Friesland Boating, de Tille 5, Koudum, Netherlands. Tel: (5142) 2607 or 2609 (English spoken).

Jo Parfitt. Chantier Fluvial du Nivernais, Péniche Johanna, 89730 Mailly-la-Ville, France. Tel: 86.40.44.77 (English spoken).

Enkhuizen Maritiem, Oosterhavenstraat 13, 1601 KV Enkhuizen, Netherlands. Tel: 31 2280 17279.

IMT Nederland, Zaadmarkt 89, 7201 DC Zutphen, Netherlands. Tel: 31 5750 42220.

Regulations

Currently, foreign-owned pleasure craft may be used in French waters for six months (not necessarily consecutive) in every twelve without payment of Value Added Tax (TVA) calculated at 18.6 per cent of the boat's marketable price. This arrangement may continue for a period of three years, after which the vessel must be exported (even for a short period) before another three-year cycle can start. Documentary evidence must be obtained from the French Customs authorities, preferably leaving registration papers with them when the boat is out of commission. This procedure was successfully followed with *Avonbay* after her entry to France in 1985. One assumes that the regulation will be abandoned with the removal of Common Market trade barriers in 1992 although at the time of writing the authorities are unable to confirm this. Visiting foreign craft may not be hired or lent to anyone: the owner/s is/are required to be the only user.

No certificate of navigational competence is necessary unless obligatory in your country of origin. None is needed by British boaters. While this book was in production, plans were announced to make a charge for use of French waterways, starting in 1991. Details were sketchy but suggested a cost of between 1,000 and 2,000 francs per year for an average-sized cruiser.

Ship's Papers

All on board should, of course, carry passports. It is preferable that the boat is registered as a British ship (under full Part 1 Registry). A simpler method of obtaining official papers is to apply for the Small Ships Register, available from the Royal Yachting Association, RYA House, Romsey Road, Eastleigh, Hampshire, SO5 4YA, England. Tel: (0703) 629962. Resulting paperwork will be used to (a) prove ownership and (b) provide details of boat, dimensions and owner/s at certain lockside check points. A current certificate of insurance with adequate third-party cover is also advised.

Customs Regulations

Duty-free allowances are the same as for any visiting tourist. In practice, you are more likely to attract attention if importing marine equipment or stores for your boat when arriving in France by car than if entering the country on your vessel.

Moorings

Fees (generally including use of water and shore electricity) will be demanded at certain town quays and marinas. Otherwise, you may select overnight moorings when in transit at any reasonable situation without payment while taking care to avoid obstructing the navigation. Study of the *Carte Guide* should identify a suitable stopping place each night. On rivers, bank protection may be of loose rock. If unexpectedly caught out by failing light, there will be circumstances where anchoring is appropriate (outside the main navigation channel and displaying an all-round white light during darkness); otherwise, make fast to a moored barge, having first asked permission and ascertained at what time they are likely to be moving next morning.

Although some owners make unofficial arrangements with lock-keepers or other local people to leave their craft on the French waterways when not in use, I always book a secure mooring in a marina. Certain hire cruiser firms will also undertake this service. Fees paid rarely exceed charges made at similar British inland harbours. The harbourmaster will generally lodge your registration papers with the local Customs Office, if asked.

Boat Handling

Commonsense will see you through most situations. If negotiating locks in company with other craft allow larger commercial vessels to enter first, following the keeper's instructions. Maintain contact with lockside bollards until any barges ahead are well clear and their (often powerful) wash has subsided. At manually worked locks you will be expected to assist with working gates and paddles. With a few exceptions, passing through locks unless authorised by the keeper is forbidden. Some canal locks are automatic with equipment activated by radar or hand-held sensors with which you are provided when entering a sequence. In the event of a breakdown, a central control office can be contacted by lockside telephone. Certain locks on the rivers Marne and Yonne have sloping sides. If applicable, ask permission to moor to a barge so avoiding contact with the banks. Otherwise, fend off with boathooks or use the vertical-sided portion of the chamber nearest the gates. Mechanised locks on larger river navigations may be contacted by VHF radio telephone when you are several km off. A simple statement (in French) may enable the keeper to prepare the chamber in advance thus saving much waiting time. VHF channel numbers are published in the *Carte Guides*. Always approach unknown banks and quays warily, sounding water depth with a boathook. Some canal basins may be badly silted.

Navigating rivers when there is floodwater should only be attempted within the limits of your engine power. An anchor should be rigged for instant use, should your motor suddenly fail. Approach river moorings against the current: this provides greater control.

Stoppages

Annual closure of waterways for repairs is normally arranged so that an alternative route is possible. A list of such *chômages* for the following year is available from the end of March on application to the French Government Tourist Office in London. Additionally, there may from time to time be emergency closures. Details of these should be sought from local navigation offices. Addresses appear in the relevant *Carte Guides*.

Sanitation

Legally, it is now forbidden to discharge loos into the navigation. In practice all commercial craft, hire cruisers and private pleasure boats do just that, in the absence of pump-out facilities for boat holding tanks.

Fuel, Bottled Gas and Water

Diesel fuel is reasonably widely available at waterside pumps as marked on the *Carte Guides*. Tanker delivery can be arranged elsewhere if substantial quantities are to be purchased. Otherwise supplies must be carried in cans from roadside garages. On *Avonbay*, we have a tank capacity in excess of 450 litres, take every opportunity to refill when half empty and have never yet run dry. Tax-free diesel oil (coloured red) must not be used on pleasure craft, even though it is often available through barge fuelling firms. Spot checks by Customs officials are not unknown. The red *fuel-oil domestique* is, however, permitted for heating appliances. As *Avonbay*'s tanks serve both engines and the central heating system, there is scope for an interesting debate! Petrol (*essence*) is less commonly found at the waterside and may have to be conveyed in cans.

Both butane and propane bottled gas (for cooking and running fridges) is much more common in France than England and may readily be purchased at marinas, garages, supermarkets and hardware stores. Pipe fittings differ from those used in England and should be replaced on arrival in France. Empty British bottles will not be accepted in exchange for full Continental ones. Try to purchase a nationally available brand (Butagas, Primagas) so that there are no problems in disposing of the empties.

Reasonably economical use of domestic water and moderately sized tanks should ensure that you never run out. Taps will be found at some locks, town quays and all marinas. They are generally threaded to accept a screw-on hose but occur in at least three different diameters. Time spent in a French hardware shop should result in purchase of all necessary adaptors; the most useful fitting is a push-on rubber one, compressed with a jubilee clip. A hose of at least 60m is recommended.

Ours winds flat onto a reel and is far more compact than the conventional type. Water is normally supplied free of charge although it is a kindness to make a modest payment to a lock-keeper, especially if he has supplied the hose.

Tipping

In the early seventies, many locks were worked by war veterans or widows: then, a small payment was much appreciated. Now, canal staff are mostly younger and more affluent. To give them less than 5 francs borders on the insulting; any more can be ruinous to the boatman. We prefer to take every opportunity to buy home-produced eggs, vegetables, flowers, wine and poultry (this last may not be oven ready; more likely it is running about when first encountered). Often, exchange of a few friendly words and willingness to help work gates and paddles is all that will be expected.

Special Equipment

In addition to gear carried on any properly equipped cruiser, the following are necessary: a powerful searchlight for tunnels even though many are illuminated; at least two boathooks, as long as can conveniently be handled and stowed (these are for sounding water depths close to the bank or rescuing objects lost overboard and are useful should you run aground -- they should *not* be used like lances to ward off other craft in a threatening and dangerous manner) plenty of light, strong rope for bankside mooring or deep locks; at least two stout steel mooring spikes and a heavy hammer; a small dinghy, either hung in davits or stowed on deck, this will provide entertainment for younger members of the crew, can act as a useful camera platform and will be invaluable should you ever run hard aground far from the shore.

Every boat will require fenders. Even rugged commercial barges will be noted hanging short lengths of tree trunk on their most vulnerable quarters. *Avonbay*'s gunwhales are ringed with tough D-section rubber fendering. In addition, we use just four spherical inflated fenders down each side when passing through locks or mooring to a hard bank. These are lifted when under way except if locks occur very frequently. We consider that any additional fendering precautions are unnecessary, unsightly and unseamanlike. To suspend arrays of canvas-draped car tyres or even horizontal planks along the topsides of a cruiser is a clear indication that the skipper is incapable of handling his craft with the required skill. Furthermore, tyres are banned by the authorities: should they be ripped off when entering a lock, they will rapidly sink, foul up the paddle gear and bring all craft movement to a halt.

A gangplank, as long as it can easily be handled and stowed, is well worth carrying for use when you cannot moor directly alongside a shallow bank. Ours consists of an aluminium ladder with a strong piece of timber fixed across the treads.

Land Transport

If ever I were to own a converted barge it would need to be sufficiently large to accommodate a small car on deck, preferably astern of the wheelhouse. Thus could be avoided all those tedious crew-fetching jaunts to railway stations and airports, using taxis, hired cars or public transport. Shopping would be transformed. At the end of a cruise, the means of returning home would be instantly available. Lacking an onboard car, we resort to taxis (cheaper over long distances than in England) or expensive self-drive hire cars which can be located in all medium-sized towns.

Bicycles are invaluable for fetching fresh bread from the nearest village each morning; sightseeing; speeding down the towpath to alert the next lockkeeper; and exercising energetic youngsters. We carry two folding ones, the maximum possible without unduly cluttering the deck. They are rarely folded, being more convenient if always ready for use. Cycles to which a large box can be fixed with an elastic 'spider' make light work of expeditions to the supermarket. Even better, is a folding shopping trolley with a pair of tough carrying bags. Ours doubles as gas-bottle carrier when necessary.

Navigation Signals

A range of visual signal boards and traffic lights will be encountered: these are designed either to warn or to command. Additionally, various sound signals will be heard from other craft and should be used in appropriate circumstances. All appear in full colour in most of the *Carte Guides* published by Éditions Cartographiques Maritimes or are available on a self-adhesive panel, 24.5x16cm, published by Les Éditions du Plaisancier.

Hours of Navigation

Pleasure craft equipped with navigation lights are normally permitted to travel during hours of darkness on pounds (*biefs*) between locks. One exception is the tidal River Seine, where there is substantial commercial shipping. Movement of hire cruisers at night is forbidden. Lock opening hours vary according to time of the year and from one waterway to another. In winter they are available 7.30am–5.30pm, gradually increasing to 6.30–7.30pm, April–September. All but the largest routes are subject to a short break at lunchtime. Certain canals are closed on Sundays. All locks are closed on the following public holidays: Easter Sunday, 1 May, 14 July, 11 November and Christmas Day. Further, there may also be closures on 1 January, 8 May, Whit Sunday and 1 November. Fuller details appear in the relevant *Carte Guides*.

Speed Limits

Again, consult the *Carte Guides*. Normally, between 6kph and 10kph on canals; 25kph on rivers. Where specifically signed, higher speeds are permitted for purposes of water skiing. Consistent travel on canals breaking the speed limit may result in you being timed between locks with resultant heavy fines. As a general rule never go so fast, especially on canals, as to produce a breaking wash on the banks. It is only good manners to slow when passing small craft, fishing punts, canoes and moored craft, even if this rule is frequently ignored by local boaters.

Shopping

Bulk supplies of food and drink are most easily obtained in supermarkets. These offer the best value and require little knowledge of French. Small village shops, on the other hand, can produce more enjoyable encounters with the locals. The use of preservatives is less widespread in France than in Great Britain. Fresh meat should be placed in the boat's fridge without delay and normally be eaten within two days of purchase, especially in warm weather.

Restaurants

Most quite small villages have at least one restaurant. As the French enjoy their food to the point of fanaticism, poor quality meals are a rarity. Eating out is an excellent and convivial way of passing the evening. Cost need never be excessive, especially if you select a low-priced establishment and choose their best menu. Conversely, it is not worth trying to economise at an expensive restaurant: the result will invariably disappoint.

Rhône Moorings

Suitable stopping places for each night can easily be found on most waterways, especially if you study the *Carte Guide* in advance. The recently canalised River Rhône is one exception, long sections of the banks being composed of unsuitable loose rock. Among good moorings, within convenient daily travel of each other are the following. (This list is not exhaustive, but all have met with *Avonbay*'s approval):

Lyon	On Saône, upstream of Pont Bonaparte
Givors	Quay, K18.4
Condrieu	Marina, K40.8
Tournon	Harbour, K90.9. Entry difficult with strong flow
Valence	Marina, K112
Le Pouzin	Quay, K133
Viviers	Quays, K166, on old river
Avignon	Marina. 2.5km upstream of K244, on town arm, just above Pont St Bénezet
Arles	Pontoon, K282.7, opposite town
Port St Louis	In basin, K323

Note At the time of these journeys, £1.00 (UK) was worth about 10.60 French francs; $1 (US), about 6.60 French francs. American readers are advised that £1.00 (UK) roughly equalled $1.60 (US). References to 'gas' apply to bottled butane and propane, used for the cooker and fridge.

SELECTED BIBLIOGRAPHY

The following publications are all relevant to the journeys described in this book. Dates are those of latest editions. The leading retailer (by mail order) in Britain is Shepperton Swan Ltd, The Clock House, Upper Halliford, Shepperton, Middlesex, TW17 8RU, England. Tel: (0932) 783319. Catalogue of new inland waterways publications, all parts of Europe. Regular list of secondhand and out of print titles.

Maps and Guides

Carte Guides, Éditions Cartographiques, Joinville-le-Pont. 1 *Seine*, Le Havre–Paris. 2 *Seine*, Paris–Marcilly. 3 *Marne*, Paris–Vitry-le-François. 4 *Yonne*. 5 *Canal de Bourgogne*. 8 *Champagne-Ardenne*. 10 *Saône*. 11 *Canal des Deux Mers*, Rhône–Bordeaux. 14 *Nord Pas-de-Calais*, Channel ports–Belgium, Canal du Nord etc. 15 *Oise-Aisne-Ardennes*. 16 *Rhône*. 17 *Canal de la Marne au Rhin*, includes Canal des Houillères de la Sarre, Strasbourg, Canal du Rhône au Rhin (Strasbourg section). 18 *Bourgogne Vol 1*, Canal de Bourgogne, Yonne, Nivernais, part of Saône. 24 *Picardie*, includes Canal de St Quentin, Oise etc. 26 *Canal de l'Est*, Liège–Corre. 21 *Carte de France*, all waterways. 23 *Carte de Belgique*, all waterways. All carry French/English/German text.
Carte Guides Vagnon, Éditions du Plaisancier, Caluire. 2 *Doubs et Canal du Rhône au Rhin*.
Le Rhin et la Moselle, Verlag Rheinschiffahrt, Bad Soden, West Germany. Very detailed ringbound charts of the navigable length of each river. Text in French/German/Dutch.
Paris, Tony. *Enterprise Guides: The Canal du Midi* (Second edition, 1988); *The Yonne and the Nivernais* (1989); *The Canal de Bourgogne* (1990). Especially useful for restaurant recommendations. (Enterprise Publications, Bideford, Devon.)

General

Edwards-May, David. *Inland Waterways of France* (Imray, St Ives, 1991) Tabulated distances, locks etc for whole system.
Liley, John. *France–the Quiet Way* (Stanford Maritime, London, 1983). Amusing and perceptive exploration by barge.
Marchant, Vernon. *Notes on French Inland Waterways* (Cruising Association, London, 1988) Much useful information.
McKnight, Hugh. *Cruising French Waterways* (Nautical Books/A. & C. Black Ltd, second ed., 1991) Detailed descriptive guide to all 8,000km of rivers and canals.
———. *The Guinness Guide to Waterways of Western Europe* (Guinness, London, 1978) Includes French section.
Michelin Green Guides (Michelin, Clermont-Ferrand) Excellent concise history and tourism. English titles: *Paris; Provence*. In French

only: *Environs de Paris; Jura; Nord de la France; Champagne; Vallée du Rhône; Bourgogne; Alsace et Lorraine, Vosges.*
Pilkington, Roger. *Waterways in Europe* (Murray, London, 1972) Still invaluable especially for mooring advice.
Sharman, Fay, *et al. The A-Z Gastronomique* (Macmillan, London, 1989) Cannot be faulted for translating restaurant menus.

Cruising and Travelogues

Massey, Hart. *Travels with 'Lionel': A Small Barge in France.* (Gollancz, London, 1988) Very readable account of buying a Dutch barge and voyaging from Paris to the south.
Morgan Grenville, Gerard. *Barging into France, Barging into Burgundy, Barging into Southern France* (David & Charles, Newton Abbot. 1972–5) Exploring by converted barge.
Pilkington, Roger. *Small Boat* series (Macmillan, London, 1961–71) Very readable exploration by cruiser. Titles include: *Alsace; France; Luxembourg; Meuse; Southern France; Upper Rhine.*
———. *Small Boat Down the Years* (Pearson, Burton-on-Trent, 1987) Recalls a range of cruises, France included.
———. *Small Boat in the Midi* (Pearson, Burton-on-Trent, 1989)
Vine, P.A.L. *Pleasure Boating in the Victorian Era* (Phillimore, Chichester, 1983) Accounts of boating pioneers, including in France.

Historical

de Roquette-Buisson, Odile. *The Canal du Midi* (Rivages, Marseille, 1983) Translated from French.
Rolt, L.T.C. *From Sea to Sea; The Canal du Midi* (Allan Lane, London, 1973) Admirable history.

In French

Beaudouin, Francois. *Bateaux des Fleuves de France* (Éditions de l'Estran, Douarnenez, 1985) Lavish study of working boats.
Descombes, René. *Canaux et Batellerie en Alsace* (Le Verger, Strasbourg-Illkirch, 1988)
Henry, Marianne et Bernard. *Voyages aux Longs Jours* (Arthaud, Paris, 1982)
Le Sueur, Bernard. *Batelleries et Bateliers de France* (Horvath, Le Côteau, 1985) Many old postcard views.
Lorenzo, Annie. *Professional? Marinier* (Massin, Paris, 1984)
Paon, Roger. *Marine de Rivière, Images de la Batellerie* (Cabri, Breil-sur-Roys, 1987)
Un Canal . . . Des Canaux (Picard, Paris, 1986) Beautiful guide to the 1986 Paris Waterways Exhibition with many historical pictures.
Vincelot, Henri. *Les Canaux de Bourgogne* (Rivages, Marseille, 1984)

Index

Page numbers in **bold** refer to illustrations